TRINITY
and
SOCIETY

Forthcoming books in the series:

Enrique Dussel, *Ethics and Community*

José Comblin, *The Holy Spirit and Liberation*

Eduardo Hoornaert, *The Memory of the Christian People*

Ivone Gebara and Maria Clara L. Bingemer, *Mary: Mother of God and Mother of the Poor*

Now being translated:

Clodovis Boff and Jorge Pixley, *Opción por los pobres*

THEOLOGY AND LIBERATION SERIES

Leonardo Boff

TRINITY
and
SOCIETY

Translated from the Portuguese by
Paul Burns

ORBIS BOOKS
Maryknoll, New York 10545

First published in this translation in Great Britain in 1988 by Burns & Oates, Wellwood, North Farm Rd., Tunbridge Wells, Kent TN2 3DR, and in the United States of America by Orbis Books, Maryknoll, NY 10545

Published originally in Brazil by Editora Vozes Ltda., Petrópolis, RJ, Brazil, under the title *A Trindade, a Sociedade e a Libertação* (third edition, 1987, *A Trindade e a Sociedade*)

Original edition © CESEP—São Paulo 1986

This edition © Burns and Oates/Search Press Ltd 1988

Library of Congress Cataloging-in-Publication Data

Boff, Leonardo.
  Trinity and society.

  (Theology and liberation series)
  Translation of: A trindade, a sociedade e a liber-
tação.
  Bibliography: p.
  1. Trinity.   2. Sociology (Christian)   3. Liberation
theology.   I. Title.   II. Series.
BT111.2.B7413   1988   231'.044   88-9884
ISBN 0-88344-623-5
ISBN 0-88344-622-7 (pbk.)

Theology and Liberation Series

In the years since its emergence in Latin America, liberation theology has challenged the church to a renewal of faith lived in solidarity with the poor and oppressed. The effects of this theology have spread throughout the world, inspiring in many Christians a deeper life of faith and commitment, but for others arousing fears and concerns.

Its proponents have insisted that liberation theology is not a subtopic of theology but really a new way of doing theology. The Theology and Liberation Series is an effort to test that claim by addressing the full spectrum of Christian faith from the perspective of the poor.

Thus, volumes in the Series are devoted to such topics as God, Christ, the church, revelation, Mary, the sacraments, and so forth. But the Series will also explore topics seldom addressed by traditional theology, though vital to Christian life—aspects of politics, culture, the role of women, the status of ethnic minorities. All these are examined in the light of faith lived in a context of oppression and liberation.

The work of over one hundred theologians, pastoral agents, and social scientists from Latin America, and supported by some one hundred and forty bishops, the Theology and Liberation Series is the most ambitious and creative theological project in the history of the Americas.

Addressed to the universal church, these volumes will be essential reading for all those interested in the challenge of faith in the modern world. They will be especially welcomed by all who are committed to the cause of the poor, by those engaged in the struggle for a new society, by all those seeking to establish a more solid link between faith and politics, prayer and action.

Contents

Abbreviations

CF   *The Christian Faith in the Doctrinal Documents of the Catholic Church.* Revised edition, edited by J. Neuner and J. Dupuis. New York: Alba House, 1982.

CT   *The Church Teaches: Documents of the Church in English Translation.* St Louis and London: B. Herder Book Co., 1955.

DS   Denzinger-Schönmetzer. *Enchiridion Symbolorum, definitionum et declarationum de rebus fidei et morum.* First published in 1854, latest edition 1976. Translations in the present work are from *The Christian Faith* (CF), from *The Church Teaches* (CT), or from the author's Portuguese with reference to the original.

LG   *Lumen Gentium.* Vatican II, Dogmatic Constitution on the Church, 1965. Translations are from Walter Abbott, ed., *The Documents of Vatican II.* Piscataway, N.J.: America Press, 1966 and London-Dublin: Geoffrey Chapman, 1966.

GS   *Gaudium et Spes.* Vatican II, Pastoral Constitution on the Church in the Modern World. Translations are from Abbott.

INTRODUCTION

From the Solitude of One
to the Communion of Three

An encounter with the divine Mystery lies at the root of all religious doctrine. This encounter evokes a deep experience embracing all our humanity: emotions, reason, will, desire and heart. The first reaction, an expression of pleasure, is praise, worship and proclamation. After that comes the task of appropriating and translating this experience-encounter, the task of devout reasoning. This is the stage at which doctrines and creeds come into being.

1. FAITH AND EXPLICATIONS OF FAITH

The Christian doctrine of the Trinity has gone through this process. In the first place came the original experience: the first disciples lived with Jesus, saw how he prayed, how he spoke of God, how he preached, how he treated people, particularly the poor, how he faced up to conflict, how he suffered and died and rose again; they also saw what happened in the community that believed in him, especially after Pentecost. With joy in their prayers and simplicity in their preaching, they proclaimed the Father, Son and Holy Spirit. Without wishing to multiply the divinity, since they all were rooted in Judaism, for which monotheism was a strict dogma, they called each of these God. Later, Christians began to think about this experience and to translate this proclamation into a formula. This gave rise to the classical expression of the doctrine of the Trinity: one God in three Persons, or one nature and three hypostases, or three Lovers and a single love, or three Subjects and a single substance, or three Uniques and one communion. What had happened? Doxology (praise) had changed into theology (reflection on God), and faith had made room for reason.

In this development, it is important to distinguish what is faith and what is explication of faith. So, saying that God is Father, Son and Holy Spirit is faith; saying that God is one nature and three Persons is an explication of faith. We welcome faith with open hearts; explications of faith can be debated and even rejected. Faith is response to divine revelation; explications of faith are the responses of reason to the questions raised by faith.

All explications of faith seek to shed light on faith so that it may become stronger and find more reasons to praise and proclaim. Explications of faith adopted by the church in its official pronouncements—from Councils, Synods and magisterial documents—are worthy of great respect. But they do not in themselves constitute faith. The act of faith, theologians have always taught, surpasses explications (formulas), reaching beyond what they seek to express without always succeeding in doing so. Any new explication of trinitarian faith should make faith more credible and acceptable, but it will do so only by taking on the whole truth present in accepted explications and going beyond them. Then what is new is not a distortion but something that can be recognized as a true expression of the treasure of faith, in which, as our Lord said, there is old and new (cf Matt. 13:52).

If, as may happen, new things come to be expressed through new explications, then they should be understood as attempts to articulate the same treasure in conjunction with the old (but not outdated) things, whose truth we willingly accept.

2. THE TRINITY AS A MYSTERY OF INCLUSION

The rationale for faith in the Trinity can better be seen when it is compared to monotheism and polytheism, in dialogue with unity and plurality. In monotheism we are faced with the solitude of One. However rich and full of life, intelligence and love this One may be, there can never be anyone else by its side. The One will be alone for all eternity. All other beings must be subordinate to and dependent on that One. Any sort of communion will be of unequals. In polytheism, as generally understood, we have to do with a plurality of divinities, of different degrees and natures, some good and some evil. The unity of the divinity disappears.

Each of these religious expressions contains an element of truth that should be recognized. There is a perception that there are both unity and diversity in the experience of the Mystery. Can there not be a unity in diversity? Can diversity not be a revelation of the richness of unity?

Faith in Father, Son and Holy Spirit—in the Trinity, that is— provides an answer to these questions. In our experience of the Mystery there is indeed diversity (Father, Son and Holy Spirit) and at the same time unity in this diversity, through the communion of the different Persons by which each is in the others, with the others, through the others and for the others. The Trinity is not something thought out to explain human problems. It is the revelation of God as God is, as Father, Son and Holy Spirit in eternal correlation, interpenetration, love and communion, which make them one sole God. The fact that God is triune means unity in diversity.

If God were one alone, there would be solitude and concentration in unity and oneness. If God were two, a duality, Father and Son only, there would be separation (one being distinct from the other) and exclusion (one not being the other). But God is *three,* a Trinity, and being *three* avoids solitude, overcomes separation and surpasses exclusion. The Trinity allows identity (the Father), difference of identity (the Son) and difference of difference (the Holy Spirit). Trinity prevents face-to-face confrontation between Father and Son in a "narcissistic" contemplation. The third figure is the difference, the openness, communion. Trinity is inclusive because it unites what separated and excluded (the Father-Son duality). Single and multiple, unity and diversity meet in the Trinity as circumscribed and reunited. "Three" here needs to be understood not so much as an arithmetical number as an affirmation that the name of God means differences that include, not exclude, each other; that are not opposed to each other, since they are set in communion; a distinction that makes for union. Through being an open reality, this triune God also includes other differences; so the created universe enters into communion with the divine.

3. GOD IS THE UNION OF THREE UNIQUES

How should we think of the unity of the Three? How, in the Christian faith, are Father, Son and Holy Spirit one sole God? Theology has provided two main explications.

The first starts with the Father. This is the way of the Greek Fathers. According to them, the Father is the source and origin of all divinity. He communicates his whole substance to the Son and the Holy Spirit. The Three are consubstantial and so one sole God. This view risks introducing a sort of theogony, that is, a genesis of God. The Father, who is uncaused, causes the Son and makes the Holy Spirit proceed from himself. It also holds the temptation to *subordinationism* (the Arian heresy): in this, the Son and the Holy Spirit would be subordinate to the Father; there would be an unequal hierarchy between the three Persons.

The second explication starts with the divine, spiritual nature. This is the way of the Latin Fathers. For them, God is above all an absolute Spirit who thinks and loves. So his supreme understanding of himself is called the Son, and his infinite love, the Holy Spirit. Or, God is the highest Good, which intrinsically expands. The complete self-surrender of himself is called the Son, and the relationship of love between Father and Son means the Holy Spirit, the thread of union between the two. This view does not entirely avoid the danger of theogony either. Surely it is applying the metaphysical principle of causality to God? Can one talk of begetting and "breathing-out" where all is eternal? Furthermore, it carries the risk of *modalism* (the heresy of Sabellius), according to which the very divine nature or absolute Spirit is manifested under three distinct modes and different embodiments, while ultimately retaining the oneness of the same absolute Spirit. Here we are left at the frontiers of pre-trinitarian monotheism.

I propose to try a third way, starting decisively from the Trinity, from Father, Son and Holy Spirit as revealed in the scriptures and as apparent from the historical actions of Jesus Christ. They co-exist simultaneously and the Three are co-eternal from the beginning. As we shall see in chapter 2, Father, Son and Holy Spirit do not emerge as separate or juxtaposed, but always mutually implied and related. Where is the unity of the Three found? In the communion between the three divine Persons. Communion means union with (*communio*). There can be unity only between persons, because only persons are intrinsically open to others, exist with others and are one for one another. Father, Son and Holy Spirit live in community because of the communion between them. Communion is the expression of love and life. Life and love, by their very nature, are dynamic and overflowing. So under the name of God we should always see Tri-unity, Trinity as union of Father, Son and Holy Spirit. In other words: trinitarian union is proper to the Trinity.

In this way, both the identical unity of the divine nature itself and the oneness of the absolute Spirit itself have a strictly trinitarian meaning: the permanent interpenetration, the eternal co-relatedness, the self-surrender of each Person to the others form the trinitarian union, the union of Persons. In order to express this union, theology, from the sixth century, embraced the Greek term *perichoresis* (each Person contains the other two, each one penetrates the others and is penetrated by them, one lives in the other and vice-versa), or the Latin *circumincessio* (*cessio* with a "c" meaning the active interpenetration of one with the others) or *circuminsessio* (*sessio* with an "s" meaning being statically or ecstatically in one another). I propose to keep the term *perichoresis* central to my reflections, using it as the structuring principle of my explication of trinitarian faith, keeping the original Greek word as there is no translation that expresses its meaning as well. In the Trinity, all is perichoretic: union, love, hypostatic relationships.

The basic reason for this choice is to be found in John 10:30: "The Father and I are one" (*hen*). Note that Jesus is not saying, "The Father and I are numerically one" (*heis*), but uses a term meaning "we are together" (Greek *hen,* as used again in v. 38: "The Father is in me and I am in the Father"). The union of Father and Son does not blot out the difference and individuality of each. Union rather supposes differentiation. Through love and through reciprocal communion they are one single thing, the one God-love. The Holy Spirit is also always together with them because it is the Spirit of the Son (Gal. 4:6; Rom. 8:9), because it reveals the Father to us in prayer (cf Rom. 8:16), because it comes "from the Father" (John 25:26), asked for by the Son (John 14:16).

This choice carries a risk of tritheism, but avoids it through perichoresis and through the eternal communion existing from the beginning between the three Persons. We are not to think that originally the Three existed on their own, separate from the others, coming only later into communion and perichoretic relationship. Such a picture is false and makes their union a later result, an outcome of communion. No, the Persons are intrinsically and from all eternity bound up with each other. They have always co-existed, never existed apart from one another.

This union-communion-perichoresis opens outwards: invites human beings and the whole universe to insert themselves in the divine life: "May they be one in us . . . that they may be one as we are one" (*hen:* John 17:21-2).

Because of its perichoresis and communion, everything in the Trinity is triadic. Each Person acts in union with the others, even when we consider actions belonging to one or attributed to one: creation by the Father, the incarnation of the Son, the coming of the Spirit. The Father creates through the Son in the inspiration of the Spirit. The Son, sent by the Father, becomes flesh by virtue of the life-giving Spirit. The Spirit comes upon Mary and fills the life of the just, sent by the Father at the request of the Son.

Using the descriptive terminology of tradition, we should say: the Father "begets" the Son in the bosom of the Spirit (*Filius a Patre Spirituque*), or the Father "breathes out" the Spirit together with the Son (*Spiritus a Patre Filioque*), or the Spirit reveals the Father through the Son, or the Son loves the Father in the Spirit, or the Son and the Spirit see each other in the Father, and so forth. In this way we should have a trinitarian equilibrium since all is triadic and perichoretically implied; all is shared, circulated, reciprocally received, united through communion.

This understanding of the mystery of the Trinity is extremely rich in suggestion in the context of oppression and desire for liberation. The oppressed struggle for participation at all levels of life, for a just and egalitarian sharing while respecting the differences between persons and groups; they seek communion with other cultures and other values, and with God as the ultimate meaning of history and of their own hearts. As these realities are withheld from them in history, they feel obliged to undertake a process of liberation that seeks to enlarge the space for participation and communion available to them. For those who have faith, the trinitarian communion between the divine Three, the union between them in love and vital interpenetration, can serve as a source of inspiration, as a utopian goal that generates models of successively diminishing differences. This is one of the reasons why I am taking the concept of perichoresis as the structural axis of these thoughts. It speaks to the oppressed in their quest and struggle for integral liberation. The community of Father, Son and Holy Spirit becomes the prototype of the human community dreamed of by those who wish to improve society and build it in such a way as to make it into the image and likeness of the Trinity.

4. WORDS HIDE MORE THAN THEY REVEAL

Faced with the ineffable Mystery, theology suffers from the acknowledged inadequacy of our human concepts and expressions. Applied to the Trinity, our terminology can have only analogical and indicative meaning; our words hide more than they reveal, however much what is revealed corresponds to the reality of the divinity.

The very expressions Father, Son and Holy Breath (Spirit), as they appear in the scriptures and in the subsequent two thousand years of theological reflection, suggest certain relationships. Hence the explications of faith in terms of "procession" of Persons: the Father *without origin,* the Son *begotten* and the Breath (Spirit) *breathed out.* These expressions, seemingly naturally, allow the principle of causality (on the Father's part) and of causal dependence (on the part of the Son and the Holy Spirit) to enter into trinitarian thought. It is difficult to combine this language with the other sort also employed by the Councils, in which none in the Trinity is earlier or later, greater or lesser, superior or inferior (cf DS 75, 569, 618, etc.); in which the divine Three are rather co-eternal (DS 616-18, 790, 800, 853) and equally immense and omnipotent (DS 325, 529, 680, 790). We need therefore to use expressions suggestive of "procession" with great care, conscious all the time that they are descriptive terms aimed at expressing the interrelationship of the Persons and also at safeguarding the differences between them. Following tradition and the magisterium, I shall use them here, but always with this basic reservation. They do have the advantage of being highly expressive of processes of life, of love, of self-communication, of union of differences.

The word "person" applied to Father, Son and Holy Spirit requires the same reservations. We use the same word for three different realities, giving the erroneous impression that they are homogenous and equivalent. This collective term (person) can express only what is common to them; whereas here our task is rather to express what is proper to each and distinct in each. So logically, we should use one word for the Father, another for the Son and another for the Holy Spirit, since each of them is unique. Yet I shall continue to use the term "persons" applied to all three, as tradition and the whole of theology have done, because there is no better alternative.

The same problem applies to the term "divine nature." It is said that this is the same in all three divine Persons, but attributed differently to the Father, the Son and the Holy Spirit. This can easily be understood modalistically; we would then be stuck in monotheism and not be expressing faith in the Trinity; or we would be running the risk of hierarchizing the three Persons and introducing inadmissible subordinations and inequalities into the Trinity. Excessive stress on the unity of essence, as found in many Western writers, can render the Trinity superfluous or deprive it of its saving meaning in history. The Trinity is a mystery communicated to us for our salvation, so that by penetrating, however little, into divine reality, we should be set free and have a part in eternal life. If we understand the divine nature, as I shall do throughout this book, as the eternal perichoresis of the Persons of the Trinity, as the love and communion intrinsic to the divine beings, then it will become easier to understand the unity which this nature guarantees: it will always be a trinitarian concept, the union of Persons bound up one with the others in eternal communion. God is one and is never alone: God is always the living-together and co-existence of Father, Son and Holy Spirit, all three existing from the beginning, revealing each other, knowing one another and communicating themselves from the beginning.

5. THE TRINITY REQUIRES SILENT ADORATION

I have now said at the outset what would be better left to the end. Faced with the awesome mystery of trinitarian communion, we should be silent. But we can be silent only after trying to speak as adequately as possible of that reality which no human words can properly express. Let us be silent at the end and not at the beginning. Only at the end is silence worthy and holy. At the beginning it would be prejudicial and irreverent.

CHAPTER I

In the Beginning Is Communion

By the name of God, Christian faith expresses the Father, the Son and the Holy Spirit in eternal correlation, interpenetration and love, to the extent that they form one God. Their unity signifies the communion of the divine Persons. Therefore, in the beginning there is not the solitude of One, but the communion of three divine Persons.

What relationship does the Trinity as understood by Christians bear to the God experienced in the history of humankind? Does it serve to confirm what we already knew, or does it bring us something new? We have to say that, in an ontological sense, it serves to confirm and amplify what we already knew; on the level of understanding, however, it brings something different.

On an ontological level (which refers to the reality in itself), the Trinity, Father, Son and Holy Spirit, is no different from what those who seek with a sincere heart have always sought and found. Whenever people have met with mystery, with absolute meaning, with something of decisive importance in their lives, they have come into contact with the true God. This true God exists as communion of Father, Son and Holy Spirit. The names can vary, but they all indicate the same reality. It may be that they have had no consciousness of God as God, let alone of a Trinity of Persons as a union of the divine Three. But this does not mean that what they have experienced is any less the triune and true God, merely that this trinitarian reality has not entered their understanding.

It is on the level of understanding that the Christian faith brings something new and different. It shows us God revealed as Father, Son and Holy Spirit. This revelation took place through the life of Jesus of Nazareth and through the manifestations of the Holy Spirit either in Jesus himself or in the community that formed around him (Pentecost). Not that there had been no previous communication of the Trinity to humanity. It had been communicated, because any true revelation of God's self must be trinitarian. But this dimension had not always been grasped by seekers after truth. Nevertheless, here and there, in the theologies of ancient Egypt, in Indian mysticism, in the works of certain great thinkers, there had been an affirmation of triads.[1] There had been intuitions that the divine mystery was a reality of communion with itself and with the universe. But it had not yet been given to men and women to verify the truth of what their intuitions, conscious and unconscious, had told them. This is where Christianity made its contribution. Through Jesus and his Spirit, humanity came to a full understanding of the perichoretic reality of God, that by the name God it should in the future understand the communion of Father, Son and Holy Spirit. What was new, and could not be deduced from any earlier principle, was this: the Persons of the Son and of the Holy Spirit had not just revealed themselves but communicated themselves in person. The God-Trinity, which had been present in human history, now through the Son and the Holy Spirit, sent by the Father, took on human history as its own and dwelt among us as in its own dwelling place. The task of theology is to try to deepen this understanding which has been handed to us.

There are three main motives for studying belief in the Trinity:

1. We need to enquire, reverently, what God is actually like. Those who feel themselves to be God's friends feel the urge to understand the mystery of God. How, being three Persons-in-communion, does God form one sole God?

2. We want to come closer to the two divine self-communications, the Son and the Holy Spirit. We have been visited by the Persons of the Son and the Holy Spirit, who took on the specific forms of Jesus (the Son) and Mary (the Holy Spirit, as I would see it). Our masculine and feminine natures are now inserted in the mystery of trinitarian communion. How do we see our

vocations or the meaning of our lives in the framework of such a revelation?

3. Finally, we need to know what type of society accords with God's plan. The form of social organization we have at present cannot be pleasing to God, since most people have no place in it. There is little sharing, less communion, and a great weight of oppression placed on the poor. They are crying out for justice and organizing themselves to throw off their shackles and liberate their lives and their creativity, to bring goodwill to all. Fromwhere do oppressed believers derive their inspiration, what guides their utopic dreams, where do they see historical embodiments of a better society?

This is where faith in the Holy Trinity, in the mystery of perichoresis, of the trinitarian communion and divine society, takes on a special resonance, since the Trinity can be seen as a model for any just, egalitarian (while respecting differences) social organization. On the basis of their faith in the triune God, Christians postulate a society that can be the image and likeness of the Trinity. Faith in the Trinity of Persons, Father, Son and Holy Spirit, can be seen to offer a response to the great quest for participation, equality and communion that fires the understanding of the oppressed. Both on the lowest levels of society and in the church there is a rejection of the exclusive type of society under which we all suffer to a greater or lesser extent.

1. TRINITY, SOCIETY AND LIBERATION

Let us look in more detail at the challenges posed by society to faith in the Holy Trinity, and to the contribution this faith can make to the process of liberation.

All societies in Latin America, and most throughout the Third World, have lived under the stigma of dependence, first on the imperial colonial powers, then on expansionist European capitalism, and now on multinational capitalism. Throughout the world, we are all living through a phase of development characterized by a deep dualism: on one side it produces a great abundance of goods, which are appropriated by already developed countries or by the ruling classes in underdeveloped countries; on the other, it imposes poverty and deprivation on the already poor countries. Development and underdevelopment are, in truth, two sides of the same coin. Both are produced by the same world-wide system of capitalist structures, which produces major inequalities in every sphere. In the Third World, we are held in underdevelopment by a capitalism which itself depends on that of the developed countries, is strongly linked to that, and excludes most of the population.

Dependence operates on every social level: in the economic order and in the social division of labour; in the socio-cultural climate, the political sphere and the religious field. The consequences visible to the naked eye are the great divisions between social classes, with conflicts of interest that continually generate open class struggles and social unrest. The rich minority becomes steadily richer at the expense of the increasingly poor majority.

The poor have many faces, as was expressively proclaimed by the bishops of Latin America meeting at Puebla, Mexico, in 1979, and in their faces we "ought to recognize the suffering features of Christ": segregated blacks, despised Indian tribes, repressed women, the poor exploited by socio-economic mechanisms, peasants, old people. . . .

Christianity has had an ambiguous presence in this contradictory process. We should not expect it to be otherwise; each group has appropriated the Christian message in the way most suited to it. The ruling classes gave it a spiritual and reductionist twist so as to be able to keep and strengthen their hold; the middle classes swayed with the tide of history: they embraced a progressive Christianity that favoured their class interests when they were in the ascendancy, and one that took on overtones of liberation when they were threatened with impoverishment. The oppressed classes have had to undergo a powerful process of indoctrination with the religious values of the ruling classes and so, contrary to their wishes, have had to experience a devotional Christianity cut off from any dimension of justice. At the same time, they have worked out their own codification of the message in terms of resistance and liberation, more in keeping with their desires. The church, or at least some of those in it, has from the beginning of colonial times denounced violations of the rights of ethnic minorities, and has undoubtedly been a factor working for better conditions of life for them. Today more than ever, it is carrying out its social mission in terms of liberation, not of conservation of the *status quo*. It is fighting for radical changes. The oppressed know they have an ally and a defender in the church. The rise of liberation theology became possible only because of the liberating pastoral mission of those churches that took the preferential option for the poor seriously.

Historical liberation, the expression in time of full salvation in God, finds practical expression in participation by the many, at all levels of social life, in the advancement of human dignity, in creating the maximum of opportunity for everyone. It will be integral and truly human if it furthers communion with God, helps to form an understanding of divine filiation and of being brothers and sisters throughout the world. This understanding takes shape in the church community of those who follow Jesus; from there it opens out to all the values humanity has produced in its encounter with God, or has created through its work, intelligence and skill.

A society structured on these lines could be the sacrament of the Trinity. It would help us in understanding the communion of the Trinity. But as long as the present social inequalities remain, faith in the Trinity will mean criticism of all injustices and a source of inspiration for basic changes.[2] If faith in the Holy Trinity is to be able to unleash its liberating potential we need to overcome certain distortions of this faith which have become embedded in the piety of the faithful and in the understanding of theologians.

The next section deals with this problem in more detail.

2. DISINTEGRATED UNDERSTANDING OF THE THREE DIVINE PERSONS

A disunited society affects our understanding of faith; it cannot create favourable conditions for an integrated expression of the mystery of the Trinity.[3]

In colonial and agrarian societies, such as exist in Latin America and many other parts of the world, the figure of the father is central and forms one of the axes around which society and culture are organized. It is the father who has knowledge and power and makes the decisions. Other members of the family are dependent on him, and are seen as lesser beings subject to him. Paternalism is the model for relationships in the family and in society at large. Paternalism makes people objects of help, never subjects of auton-omous action. That type of help maintains dependence and impedes development of personal and social freedoms.

This type of patriarchal and patrimonialist (on the political level) society projects an image of God that suits it, since it buttresses its existence and legitimizes its behaviour. God is represented as the almighty Father, supreme Judge and absolute Lord of life and death. Besides this God there is really no room for a Son and Holy Spirit with whom he would be in communion. Jesus himself appears as "my Father" or "Father of great power," as he is represented in so many baroque churches in Spain and Latin America. Human beings are made to feel servants rather than children, submissive servants who have to conform to the will of their Father in heaven. A religion of the Father alone is dominant, and the relationship is a vertical one.

In more modern and democratic environments, characterized by horizontal relationships, emphasis is placed on the figure of the "leader" of political parties or social movements. Personal endeavour is highly valued and charismatic figures become sources of guidance and inspiration. The extreme expression of this has been seen in the rise of fascism, with its *duce, Führer* or *caudillo,* projected as "big brother," "guide" or "companion." This context gives rise to another image of God, this time identified with the figure of Christ. In several Christian societies, especially in recent movements within Christianity, Christ is proclaimed "Brother" or "Chief." This goes with a markedly emotional, juvenile piety, full of enthusiasm for the "leader" Jesus of Nazareth. Following Christ here means adopting his heroic and humanitarian attitudes, generally dissociated from human conflict and from any deep relationship with transcendence (the Father), from which Jesus in fact derived his commitment to the Kingdom and the humble of the earth. This is religion of the Son alone, and its relationship is horizontal.

Finally, there are large sectors of society, among the well-off and the poor, in which the dimensions of subjectivity and personal creativity are over-valued. This is particularly true of charismatic groups. People from the middle and upper classes, who enjoy the benefits of an individualistic social system working in their favour, tend to find that the Christian charismatic movement, with its inward-looking spirituality, satisfies their religious needs for inner peace, for resolving conflicts, for not feeling alone. Members of the poor and oppressed classes, denied any participation in society, find that charismatic sects and religious renewal movements can provide them with means of expressing their needs for freedom, respect and recognition. We then find the confusing gamut of religious experiences, sects and movements whose dominant feature is the expression of human subjectivity and individuality, expressed in "witnessing": "God enlightened me . . . ," "God gave me these words of wisdom . . . ," "the Spirit led me" and so on. The extreme forms of this charismatic, inward-looking religion are fanaticism and anarchy. This is religion of the Spirit alone and its main relationship is with the inner self.

These three forms of religious expression indicate lack of cohesion in society and, consequently, lack of cohesion in experiencing the Christian God as a Trinity. The verticality (of the Father), horizontality (of the Son) and interiority (of the Spirit) cannot co-exist in understanding, but are juxtaposed. This can give rise to pathological expressions of a principle in itself true.

A Christianity too much focused on the Father without communion with the Son or interiorization of the Spirit can give rise to an oppressive image of God as terrifying mystery, whose designs seem unforeseeable and absolutely hidden. A Christianity fixated on the Son without reference to the Father and union with the Spirit can lead to self-sufficiency and authoritarianism in its leaders and pastors. Finally, a Christianity excessively based on the Spirit without links to the Son and his ultimate reference to the Father can favour anarchism and lack of concern.

A society cannot organize itself on the basis of oppression by the normative (the image of the Father alone), nor of domination by its leaders (the figure of the Son alone), nor of the anarchy and insensitivity of its "creative spirits" (the figure of the Holy Spirit alone). No individual or society can subsist without upward reference and without memory of its origins (the Father); in the same way no one (in personal or social terms) lives without cultivating sideways relationship and solidarity (the Son); finally there is no person or society that can organize life without respecting the personal dimension and without cultivating the inner regions (the Holy Spirit) where creativity comes from and where the dreams that can transform history are worked out.

Individuals need to remain always within a network of relationships, and society needs to be a conjuncture of relationships of communion and participation. Only in this way can both avoid pathologies. The disintegration of trinitarian understanding is due to our losing the memory of the essential perspective of the triune God: the *communion* between the divine Persons. Upwards, outwards and inwards must co-exist and so open the way for us to achieve a right representation of the Christian God. In other words, the Father is always in the Son and the Holy Spirit. The Son is interiorized in the Father and in the Spirit. The Spirit unites the Father and the Son and is totally united to them. Finally, the whole Trinity contains creation in itself. Communion is the first and last word about the mystery of the Trinity. Translating this truth of faith into social terms, we can say: "the Trinity is our true social programme."

3. DIFFICULTIES INHERENT IN MONOTHEISTIC FAITH

There are huge difficulties in the way of really holding this concept of Trinity-communion, stemming from the predominance of belief in a single God and Lord. The weight of monotheism, that is, of proclaiming the unity and oneness of God, is so great because it is rooted in both the historical-social order (the centralization characteristic of the modern age) and in the religious order (the organization of churches on the principle of authority), and these two roots continually feed it. We need to go a little deeper into this aspect, since it throws up formidable obstacles in the way of the process of liberation based on faith.[4]

(a) The Judaic Inheritance

At the outset, Christianity inherited the great *Judaic tradition,* which was also that of Jesus. The central tenet of the Old Testament and of historical Judaism consists of the affirmation of faith in Yahweh as the one and only true and living God. This affirmation has always been sealed with the blood of martyrs. How then can we maintain a triad beside or together with this oneness of God? It has always been maintained that God is absolutely whole, without division or multiplication. If this were not so, there would be a multiplicity of gods and we would be back in polytheism.

Christian faith in the Trinity has to assimilate, in a proper fashion, the faith of our fathers in faith—Abraham, Isaac, Jacob, Moses and all the prophets and teachers. When we speak of a trinity, we are not multiplying God. However, we are not just affirming the oneness of God; rather we are insisting on the unity of the three divine Persons. We seek to say that this unity is produced within an absolute communion.

Furthermore, early Christianity had to face the full panoply of the Greco-Roman pantheon. Nothing could be better fitted to oppose *polytheism* than the profession of monotheism. Professing a trinity, without a proper understanding of its unifying communion, still meant holding to a sort of polytheism. The many gods would be reduced to the three, those of the Trinity. This would still have left polytheism essentially intact. Apologetic and pastoral pressures argued for insistence on a strictly monotheistic approach in the face of the prevailing polytheism, but this stress on monotheism in fact led to a weakening of Christian understanding of the originality of a triune God. The most immediate consequence of this was that most theological accounts of the Holy Trinity started from the idea of one God in order to arrive at the notion of the triune God. Monotheism remained the matrix from which the doctrine of the Trinity was struck. Should it not have been the other way round? After all, the only God who really exists is called Father, Son and Holy Spirit.

(b) The Greek Inheritance

Then Christian thought inherited the great structure of *Greek architectonic thought*. Both classical and modern (think of Einstein) thinkers have been deeply impressed with the harmony and order of the universe. The undeniable reasonableness of everything demands the existence of the supreme Intelligence; the multiplicity of causes requires an ultimate Cause; numberless beings suppose an absolute Being. Proposing the existence of a Supreme Being means that it will be present in all beings, shining through them and being revealed in them. Therefore, the Greeks saw the whole of reality as making up the great sacrament of the ineffable presence of the Supreme Being. God is this Supreme Being, the ultimate Cause, the infinite Substance. Unlike the world, which is changeable, God is immutable; unlike beings who are mortal, God is immortal; unlike events which are fleeting, God is necessary. Everything, in the hierarchy of beings, leads to the end point of untransferable convergence: the many lead to the One and everything derives from the One. In this way the whole order of being is presided over by the monarchy of the one Supreme Being.

This philosophical stream of thought fed into and strengthened the Old Testament belief in the oneness of Yahweh-God. Christian theologians, especially the great scholastics (Thomas Aquinas, Bonaventure, Albertus Magnus), incorporated this impressive Greek philosophical construct into their summas. It is no coincidence that, from St Thomas onwards, Western theology has dealt first with the one God and only after that with the triune God. It thereby systematizes both the Old Testament tradition and the Greek philosophical tradition in the Christian novelty of God the Trinity.

It is, however, possible to criticize this philosophical approach as failing to take account of the whole of reality. It starts with an inconclusive appreciation of the harmony and order of creation. But reality has another face as well: it includes disorder, absurdities inaccessible to reasonable analysis, violence, conflict, sin. The cry of innocent Job and the sorrowing of fallen Adam cannot be forgotten. How can one think of God as Supreme Being and ultimate Cause from the depths of the experience of suffering?

This question forced Christian thinkers who followed this approach to work out a theodicy, to justify God in the face of the harsh reality of suffering, especially that of innocent people. How can one simultaneously maintain the two affirmations: of the goodness of God and of the evil of parts of the world? However many reasons one can think of, suffering is not suppressed, nor evil put right. Affirming the goodness of God does not make the open wound stop bleeding. Denying the existence of God because of the absurdities manifest in the world does not solve the problem either, since without God suffering goes on, worse because there is no hope.

The Book of Job offers a possible way out: faith in God leads to protest against suffering and a commitment to fight for its eradication through the practice of solidarity. The theology of the Suffering Servant in the Old Testament shows that God is not indifferent to the suffering of God's children. God even took it on and redeemed it.[5]

(c) The Inheritance of Modern Thought

This question has been thoroughly debated in modern thought, which has tended to reinforce the persistence of an a-trinitarian monotheism. We say: the world is not as it should be, but human effort can put it to rights. The point of departure for thinking about God is not so much the world as human beings in their actions. The word "God" takes on meaning as a result of human enquiry into the depths of personality and the mystery of existence. What is the ultimate meaning of action? That it defines human beings as persons and their spirit as freedom.

If human beings are seen as persons, then God is the absolute Person; if as spirits, then God becomes the infinite Spirit; if humanity is a mystery, then God is the ultimate Mystery. This supreme personality communicates itself, enters into dialogue with human beings and appears on the stage of human history. But this thought-process does not go beyond monotheism—the one and only unique Person, the unique and supreme Spirit. This tendency has been reinforced with the growing need to combat atheism, the systematic denial of an ultimate source, a meaning for meanings, an infinite understanding. The need to respond to atheism has led Christians to be more concerned with *one* God, on the basis of philosophical and anthropological arguments, than with witnessing to the Trinity as absolute communion of the three divine Persons.

It is not surprising, then, that Immanuel Kant should have written: "The doctrine of the Trinity provides nothing, absolutely nothing, of practical value, even if one claims to understand it; still less when one is convinced that it far surpasses our understanding. It costs the student nothing to accept that we adore three or ten persons in the divinity. One is the same as the other to him, since he has no concept of a God in different persons (hypostases). Furthermore, this distinction offers absolutely no guidance for his conduct."[6] This observation shows that the Trinity, for most people, has become a problem in logic and has ceased to be the mystery of our salvation. It has been reduced to a curiosity rather than being a reality that matters to us because it sheds light on our own existence

and tells us the ultimate structure of the universe and of human life:
communion and participation. And such an understanding has
consequences for social and personal behaviour, as we shall go on
to see.

4. POLITICAL DANGERS OF AN A-TRINITARIAN MONOTHEISM

If Kant could see no practical consequences stemming from the
mystery of the Trinity, others have shown the dangerous consequences, in the political and religious spheres, of a monotheism
detached from a trinitarian concept of God.[7] Strict monotheism
can justify totalitarianism and the concentration of power in one
person's hands, in politics and in religion. There is a strange dialectic at work here: authoritarian theories can lead to acceptance of a
rigid monotheism, just as theological visions of an a-trinitarian
monotheism can serve as an ideological underpinning of power
concentrated in one person: dictator, prince, monarch or religious
leader.

These consequences are not confined to the field of speculation.
In the early centuries of Christianity, there were those who worked
out correspondences such as these: just as Israel is the one people
mediating faith in the one God, so humanity, at present divided into
many nations and tongues, will return to being a single humanity
under the empire of a single political lord; just as there is one Lord
in heaven, so there should be one Lord on earth; just as there is only
one God, so one royal house and one monarchy should rule on
earth.[8] This is how the Christian emperors justified their absolute
rule.

In more modern times, absolute monarchs were justified like
this: the king enjoying absolute power is the image and likeness of
the absolute God. Just as God is above all laws (*"Deus legibus
solutus est"*), so the prince too is above all laws (*"princeps legibus
solutus est"*). So laws come to depend on the will of the sovereign,
not on truth and justice. Again, Christian absolute monarchs
found a theological justification.

This rigid understanding of monotheism led to excessive power
on one hand and submission on the other, to absolutism coupled
with dependence and slavery. The exercise of freedom as a collec-

tive endeavour was forbidden; the sovereign alone was free, the rest slaves. This type of ideology holding sway at the apex of society greatly delayed the spread of democracy to the bulk of the people, with results we are still suffering from today.[9]

A-trinitarian monotheism can also pave the way to an inflexible concept of *church unity* and a monopolistic view of sacred power. Just as there is only one head in heaven (God), so there should be only one head on earth to represent God, the pope. St Ignatius of Antioch (d. 104) argued for the unity of the church community as follows: one God, one Christ, one bishop, one local community. The function of the pope was understood as service to unity, but this unity was widely understood in monarchical, monotheistic terms: one church, one pope, one Christ, one God. At times the pope was seen as a visible God on earth, the *"Deus terrenus."*[10] Anyone who dared to break this mould of unity risked excommunication or had to submit completely. The corollary was that the pope enjoyed *suprema potestas* and was not subject to the laws of the church.

This concept produced a pyramidal model of the church, with power concentrated at the top (the hierarchy) and complete powerlessness for the rest (the laity). Unity conceived and structured in this way is not conducive to the emergence of a community of brothers and sisters in any real sense, or to a wholly ministerial church.

There is another political derivation of monotheism whose developments are still widely apparent in many cultures: patriarchalism and paternalism. The one God was represented as the great Patriarch, supreme Father and absolute Lord. The characteristics of absolute rulers in our cultures were attributed to him, in the family sphere (the domination of the father) and the social (the absolute role of the emperor or prince). In this way, the sociohistorical domination of fathers over their families, males over females, masculine attributes over feminine ones, found its theological-ideological justification in a one-sided representation of God. God was seen as Father only, and not also as Mother of infinite tenderness or eternal Father and Mother together. The exclusive attribution of the father-figure to God prevented women and men sharing the same integrating and humanizing religious experience.[11]

These political and religious distortions could be thoroughly corrected by a return to the triune God of Christians. The Trinity has important consequences, unsuspected by Kant, victim as he was of his one God, the postulate of logical reasoning. Dictators and tyrants could never draw arguments to legitimize their absolutism from the God-Trinity, because this is not the oneness of a single source, but the unity of three divine Persons, eternally involved in full communion, with no distinction between them on grounds of the prevalence of one over the others. This complete communion of three Persons, the full perichoresis of one in the others, for the others, by the others and with the others, destroys the figure of the one and only universal Monarch, the ideological underpinning of totalitarian power. Only a human community of brothers and sisters, built on relationships of communion and participation, can be a living symbol of the eternal Trinity.

In the same way, communion (Latin *communio,* Greek *koinō- nia*) is a far more adequate basis for understanding the inner structure of the church than *potestas sacra.* As a network of communities living in communion with their brothers/sisters and all participating in its benefits, the church can be built on the model of the Trinity and become its sacrament in history.

The unity of the church is built not so much on the sacred power placed in the hands of Peter and his successors as on the Trinity itself, as Jesus indicated in his final priestly prayer: "May they all be one. Father, may they be one in us, as you are in me and I am in you, so that the world may believe it was you who sent me" (John 17:21). Nowadays, the idea of communion and mutual insertion in a whole is gaining ground as a basis for dynamic and integrating unity. God is not a solitary power, but an infinite love opening out to create other companions in love.

A model of a truly liberated church, one that could serve as a principle for liberation, can be projected from the mystery of the communion between the three divine Persons. This would be a church, a community of brothers and sisters, gathered round the Son sent by the Father of all goodness for the purpose, in the dynamism of the Spirit, of bringing forward, deliberately and with full commitment, that Kingdom of God that is found wherever justice and freedom triumph in the personal and social spheres. Such a church, inspired by the communion of the Trinity, would be characterized by a more equitable sharing of sacred power, by dialogue, by openness to all the charisms granted to the members of the community, by the disappearance of all types of discrimination, especially those originating in patriarchalism and *machismo,* by its permanent search for a consensus to be built up through the organized participation of all its members.

5. THE INTEGRATING UNION OF THE THREE DIVINE PERSONS

If we are to escape from the impasse brought about by a strictly monotheistic concept of God, whether pre-trinitarian (as in ancient religions and Judaism) or a-trinitarian (not taking the Trinity of Persons into account), we need to get back to the Christian God, to Father, Son and Holy Spirit. The eternal Persons co-exist one within the others. A dynamic of life and love unites them in such a way that they form themselves into an integrating, full and complete union. This is the union of perichoresis (which we shall examine in more detail later), the unity proper to a Trinity of equally eternal, omnipotent and loving Persons. This unity is formed by the essential openness of one Person to another; or more, by the interpenetration of one by the others so that one cannot be separated from the others. This unity opens outwards, embracing the just, sinners seeking forgiveness and the whole universe. The trinitarian concept of God provides us with an overall understanding of the divine mystery. All human beings move in a triple dimension: of transcendence, immanence and transparence.

Through *transcendence* they reach up (or down), to their origins and ultimate references. The Father emerges from this undertaking, since he is the God of the unoriginated origin, of the unpredicated principle, of the source from which all things flow. He is their final reference.

Through *immanence* they meet themselves, the world that has to be organized, the society they have built vertically and horizontally. Immanence forms the space of human revelation. The Son is the revelation of the Father above all else; in his incarnation he took on the human condition as it is, in its grandeur and misery. He seeks a brotherly and sisterly (horizontal) society, but one that recognizes where it comes from (vertical).

Through *transparence* we seek to unite transcendence with immanence, the human world with the divine world, to the point where, while maintaining their difference, they become transparent to one another. We seek to experience God's gift through human effort; we long for new hearts and the transformation of the world. The Holy Spirit provides divine and human inspiration, transfiguring all things.

What would human beings be without the Father, without being rooted in something greater than themselves, without being bound up in a mystery of tenderness and welcome? Or what would they be without having the Son, without knowing where they came from, without every moment welcoming life as a gift, without being able to love the maternal Father or the paternal Mother? What would become of them without loving relationships, without being able to open up to another? Or without the Holy Spirit, without that life of the heart, that strength to be and to transform creation? Without the Spirit, we can neither believe in Jesus nor hand ourselves over in trust to the Father. Without the Trinity we wander vaguely through a dark and oppressive world, alone, without direction and without heart for the journey.

Just as transcendence, immanence and transparence form the dynamic unity of our existence, so, analogously, Father, Son and Holy Spirit are integrally united in full, reciprocal and essential communion. Every human person is an image of the Trinity; sin produces a break in this reality, but without destroying it totally. Human society has been eternally willed by God to be the sacrament of trinitarian communion in history; social or structural sin detracts from this vocation, which still persists, however, as a call to be heeded through the processes of liberation in history which seek to create conditions in which Father, Son and Holy Spirit can be signified in time.

CHAPTER II

How the Holy Trinity Was Revealed to Us

It has often—and rightly—been said that the mystery of the Trinity forms the heart of Christianity, since it concerns God as God is, as Father, Son and Holy Spirit. That being so, we would expect this basic truth to be clearly expressed in the documents on which our faith is grounded, the scriptures. In fact, the scriptures do not give us the terms used by the churches to express their faith, such as three Persons, one nature, proceeding, sending and so on. This does not mean that the scriptures do not give us a revelation of the Trinity: they do, fully, but in a different way. This obliges us to distinguish carefully between the *doctrine* of the Trinity and the *reality* of the Trinity.

1. DOCTRINE AND REALITY

Trinitarian doctrine is the systematic working out by human intelligence of the trans-subjective reality of the Trinity. Doctrine supposes revelation of the Trinity as Trinity and involves human endeavour to deepen understanding of the mystery. In this sense, trinitarian doctrine has its own long history, with various tendencies in it, which have produced an immense accumulation of reflections, deviations and definitions established by the community of faith over the centuries.

The reality of the Holy Trinity is independent of doctrines. The

Father, Son and Holy Spirit have always been present in the history of men and women, communicating their love, taking human endeavours into the divine communion of the three Persons. In other words, the reality of the Trinity is not just something expressed in doctrines or in phrases we might happen across in the scriptures. It is first and foremost a fact; only after this is it a doctrine about this fact. Because it is primarily a fact that has always been present in human life, at all stages of its evolution, we can talk of the emergence of an understanding of the Trinity in history, reaching its fullness in the New Testament.

So we find preparatory revelations of the trinitarian reality before the Christ event, both in the deeds and sayings recorded in the Old Testament, and in other world religions and historical events. The presence of the Trinity in history was gradually uncovered, through devout reflection, till Jesus Christ and the Holy Spirit revealed it to us fully, through entering into hypostatical relationship with us. The New Testament witnesses to the incarnational presence of Christ and the life-giving presence of the Spirit, both through the events themselves and the texts that show the meaning of these events.

2. THE TOUCH OF THE FATHER'S TWO HANDS: THE SON AND THE SPIRIT

Jesus Christ showed himself to be the Son of God the Father through his words, prayers, liberating actions, death and resurrection through the power of the Spirit. He revealed the Trinity to us. So did the Spirit, present in Mary, forming the holy humanity of Christ, coming down on Jesus at his baptism, making him the lasting bearer of the Spirit, filling the hearts of the Apostles with fire, showing us the Abba-Father and the mystery of the Son of God.

St Irenaeus (d. 208) described the Son and the Spirit as the two hands of the Father, touching us and moulding us to his image and likeness.[1] They were sent into the world to set up his tent amongst us, to take on our human condition in order to save us and bring us into the communion of the Trinity. Their sending is an absolute revelation of God, because it implies that the Son and the Spirit communicated themselves completely, without reservation. It brought about a new time for us and also for them. Listening to them, watching their actions and attending to their communications, we discover the dense presence of the three Persons of the Trinity. Without the infinite tenderness of the Father sending the Son in union with the Spirit, our ideas about the Trinity would be mere speculations or affirmations with no concrete basis for verification.

This fact was initially welcomed as it should be: in praise and joy in hearts opening out to give thanks and celebrate. So the *liturgy* became the first setting in which faith in the Trinity was expressed. Doxologies (prayers of praise and glory—the meaning of the Greek *doxa*), which we still use in our celebrations, are the earliest testimonies of the recognition of the Trinity in the faith of the believing communities. Everything proceeds from the Father through the Son in the Holy Spirit and is to be given back, in praise and thanksgiving, to the Father through the Son in the Holy Spirit.[2] St Justin, the first Christian philosopher (d. 167), tells us: "We . . . in everything we take as food, bless the Creator for all through his Son Jesus Christ and through the Holy Spirit."[3]

Sacramental practice, particularly of baptism and the eucharist, forms the second setting for professing faith in the Trinity. Matthew's Gospel already speaks of the early church's practice of baptizing "in the name of the Father, and of the Son and of the Holy Spirit" (28:19). The oldest eucharistic anaphoras, such as that in the *Tradition of the Apostles,* are equally trinitarian in expression. Baptismal and eucharistic practices led to the first insinuations of *professions of faith* in the truth of the Trinity. Paul concludes his second letter to the Corinthians with: "The grace of our Lord Jesus Christ, the love of God [the Father] and the fellowship of the Holy Spirit be with you all" (13:13).

The third setting in which the truth of the Trinity came to be fully understood was that of *theological reflection* on the nature of Christ and the Holy Spirit. By defining, after long and deep discussion, that Jesus who died and was raised again was the Son of God, of one nature with the Father, and also by defining that the Holy Spirit, Lord and giver of life, was of one nature with the Father and the Son, Christian thinkers of the fourth and fifth centuries effectively laid down a doctrinal formulation of the Christian God.

In this way, the Holy Trinity came to be seen as the underlying meaning of the saving visitation of the Father through his Son incarnate in Jesus Christ and through his Spirit who inspires his followers and the church. If we do not accept the Trinity in this way, it becomes totally impossible to proclaim what the faith of the Apostles and of all Christian centuries has professed of Jesus Christ and his Spirit, that they are truly God present in the flesh of our history, the emissaries of God the Father.

We need to look next in more detail at how the Trinity was revealed in the words of Jesus and the activity of the Spirit.[4] The rest of this chapter does not pretend to be an exhaustive study of the subject; it merely draws out the essentials.

3. JESUS, THE SON, REVEALS THE FATHER OF INFINITE GOODNESS

What Jesus told us about God is not an explanation of what other sources tell us. In answer to the common question: Who is God?, Jesus did not provide a doctrinal exposition. He shows *who* God is by showing *how* God acts.

(a) Political Symbolism: The God of the Kingdom

How does God act? In order to explain this, Jesus uses a figure of political symbolism. He speaks time and again of the Kingdom of God. God acts to build and bring about this Kingdom. "Kingdom" does not mean a territory but the way in which God acts, the means by which God makes himself Lord of all creation; it therefore refers to the exercise of God's power to liberate from everything that denies or rebels against God and to bring God's final plan to fruition: a life of sharing, solidarity and justice. This lordship of God will not resemble the rule of the satraps of ancient times or that of the absolute monarchs of more recent times, alone in their solitary exercise of power; it will be the feast at which all sit together to celebrate, the new city in which all are brothers and sisters, with God in the midst of these sons and daughters, serving them all. So images of communion and sharing describe the form God's rule will take.

Jesus sees himself as both proclaiming and bringing about this

Kingdom, as an essential part of it: "If I cast out devils by the finger of God, it is a sign that the Kingdom of God has certainly come amongst you" (Luke 6:20). Jesus' practice is what brings the Kingdom about because it consists of fellowship with the poor, reconciliation with sinners, sharing his life with all, particularly with outcasts, and service without discrimination to all he meets. This practice shows that the nature of God is communion and not the solitude of One: it is a pouring-out of life to those who feel most threatened, such as the sick and the poor. This communion is clearly shown in the relationship between Jesus and his God.

(b) Family Symbolism: **Abba,** *the Best and Kindest of Fathers*

The Gospels preserve the originality of Jesus' relationship to his God.[5] This is something extremely intimate and unique; thus Jesus describes God with a word drawn from the language of family relationships, *Abba,* a childish expression of affection for a father. Jesus invoked his Father in his prayers, nearly always made alone (see Mark 1:35; 6:46; 14:32-42; Luke 3:21; 5:16; 6:12; 9:28; 11:1).

This Father is revealed as being infinite in goodness, since he does not wait for men and women to seek him, but goes himself in search of sons and daughters, especially among the strayed and suffering. So, in Jesus' parables, he is presented as someone who "loves the ungrateful and the wicked" (Luke 6:35), the God of sinners and not of the just (Luke 15:7), who rejoices over the return of the prodigal son (Luke 15:11-32) and the finding of the lost drachma (Luke 15:8-10) and the lost sheep (Luke 15:4-7; Matt. 18:12-14). Of course he is also a kind Father to the children who obey him and stay at home with him (Luke 15:31); nevertheless, he shows himself especially merciful to the disinherited and lost, as best shown in the parable of the prodigal son.

Jesus' experience of intimacy with the "little Father" is not expressed in doctrine, but in practice. In imitation of his Father in heaven, he took the part of all those the world despises; they are to be the first to hear his message; our behaviour toward them will decide our fate at the last judgment (Matt. 25:31-46). Jesus both relates to this Father by praying to him, thereby pointing to a distance and difference between them, and acts for him in bringing about the Kingdom, thereby identifying himself with the Father.

All who pray to God as children to their Father are truly children of God (Matt. 11:25-7; Mark 12:1-9; 31:32). Jesus refers to himself as "the Son" to express the relationship he himself feels to the Father.

4. IN JESUS, THE ETERNAL SON MADE FLESH IS REVEALED

Rather than explicitly proclaiming himself Son, Jesus acted and lived as Son of God. He acted with an authority that set him in the sphere of the divine. This did not go unnoticed by the Jews, who finally condemned him not just because of changes he introduced in interpreting tradition and legal precepts, but because they realized that the supreme authority he took on was that which belonged to God. Jesus did not just represent God in the world; he made God visible and touchable in all God's goodness and mercy. He forgave sins, introduced new teachings going beyond the Law and tradition, things that belonged exclusively to God (Mark 2:28). The Jews were quite right in seeing that he "made himself God's equal" (John 5:18).

More than this, Jesus asked for faith in himself. It is true that this faith is bound up with stories of miracles and healings, but it was in just such situations that he showed, in time and space, exactly what is meant by being the Son of God. Those who benefitted from his liberating acts (the leper, the blind man, the woman with a haemorrhage, and others) realized that they were dealing with the personalized power of God, who heals and saves. Jesus acted as one who had the source of divine power within him. He did not ask the Father for the power to perform miracles, but acted miraculously as one who holds God's power. In his person and actions, what is impossible to creatures became possible to him (Mark 10:27).

Rather than looking for phrases in which Jesus shows his consciousness of being the Son (such as Matt. 11:25-7; Mark 12:1-9; 13:32), we should concentrate on his actions, which speak more generally and persuasively. So let us look at two passages which show Jesus' relationship of Son to his Father-God.

The first is Luke 10:21-2 (also in Matt. 11:25-7): "It was then that, filled with joy by the Holy Spirit, he said, 'I bless you, Father,

Lord of heaven and of earth, for hiding these things from the learned and the clever and revealing them to mere children. Yes, Father, for that is what it pleased you to do. Everything has been entrusted to me by my Father; and no one knows who the Son is except the Father, and who the Father is except the Son and those to whom the Son chooses to reveal him.' "

The first thing to note here is the presence of all three divine Persons. It is the Spirit who shows us the presence of the Son in the humble figure of Jesus of Nazareth. The Son, in turn, reveals the Father. It is through praise, not speculation, that we come to grasp this mystery. So the context in which this revelation of the blessed Trinity is given to us is a liturgical and doxological one. Here all, including the learned and clever, have to learn how to pray to God as children do, calling God "Father." They have to forget that they are learned and clever, because their learning and cleverness cannot grasp the communion of Three without multiplying God. Without devotion, reflection reduces the truth of faith and prevents access to its understanding; only those who make themselves like children can understand revelation.

"Everything has been entrusted to me by my Father": this "everything" needs to be taken in its strongest sense. First, the Son receives the Father's mission to install the Kingdom that is the Father's Kingdom. Then he receives full knowledge of who the Father is so that he can communicate it to others. Finally, what makes the Son be the Son is received from the Father. This is an indication that the Son is on the same level of reality as the Father.

"No one knows who the Son is except the Father, and who the Father is except the Son and those to whom the Son chooses to reveal him." This passage describes an exclusive knowledge; there is a secret mutual relationship between Father and Son which is not accessible to a third party. The Father is anterior to the Son; his knowledge of the Son stems from the fact of his having given the Son his origin. The Son receives everything from the Father, and only the Son is in a position to know the Father because he has received everything. Knowledge here does not just mean an intellectual process; more than anything else it is a recognition, a meeting of two intimacies and of two sides of the same process of communion and mutual surrender. So the Father can express his knowledge in the form of love: "This is my Son, the Beloved" (Matt. 3:17), and Jesus in turn can refer to "my Father and your Father" (John 20:17).

It is only the Son who can reveal the Father to others. He is the permanent and necessary road to the final mystery we call Father. From now on we cannot speak of the Father without first speaking of the Son. He alone can provide a true guide to how the Father acts and so to what he is. Therefore, in order to know the Father, we must see how the Son acts. His actions and words give us access to the Father. This is not an abstract and metaphysical approach; rather, in it the Father is revealed through a history, by way of a revealing gesture through the course of his Son's life among his sons and daughters. Yet we cannot believe in the Son purely in terms of profession of faith, devoid of ethical content. We discover Jesus as Son through following him. This discovery makes us love the person of the Son and also that of the Father to whom the Son constantly refers us. Ethic leads to ontology; following to believing. Jesus himself laid down this order for us: "Why do you call me, 'Lord, Lord' and not do what I say?" (Luke 6:46).

The second basic text belongs to the theology of St John, the apostle who saw more clearly than any other the secret of Jesus as Son of God: "The Father and I are one" (10:30); "May they all be one. Father, may they be one in us, as you are in me and I am in you, so that the world may believe it was you who sent me" (17:21). The text of 10:30 does not use the Greek *heis,* meaning "the same person," but *hen*, meaning "one and the same thing," i.e. sharing one reality of communion. This communion is brought out better in 17:21, where it is expressed as one being "in" the other; each is itself, not the other, but so open to the other and in the other that they form one entity, i.e. they are God. It has been the task of theology to give deeper, trinitarian expression to this affirmation, a task carried out intensively from the third to fifth centuries, and continuing down to our day.

5. THE HOLY SPIRIT IS REVEALED IN JESUS' LIFE AND WORKS

More than in his words, it is in Jesus' actions and his liberating practice that the Holy Spirit is revealed. His own references to the

Spirit are few (see Mark 3:28-30; John 14:16ff), but this does not mean that the reality of the Spirit is not made plain throughout.[6] The Gospels, Luke in particular, do not show him as a charismatic occasionally possessed by the Spirit. The very incarnation of the Son is presented as the work of the Spirit (Luke 1:35; Matt. 1:20), so Jesus is full of the Holy Spirit from the start. The Spirit comes down on him when he is baptised by John in the Jordan (Mark 1:9-11; Luke 3:21-2; John 1:32-3); he launches his messianic programme with the quote "the spirit of the Lord has been given to me" (Luke 4:18). He is "led by the Spirit" into the wilderness to be tempted, and returns to Galilee "with the power of the Spirit in him" (Luke 4:1, 14). The Spirit provides the "power" (*dynamis*) and "authority" (*exousia*) with which he performs his liberating miracles and works (Mark 3:20-30). He explicitly states: "If it is through the Spirit of God that I cast devils out, then know that the kingdom of God has overtaken you" (Matt. 12:28).

This power of the Spirit in Jesus springs forth in a way that leaves even him surprised, as in the case of the woman with a haemorrhage: "Immediately aware that power had gone out from him . . . " (Mark 5:30). It is the power in Jesus yet at the same time different from Jesus, that the apostolic community was to call the presence of the Holy Spirit. This presence of the Spirit was evident in the resurrection event; there the bodily Jesus was totally transfigured by the power of the Spirit. In Pauline language, he became a spiritual body, that is, a reality that has taken on the characteristics of Spirit, which implies the fullness of divine life (see 1 Cor. 15:45).

So we can say, to sum up, that Jesus reveals a God-Father through this God-Father bringing about his Kingdom, showing his mercy and setting men and women free. He reveals himself as Son by, in the name of the Father, giving a start to the Kingdom in history, a Kingdom of freedom, of communion with outcasts and full confidence in the Father. In this task he also shows the liberating action of the Spirit, castigated by his enemies as the work of Beelzebub (Mark 3:22), the work of the unclean spirit and not of the Holy Spirit. The Trinity cannot be understood outside this liberating context; it is not a theological curiosity with its own intrinsic interest; it is always a reality of communion which redeems us, sets us free and gives us back our humanity enriched and full.[7] So the Trinity is a saving mystery, revealed for our salvation.

6. THE SPIRIT REVEALS THE SON AND THE FATHER

The Spirit is the second of the hands which the Father reaches out to save us. Like the Son, it has set up its tent in our midst, first in Mary at the time of Jesus' conception (Luke 1:35: "The Holy Spirit will come upon you"), then in Jesus at his baptism, finally in the whole apostolic community grouped round Mary at Pentecost (Acts 2).

How do the actions of the Holy Spirit reveal the mystery of the Trinity? Both the Pauline and Johannine conceptions of the Spirit are complex and not always clear.[8] But both convey a master theme underlying the most varied expressions: the Spirit leads us to discover Jesus as Son of God and allows us to cry "Abba, Father."

In the first place, the Spirit is shown as God: throughout the course of revelation, the Spirit provides the activating *power* of God in history. In this sense, it signifies God acting, innovating, opening new paths in history together with men and women and creation. With few exceptions, the Spirit was always accepted as God, whereas Jesus was not so accepted.

So the work of the Spirit consists basically in revealing the Son to all and in working out the liberating action of the Son. We come to the Son through the Spirit, which is why it is rightly called the Spirit of Christ (Rom. 8:9) and also Spirit of the Lord (2 Cor. 3:17; Phil. l:19) and Spirit of his Son (Gal. 4:6). The Spirit provides as it were the setting in which the baptized meet the Son, forming one body with him (l Cor. 12:13). Consequently, the functions attributed to the Spirit are interchangeable with those of the Son. Both are present in the baptized (1 Cor. 1:30; 2 Cor. 5:7 and Rom. 8:9); both the Son and Spirit reside in the hearts of the faithful (Rom. 8:10; 2 Cor. 13:5; Gal. 2:20; Rom. 8:9; 1 Cor. 3:16). So the baptized are said to have been infused with the peace, charity, glory and life of both Spirit and Son.

The Spirit is also the one who "reaches the depths of everything, even the depths of God [the Father]. . . . The depths of God can only be known by the Spirit of God" (1 Cor. 2:11). The Spirit leads us to God whom we recognize as Father. The trinitarian theology of St John tells us why: because the Spirit comes "from the Father" (15:26), and the Father sends the Spirit at the request of the Son

(14:16). The Spirit gives us access to the Father because the Son sends the Spirit (16:8) on behalf of the Father (15:26).

The Spirit communicates no other truth besides that of the Son; it takes what is of Jesus and makes it known to us (John 16:14). Under its guidance and by its light the mystery of the Son of the Father becomes no longer a past event but always present as the experience of salvation for every generation.

In the New Testament evidence, the Spirit is shown as a divine Someone who acts personally, inspires, consoles, intercedes for us, teaches us the spirit of prayer, the feeling of being children of God, the experience of God as Father and the many charisms/services for the good of the whole community (see Rom. 8:9-11:27; Gal. 4:6; 1 Cor. 12:8, 11, etc.). As the exegete F. J. Schierse writes: "for him to be a 'person' in dogmatically accepted terms (a distinct individuality related to the other Persons), it suffices for the Spirit to designate a relatively different reality from the Father and the Son, but essentially equal to them."[9] This is what happens in all the New Testament evidence taken together: the Spirit is met together with the Father and the Son; and, historically, through the constant reiteration of the message of Jesus and the strength of his openness to the Father, the Spirit takes us deeper and deeper into the mystery of the Trinity.

7. TRIADIC FORMULAS IN THE NEW TESTAMENT: INDICATIONS OF UNDERSTANDING

There is still no *doctrine* of the Trinity in the New Testament. But there is evidence of a slow development of understanding that Jesus Christ, the Father and the Spirit are equally God. Indications of this understanding appear here and there in "triadic formulas."[10] These cannot be lumped together to provide comprehensive proof of revelation of the Trinity, but they nevertheless witness to the original experience of the community with reference to the reality of God. What emerges is the presence of a faith in the Trinity, as seen in doxologies and catechesis, particularly for baptism; these are the settings for these triadic formulas, the basis for a trinitarian reference to our Christian reading of God. Let us look at the main passages:

(a) Matthew 28:19

"Go, therefore, make disciples of all the nations; baptize them in the name of the Father and of the Son and of the Holy Spirit."

This baptismal formula is explicitly trinitarian; it is not found in any of the other Gospels and constitutes a peculiarity of Matthew. Scholars are virtually unanimous in declaring that the formula does not go back to the risen Christ. It represents the doctrinal crystallization of the community of the evangelist which had already reflected deeply on the meaning of the most important rite in the early church, baptism. At first, baptism was performed "in the name of Jesus Christ" (see Acts 8:16; 19:5; 1 Cor. 13:15). The name represents the person, so being baptized in the name of the Father, the Son and the Holy Spirit means introducing those who are baptized into the communion of these three Persons and entrusting them to their special protection. We know from the *Didache* and St Justin (our earliest witnesses) that a special catechesis on the Christian mystery was given before baptism. In this initiation process the catechumens learned that the Father sent his Son into the world and that the Spirit was poured into the hearts of the faithful. Paul sums up this early teaching in his letter to the Galatians: "You are, all of you, sons of God through faith in Christ Jesus. All baptized in Christ, you have all clothed yourselves in Christ. . . . The proof that you are sons is that God has sent the Spirit of his Son into our hearts: the Spirit that cries, 'Abba, Father' " (3:26-7; 4:6). Matthew's formula would certainly have been current in the communities for some years before being incorporated into the evangelical tradition and finding its present place in his Gospel. The early communities had no hesitation in putting such phrases into the mouth of the risen Christ, since they were convinced that he was present in their midst ("And know that I am with you always; yes, to the end of time"—Matt. 28:20), leading the faithful into greater understanding of his mystery. This understanding already supposed the divinity of the three Names, without yet reaching a doctrinal formulation of this conviction. But it is characteristic that by the year 85, about when Matthew's Gospel was written, his community would already possess a clearly trinitarian formulation of its faith.

(b) 2 Corinthians 13:13

"The grace of the Lord Jesus Christ, the love of God and the fellowship of the Holy Spirit be with you all."

This triadic formula, still widely used in the liturgy, undoubtedly had its place in the celebrations of the early church. Paul took it from there and, with minor variations, used it in his letters (see Rom. 16:20-21; 1 Cor. 16:23; 1 Thess. 5:28; 2 Thess. 3:18). Jesus Christ is referred to as "grace" because God's love is shown in him (see Rom. 5:7; 8:39), and, in biblical language, grace and love are synonymous; "the love of God" is the Father's part, since for Paul and the New Testament writers in general, God is always in the Father's place: this Father "so loved the world that he sent his only Son"; the "fellowship" of the Holy Spirit: the Spirit confers innumerable benefits on the community and also fellowship (communion) amongst them all for the good of all (see 1 Cor. 14:5). This formula looks forward to the doctrine of the Trinity, and its frequent use in the liturgy undoubtedly hastened the formulation of that doctrine.

(c) 2 Thessalonians 2:13-14

"But we feel that we must be continually thanking God for you, brothers whom the Lord loves, because God chose you from the beginning to be saved by the sanctifying Spirit and by faith in the truth. Through the Good News that we brought he called you to this so that we should share the glory of our Lord Jesus Christ."

These verses show how in Paul's mind everything is built around the three sources of grace and salvation: the Father, the Son and the Holy Spirit. We cannot call this a clearly trinitarian formulation, but it does express a thought in trinitarian form. Without this thought, trinitarian expressions, first in celebrations (doxologies) and then in theological reflection, could not have come into being.

(d) 1 Corinthians 12:4-6

"There is a variety of gifts but always the same Spirit; there are all sorts of services to be done, but always to the same Lord;

working in all sorts of different ways in different people, it is the same God who is working in all of them."

The context is ecclesial: Paul takes account of the profusion of services and ministries that grew in the community through its adherence to Christ, the Son of God, in the enthusiasm brought by the Spirit. It is impossible to speak of the life of the community without invoking the three living principles behind all Christian innovations: the Father, the Son and the Holy Spirit. In the same way it is impossible to speak of the manifestations of the Spirit without reference to Christ, whose Spirit he is, and to the Father, who encompasses all things. This is not overt trinitarian doctrine, but paves the way for its emergence in the future.

(e) Other Pauline Triadic Texts

There is a significant series of Pauline texts which, while not directly trinitarian in themselves, yet indicate trinitarian thought that was later to be developed into doctrine.[11] These texts are not just significant for what they are in themselves, but for the importance they had for later theological reflection, in the Fathers and others. Hermeneutically, the significance of a text lies not only in its contextual meaning but also in the practical and theoretic developments to which it gives rise. These are the principal such texts:

Galatians 3:11-14: "The Law will not justify anyone in the sight of God. . . . Christ redeemed us from the curse of the Law . . . so that through faith we might receive the promised Spirit."

Galatians 4:6: "The proof that you are sons is that God has sent the Spirit of his Son into our hearts: the Spirit that cries 'Abba, Father.' "

2 Corinthians 1:21-2: "It is God himself who assures us all, and you, of our standing in Christ, and has anointed us, marking us with his seal and giving us the pledge, the Spirit, that we carry in our hearts."

2 Corinthians 3:3: "It is plain that you are a letter from Christ, drawn up by us, and written not with ink but with the Spirit of the living God, not on stone tablets but on the tablets of your living hearts."

Romans 14:17-18: "The kingdom of God does not mean eating or drinking this or that, it means righteousness and peace and joy brought by the Holy Spirit. If you serve Christ in this way you will please God and be respected by men."

Romans 15:16: "He has appointed me as a priest of Jesus Christ, and I am to carry out my priestly duty by bringing the Good News from God to the pagans, and so make them acceptable as an offering, made holy by the Holy Spirit."

Romans 15:30: "I beg you, brothers, by our Lord Jesus Christ and the love of the Spirit, to help me through my dangers by praying to God for me."

Philippians 3:3: "We are the real people of the circumcision, we who worship in accordance with the Spirit of God; we have our own glory from Christ Jesus without having to rely on a physical operation."

Ephesians 2:18: "Through him [Christ] both of us [Jews and pagans] have in the one Spirit our way to come to the Father."

Ephesians 2:20-22: "You are part of a building that has the apostles and prophets for its foundations, and Christ Jesus himself for its main cornerstone. As every structure is aligned on him, all grow into one holy temple in the Lord; and you too, in him, are being built into a house where God lives, in the Spirit."

Ephesians 3:14-17: "This, then, is what I pray, kneeling before the Father, from whom every family, whether spiritual or natural, takes its name: Out of his infinite glory, may he give you the power through his Spirit for your hidden self to grow strong, so that Christ may live in your hearts. . . ."

(f) Triadic Formulas in Other New Testament Writings

The triadic model is not confined to St Paul, but appears in other New Testament writings. There is no need to analyze them here, since their trinitarian content is slight. But they show the presence of a way of thinking that always associates the divine Three with the work of salvation. These are familiar texts such as Titus 3:4-6; 1 Peter 1:2; Jude 20:21; Revelation 1:4-5; Hebrews 6:4. In the third and fourth centuries, the Fathers translated the early experiences of faith, of celebration and of catechesis of New Testament communities into doctrines with definite expressions of the unity of nature and communion and trinity of three Persons in the mystery of the Christian God. This is not to suggest that what had been obscure in the New Testament became clear in patristic theology. Far from it: the mystery of the Trinity will always be obscure in any form of expression. But Christian thought must always work on these first suggestions of the awesome mystery of the Father, Son and Holy Spirit. The New Testament passages constitute the supreme revelation of the Mystery.

8. CHRISTIAN RE-READING OF THE OLD TESTAMENT: PREPARATION FOR REVELATION

On the basis of their trinitarian understanding, Christians can make their own specific reading of the past, of other world religions as well as of the Old Testament in order to discern traces of and preparation for the full revelation which came about with the Christ-event in the New Testament.

The presupposition is this: if the one true God is the Trinity of Persons, then any historical revelation of God implies a revelation of the Trinity. Such a revelation may not have been adequately understood as a revelation of the Trinity, but this does not remove its authenticity. This authenticity means that here and there intimations and vestiges appear, pointers to the tri-personal nature of the mystery of God.[12] Christian re-reading of the Old Testament in particular is based on this understanding.

The authors of the Old Testament conscientiously proclaim the oneness of God, based on their experience of God's saving work on behalf of Israel in history, which in turn shows God's creative action in the universe. Yet this monotheism is far from the rigidity of the "absolute Subject" of modern thought or the deist concept in which the ultimate principle of the universe is removed from the course of history and the destiny of creation. Yahweh is a God who reveals himself, makes an alliance with his people, frees the oppressed from their oppressions and raises hopes for a Kingdom of peace and freedom. This is a God of passions and an infinite love of humankind. In a word, Yahweh is essentially a living God, the Creator of life and protector of those who feel their lives threatened (see Ps. 42:3; 84:3; Jer. 10:10; 23:36; Deut. 6:27). Because God is living, God can be seen to develop, in ways that Christians regard as indications of revelation of God's tri-personal nature. The most impressive figure in this development is that of the "angel of Yahweh" who accompanies the people, helps the oppressed and shows God's wisdom and power (see Exod. 14:19; Gen. 16:7; 1 Kings 19:5; 2 Kings 1:3; 2 Sam. 14:20). Sometimes he appears distinct from God, sometimes identified with God (Gen. 31:11, 13; Exod. 3:24). The three men who appeared to Abraham at the Oak of Mamre in Genesis 18, and who had such an influence on patristic thought and trinitarian iconography (Rublev's famous fifteenth-century icon, for example), embody a mysterious reality, open to interrogation concerning the divine nature.[13]

In the later Old Testament writings there are three kinds of personification of Yahweh which are of great interest for foreshadowing trinitarian revelation in the New Testament. First, divine Wisdom is personified, at large in the world and humanity. In the Wisdom writings, "she" comes to take on a virtually autonomous existence: see Proverbs 1:20-23; 8; 9:1-6; Job 28; Ecclesiasticus 24; Wisdom 6:12-8:1. Associated with Wisdom there is also the personification of the Word of God (Ps. 119:89; 147:15ff; Wisd. 16:12). On one hand the Word reveals the sovereignty of God, who creates everything through the Word; on the other hand God shows himself to men and women as guidance, judgment, salvation, brought about through the power of the Word. Finally, the Old Testament hypostasizes the Spirit of God. Basically, the Spirit is God's power and presence in creation and history. This power is seen in creation, in political leaders, in the prophets, and most obviously in the Messiah, the privileged bearer of the Spirit (see Isa. 42:1-3; 61:1-2); there will come a time when all will possess the Spirit (Isa. 4:4-6), who will renew hearts (Ezek. 36:26-7), bring about a new creation (Ezek. 11:19; 18:31; 36:26; 37:1-14). It is through the Spirit that Yahweh is with his people. As New Testament faith was to put it: the Spirit will be set like a temple in the midst of the community of the faithful who are the true people of God.

What we have in these and other Old Testament insights does not amount to a revelation of God as three Persons. What they show is God growing closer to Israel, with no loss of transcendence, entering more and more into history and into the hearts of the faithful, into deeper self-communication to them. God's self-bestowal in this way is shown in the New Testament in the expressions of the Son and the Spirit sent by the Father for the life of the world. The

Old Testament has its own intrinsic value, since it is the witness to the historical revelation of God to Israel. But its inner dynamic is more complete if we read it on the basis of the final manifestation in Christ and the Spirit attested by the New Testament. Then we can join the theological prayer of St Epiphanius: "Unity is taught by Moses; the prophets proclaim duality; in the gospels we meet the Trinity."[14]

CHAPTER III

Efforts at Understanding the Truth of the Trinity

The foregoing shows that faith in the Trinity of Father, Son and Holy Spirit was originally an experience rather than a doctrine worked out by human intelligence. The faithful were baptized in the name of the Father and of the Son and of the Holy Spirit, as early witnesses testify; that witness is embodied in the last verses of Matthew's Gospel.

With baptism, usually administered to adults, went the profession of faith, regarded as a "rule of faith" since it expressed the basic framework by which the community was identified. It was also called the *redditio symboli,* "recitation of the symbol"—*symbol* here used in its technical religious sense of creed, the formulas in which the church sums up its faith. We know many of these ancient creeds:[1] one of the best known goes back to the second century and is no less than the baptismal profession of faith of the church of Rome. It is still recited by parents and godparents at baptisms today. It goes like this:

> I believe in God the *Father* almighty, creator of heaven and
>   earth,
> And in Jesus Christ, his only *Son* our Lord;
> Who was conceived by the Holy Spirit
>
> Born of the Virgin Mary, suffered under Pontius Pilate, was
> crucified, died and was buried; on the third day he rose

again from the dead, ascended into heaven, where he is seated at the right hand of God the Father almighty, from whence he will come to judge the living and the dead.

I believe in the *Holy Spirit,* the holy Catholic Church, the communion of saints, the forgiveness of sins, the resurrection of the dead and life everlasting. Amen (DS 12).

The trinitarian concept is obvious and deliberate. Yet till the third century, few worried about the problems underlying such formulations: how did the three Persons relate to biblical faith in the strict oneness of God? Are they simply juxtaposed? What sort of relationship exists between Father, Son and Holy Spirit? Is there a definite order in their relatedness? All this was celebrated, proclaimed and believed rather than thought out.

1. ERRONEOUS WAYS: STIMULI TO TRINITARIAN DOCTRINE

From the middle of the second century onwards, large numbers of educated Christians began to appear, particularly in Alexandria, which was then a great centre of study and debate.[2] These were well versed in the philosophies of the time: Platonism, neo-Platonism, Stoicism; they were acquainted with Gnosticism, perhaps Christianity's greatest rival at that time. Gnosticism taught a way of liberation based on knowledge of the mystery of our existence: where we come from, where we are going and our present situation. A syncretic amalgamation of all kinds of religious and philosophical elements, it appealed to the imagination and creative speculation.

The Christian intellectuals—Justin, Clement of Alexandria, Athenagoras, Origen and others—who breathed this atmosphere found themselves faced with two main tasks:

The first was to reflect on the faith they celebrated, in terms of its own problems, within the church. Reflection requires intellectual rigour; it asks: what exactly do we mean when we proclaim that the Father is God, the Son is God and the Holy Spirit is God? Exaltation in liturgy, and even verbal excesses in piety, can be tolerated, since when we pray we are not concerned with niceties of language. But as soon as we seek to know the truth about God, then theology emerges as a discipline of thought and form, its first concern being to express a clear concept in an exact term.

Reflection has to use the instruments proper to each culture. In this case, Christian intellectuals saw themselves as the heirs of the theoretical methods of Judaism and Greco-Roman culture. Into these frameworks they tried to fit, on a critical level, what their faith expressed on a spontaneous level. Prayer and celebration predominantly use images with a strong affective charge and their own power. So the images of Father, Son and Holy Spirit (wind or breath, by derivation) have a powerful effect on our imagination. They impose certain attitudes and bring together certain affective contents; this is the way in which we establish our relationship and encounter with God.

Reflection, through its own internal conceptual demands, dispenses with images. It introduces concepts with the minimum of affectivity and the maximum of intellectual understanding. It has a certain inevitable formalism, which is not the case with the experience of faith in the Trinity (in baptism, the liturgy, the eucharistic celebration), which embraces many images and a rich charge of symbolism. Reflection leaves all this affective richness behind and projects thought-patterns with reason and coherence. It does not need concrete examples, but remains on the abstract and even contemplative level. There is a certain price to be paid, it must be said, in terms of loss of devotional fervour and pressure for conversion, for the sake of greater clarity. Theological formulations of the Holy Trinity were to be characterized by heights of abstraction and conceptual formalism unprecedented in Western history. A trinitarian doctrine was emerging alongside faith in the Trinity, and this chapter will examine the main articulations of this doctrine.

The second task facing these Christian intellectuals was to confront problems arising outside the church. Serious objections were raised on three sides: by traditional Judaism, by Greek polytheism and philosophy, and by Gnosticism. All called on them to demonstrate the logic of the Christian way of referring to God as Father, Son and Holy Spirit. The Trinity had to be upheld and defended against Jewish monotheism, Greek polytheism,[3] the doctrine of emanations and mediations of neo-Platonism, and the theogonic speculations of the Gnostics. From being theologians, the Christian intellectuals had to become apologists.

The doctrine of the Trinity was forged from this double effort: theological (aimed within the church) and apologetic (aimed outside the church, against objections from the prevailing culture). It did not appear overnight, but was the outcome of many faltering steps, with innumerable disputes over terminology and the emergence of several heresies. Heresies are doctrines which do not allow faith to find itself in them or devotion to recognize itself in them, or formulations which contradict the normative data of the scriptures. They constitute a grave danger to faith; nevertheless, they also enable theology to move forward,[4] since their refutation requires careful study and a more precise deepening of faith itself. At times, it was heresies themselves that produced concepts which came to be embodied in orthodox teaching. The doctrine of the Trinity itself is an example of this, since some of its key words come from heretical sources. So the term *Triad* (Trinity) was first used by Theodotus, a monarchian heretic (affirming the absolute oneness = monarchy of God) in the middle of the second century. It was taken up by Theophilus of Antioch, a great second-century apologist, and so passed into the theological language of orthodoxy.[5] Tertullian (d. 220) took the technical expression *prolatio* (prolation) from Valentinian gnosis, to express the procession of the Son from the Father. And the key word of trinitarian doctrine, *homoousia* (one single nature), was taken from the Gnostics Ptolemy, Theodotus and Heraclion.[6]

Now we can go back to our question: is professing that Jesus is the Son of God, God made flesh, or proclaiming that the Holy Spirit is God, just an excess of devotion and so a rhetorical figure of exaltation, or does it really have an objective content? Is God really Father, Son and Holy Spirit, or are we dealing with an anthropological problem, a characteristic tendency of human thinking always to see its prime concerns in terms of three—God actually being one and only one, and appearing to be three only *to us*? All this had to be resolved by Christian thinkers of the second to fourth centuries. Let us look at three attempted solutions that were seen then as erroneous, but which still constitute major temptations to the way in which we represent the mystery of the Holy Trinity.

(a) Father, Son and Holy Spirit, Three Modes of Appearance of the Same God?—Modalism

Christians saw themselves as heirs of the Old Testament faith according to which God was one and unique and dwelt in inaccessible light. On the other hand, they called the dead and risen Christ God. How to reconcile these two propositions? Some Christian theologians in Rome—Noetus and Praxeas in the second century and Sabellius in the third—resolved the problem in this manner: God is indeed one and unique. He founded a cosmic monarchy, since he alone is Lord over all things. It is through him that kings reign and governors govern. So, in his communication through history, this one God showed himself through three modes of revelation (hence "modalism," as Harnack called this heresy in the last century). One and the same divinity appears under three aspects (*prosopa*) and dwells in our midst in three different manners (*idia perigraphē*), as Father, Son and Holy Spirit. The one God in the aspect of creator and lawgiver is called Father, in the aspect of redeemer is called Son, and in the aspect of sanctifier and giver of eternal life is called Spirit. So the one God would have three pseudonyms. God is indivisible; there is no communion of three Persons in God; there is the divine oneness projecting itself to us through three different modes. Given this understanding, can we calmly and devoutly go on calling Jesus God? Are Father, Son and Holy Spirit not three *words* to describe the same one divine reality? This means that modalists could equally say: the Father was incarnate, suffered and died on the cross (*patripassionismus*) as the Son was incarnate, suffered and died on the cross.

This interpretation strongly upholds the unity and oneness of God, but it does away with the Trinity, which becomes just a word, not a reality. It allows us to think of God without Christ and Christ without God. It does not advance beyond Judaism and fails to teach the Christian novelty of three divine Persons forming a unity of communion between themselves.

(b) The Father Is the Only God, So the Son and the Holy Spirit Are Subordinate Creatures—Subordinationism

The problem is the same: we proclaim our faith in one God and at the same time proclaim Jesus Christ as God in our devotions and liturgies. So, prudent veneration should be shown to Jesus Christ, but not to the point of equating him with God, since such an excess would destroy the true meaning of God. He can be *like* God (*homoiousios*), but never *equal* to God (*homoousios*). He is the first creature, the prototype of all creatures, but not God.

This is how some Christians thought, among them Paul of Samosathos, Bishop of Antioch in 260, and the theologian Arius (d. 336) in Alexandria. Furthermore, there are sayings of Jesus in the New Testament which openly suggest the subordination of the Son to the Father: John 14:28, "The Father is greater than I"; see also Matthew 19:16; Mark 10:17; Luke 18:18; Acts 2:36; 1 Corinthians 15:20-28; Philippians 2:5-11. To sustain the two current pious affirmations of the oneness of God and the divinity of Jesus, Arius had recourse to Platonist religious philosophy, very much alive in Alexandria. This held God to be an indecipherable and absolutely transcendent mystery, intrinsically unutterable and incommunicable. To make contact with the world, God made use of a mediator, who is the Word. This Word is not God, though it belongs to the sphere of the divine; it is the first of creatures and the exemplar of all creatures, despite the fact that John, in the first verse of his Gospel, identifies Jesus, Son of God, with the Word and states: "and the Word was God."

Arius and his disciples stressed the fact that Jesus was a most perfect human being, since in him the Word had pitched its tent, and he was filled with the Holy Spirit. He reached the pinnacle of human perfection, to the point where he deserved a divine name. The Father *adopted* him as his Son, but compared to the abyss of mystery that is the Father, the Son remains subordinate (*subordinationism,* because he was created or generated by the Father, or *adoptionist subordinationism,* since he deserved to be adopted by the Father). Jesus is seen as the creature most like the Father that one can conceive of, without yet reaching equality of nature with the Father. In this way, this tendency—still current today—tried to do justice to both devotional affirmations of the people of God: God keeps his oneness, with no equal at his side, and at the same time has a First-born, the height of perfection, divine in that he was adopted by God and chosen by him as mediator, saviour and only channel for human access to the mystery of the One.[7]

After much discussion, the Council of Nicaea (325) solemnly defined that Jesus Christ, Son of God, is "from the being (*ousia*) of the Father, God from God, Light from Light, true God from true God, begotten, not made, one in being (*homoousios*) with the

Father, through whom all things were made, those in heaven and those on earth" (DS 125, CF). This definition, binding on all Christians, set the course for Christian understanding of God. God could no longer be thought of as the solitude of the eternal One. The unity of God is something proper and specific, being made up of a unity of Persons ever interacting with each other. This is not simply a repetition of the Old Testament idea of unity; if Christianity has adopted biblical monotheism, it is within this unique communion of Persons, since only they exist as Father, Son and Holy Spirit. The Lordship of God no longer means a heavenly monarchy, with the political and religious consequences that derive from this. The Lordship of God is seen not in domination of one over others, but in communion of all with one another, in mutual giving and freedom.

(c) Father, Son and Holy Spirit as Three Gods—Tritheism

The victory over strict monotheism (pre- and a-trinitarian) and subordinationism, which was a victory for the faith of the people of God over the mystifying speculations of theologians,[8] left one way still open for a new error to creep in: tritheism. Tritheism proclaims three divine Persons, accepts the Father, Son and Holy Spirit, but as three independent and autonomous substances. It leaves out the relationship between them and communion as constitutive of a divine Person. So it leads to the Trinity being affirmed as faith in three gods. These three are added together, without any idea of one Unique, who cannot be added to, standing, as it were, behind them. The philosophical incongruity of the idea of the co-existence of three absolutes, three eternals, three creators, implicit in a profession of three gods, is not taken into account.

Faith in the Trinity affirms the objective existence of three Ones, Father, Son and Holy Spirit, but does not believe them separate and unrelated. Faith in the Trinity sees the Persons eternally related in an infinite communion. So we can say: the three Persons form one communion. Perichoresis (circumincession—the interpenetration of the Persons) is not added to the constitution of the divine Persons; it is at their origin, simultaneous with them and constitutive of them.

Tritheism persists in a hidden form whenever the unity of the three Persons is weakened, as in the teaching of Joachim of Fiore (d. 1202). According to him, the unity of the Persons results from the collective union between them by virtue of the love they bear each other, like the union between Christians in a church, or citizens making up a nation. This asserts the distinction between them, but fails to take adequate account of their essential perichoretic communion. The risk of tritheism is but a step away.[9]

These three errors do not belong just to the past; they can still be found in the thought and language of many of the faithful today, and even in those who exercise the ministry of the word in the church. It is possible to believe what is right, but express it erroneously. We often tend to speak of God like Jews or Muslim, taking no account of the revelation of the Trinity, which as Christians we must accept; or we speak of Father, Son and Holy Spirit, but in such a way that they seem to be three gods, with three consciousnesses, three wills and three intelligences distinct from each other and merely juxtaposed; or we refer to the Son and the Holy Spirit as though they were lesser realities, subordinate to the real God, who is then reduced to the Father.

2. THEOLOGIANS WHO CREATED TRINITARIAN LANGUAGE: ON THE RIGHT ROAD

Let us now look at some of the theologians who taught us to speak correctly about the divinity of Father, Son and Holy Spirit, avoiding the errors described above. They had to engage in a tremendous battle, not only of words and formulas, but also of political interests unrelated to theology. This goes to show that reflection is never divorced from life, but always involved in all dimensions of human meaning and existence.

(a) The Starting-point, the "Economic" Trinity: St Irenaeus

St Irenaeus is considered one of the greatest bishop-theologians of the early church. Bishop of Lyon, he was born c. 125 and died in 202. His writings, *Adversus haereses* and *Demonstratio predicationis apostolici,* bear witness not only to the people's faith in the Trinity, but also to deep thought about the mystery.[10]

The first trinitarian theologians seem to have been the Valentinian Gnostics.[11] Their speculations lost themselves in consideration of the procession of the divine Persons, mixing biblical elements with theogonic and cosmogonic mythologies. They lacked the control of New Testament revelation. Reflection on the Trinity in itself, without continual reference to the "economic" Trinity, that is, the Trinity as it is shown in our history, generally loses itself in flights of fancy. St Irenaeus had to confront the showy speculations of the Gnostics. His importance, still felt today, lies in his (almost positivist) insistence that one had to start from actual faith (the "rule of faith") and the evidence of the Bible. Taking these as his starting-point, he pursued a devout investigation into the eternal essence of the Trinity.

In his *Demonstratio . . .* he writes:

This is the rule of our faith, the foundation of the building and what gives support to our conduct:

God the Father uncreated, who is uncontained, invisible, one God, creator of the universe; this is the first article of our faith. And the second is:

The *Word of God,* the Son of God, our Lord Jesus Christ, who appeared to the prophets according to their manner of prophecy and according to the state of the economies of the Father; by whom all things were made; who, furthermore, in the fullness of time, to gather all things into himself, became man among men, visible and palpable, to destroy death, bring life and achieve a communion between God and man. And the third article is:

The *Holy Spirit,* through whom the prophets prophesied and the Fathers learned concerning God and the just were led in the paths of justice and who in the fullness of time was poured out in a new way on our humanity to make men new over the whole world in the sight of God.[12]

This brief body of trinitarian doctrine lays stress on the salvific dimension of the Trinity. This is ultimately what matters, since God's revelation as Father, Son and Holy Spirit is made through God's saving actions. But Irenaeus does not confine himself to this aspect. With special reference to the Son, he stresses his pre-existence and true communion with the Father: "You, man, are not uncreated, you do not co-exist from all time with the Father like his own Word. . . ."[13] "Not only before Adam, but before the whole of creation, the Word glorified the Father, remaining in him, and being in turn Himself glorified by the Father."[14] He does not stop at this inter-relatedness, but goes on to include the Holy Spirit: "This God is glorified by his Word, who is his eternal Son, and by the Holy Spirit, who is the Wisdom of the Father of the universe."[15]

As one of the initiators of theological language about the Trinity, St Irenaeus is not always free from a certain ambiguity of expression, and sometimes suggests modalism or subordinationism. But overall, his thought makes a clear distinction between the three divine Persons.

(b) The Trinity Is a Dynamism of Communication: Origen

Origen, one of the great theological geniuses of Christendom,[16] who taught in Alexandria and died about 254, saw the Trinity as an eternal dynamism of communication; it should not be thought of as a reality complete in itself but as a process in everlasting realization. God is one (*monas*) but not alone. As light gives brightness, so the Father originates the Son (*Logos*), and Father and Logos originate the Holy Spirit. Origen was the first to use the word *hypostasis* (individual) to characterize the three divine Persons in God.[17] The distinction between the Persons is everlasting, thereby leaving modalism behind, but his understanding of the dynamism of the Trinity produces a strong tendency to subordinationism: the Father lets the Son come out of himself, and then the Holy Spirit. They are not three origins, but rather the Son and Spirit are derivations of one origin of all divinity and action, the Father. This view of the Trinity as a play of relationships and communications based on three distinct Persons became a fruitful source for later development of trinitarian thought.

(c) "Tres unum sunt, non unus": *Tertullian*

Tertullian, who lived from 160-220, was the chief creator of the language of trinitarian orthodoxy, avoiding the pitfalls of both modalism and subordinationism. Lay theologian, brilliant linguist and jurist, from Carthage in North Africa, he was responsible for 509 new nouns, 284 adjectives, 24 adverbs and 161 verbs, so it is not surprising that he coined the term *Trinitas* and the formula which came to express true faith in the triune God: "one substance, three persons."[18] This is not the place for detailed examination of his thought.[19] Suffice to note his intuition and the terminological rigour he introduced, since it has served as model for all later evolution of trinitarian thought.

His central thesis was: "*unitas ex semetipsa derivans Trinitatem*"[20]: "the Trinity derives from unity in itself." How is this? Tertullian replies: God is not just single, but one. In other words, God is not an entity closed in on himself, but a reality in process, a "self-distribution" (*dispensatio* or *oeconomia*) constituting second and third Persons who form part of God's substance and action. These two Persons (distinct individuals) are distinct but not divided (*distincti, non divisi*), different but not separate (*discreti, non separati*). This process is eternal, since the Father is always generating the Son out of himself (*prolatio*); the same Father through the Son also eternally originates the Holy Spirit. There is an order in this process of communication: the Father is the totality of the divine substance; the Son and Holy Spirit are *portiones totius,* individual communications (Persons) of this substantial whole.

Substance is what embodies the unity of the divine Three; *person* denotes what distinguishes them. In God, therefore, there exists the unity of equal substance *in* Father, Son and Holy Spirit, and the diversity of Persons *of* Father, Son and Holy Spirit, which derives from this same substance. This substance, by eternally communicating itself, maintains communion and unity with its communications. In other words, the unity of God is always a unity of Persons; the oneness of God results from the Three.

This divine process of unity and diversity is reflected in creation. The Word is expressed in history and takes on our flesh. The Spirit gives life to creation and creatures. Both lead all things back to the Trinity and then God will be all in all.

Tertullian laid down the basic lines of trinitarian understanding. He did not, however, work out the relationship between the three Persons, something that became possible only after the conciliar definitions of Nicaea in 352. His, though, was the acute vision that pointed out the path to follow so as not to lose sight of the specificity of the Christian God.

(d) The Divine Persons as Interplay of Relationship: The Cappadocian Fathers

What was lacking in Tertullian—reflection on the relationship between the three divine Persons—was developed by the Cappadocian Fathers.[21] These are the three great theologians of Cappadocia in Asia Minor: St Basil the Great (330-97), his blood brother Gregory of Nyssa (d. 394) and their friend Gregory Nazianzen (329-90). They took not the unity of the divine nature but the three divine Persons as their starting-point, seeing them as the basic reality. The unity that forms the essence of the Persons springs from the communion and relationship between them. The Persons (*hypostaseis* in Greek) mean their singular, specific and individual existences, but if we stop there we run the risk of tritheism (three gods). To avoid this, we need to consider the peculiarity of each Person, which is always defined in relation to the others, beginning with the Father, source and origin of all divinity.

So the peculiarity of the Father is to be *"ungenerated,"* not generated by anyone, and to form the source of all divinity; the peculiarity of the Son is to be eternally *"generated"* by the Father, receiving all his substantial reality from the Father; the peculiarity of the Holy Spirit lies in the fact of *"proceeding"* from the Father in a way different from the Son (not being another Son) or through the Son.

The Cappadocians restrict their differentiation of the three Persons to a purely formal level. They do not attempt to describe what makes up the nature of each of the three Persons, seeing this as the ultimate mystery inaccessible to human reason, however inspired by faith and piety. They state that the communion between the three is full, since the Father does everything by the Word in the Holy Spirit. The Trinity can only be conceived of as an interplay of mutual relations of truth and love.

Their great contribution was to clarify teaching about the Holy Spirit being truly God, one of the divine Persons. There had always been a difficulty in tradition on this point. The scriptures speak of the Spirit as wind, tongue of fire, dove; the Spirit is poured out into our hearts, comes down from heaven, and so on, expressions that cannot really be taken as defining the Spirit as a divine Person. Despite this, Jesus refers to the Spirit as advocate, as paraclete—as a *someone.* In 380 Gregory Nazianzen preached a famous sermon summing up interpretations current at the time: "for some the Spirit is a force, for others a creature, for yet others God. . . . Others accept the Trinity as we do, but at the same time claim that only the first Person is infinite in substance and power, that the second is infinite in power but not in substance, that the third is not infinite in either."[22] The followers of a certain Macedonius (d.362), also known as "pneumatomacheans," openly denied the divinity of the Holy Spirit. At the first Council of Constantinople, thanks to the collaboration of Gregory of Nyssa and Gregory Nazianzen, all doubts were removed with the solemn definition: "(We believe) in the Holy Spirit, the Lord and Giver of life, who proceeds from the Father, who together with the Father and the Son is adored and glorified, who has spoken through the prophets" (DS 150, CF). And here we have the establishment of orthodox faith in the Trinity as unity of three Persons, Father, Son and Holy Spirit.

(e) A Systematic Exposition of the Mystery of the Trinity; the Persons as Respective and Eternally Related Subjects: St Augustine

The intuitions of the Cappadocians on the interplay of relationship received their fullest expression in the work of St Augustine of Hippo (354-430), who spent many years on the composition of his masterly fifteen-book work *De Trinitate.* His teaching was a source of inspiration for all Latin theologians coming after him. For Augustine, God, in the absolute sense, is not the Father, as for the majority of Eastern theologians, but the Trinity, Father, Son and Holy Spirit. His work is full of expressions such as: "The Trinity is the only true God"[23] or "God is the Trinity."[24]

His approach to the problem combines daring with devotion: how are we to believe in one God and a Trinity of Persons? Does proclaiming the oneness of God not preclude any personal differentiation? And does not maintaining personal differentiation (Trinity) do away with God's oneness? To resolve the problem,

Augustine adopts the category of relationship used by the Greek Fathers. Unity belongs to the divine substance (essence or nature), which co-exists in each of the divine Persons, making the three consubstantial. This divine substance, however, exists in such a form that it must necessarily and eternally subsist as Father, Son and Holy Spirit. The three Persons are three relationships which coincide with the divine substance. These relationships neither develop nor define the substance, but reveal the substance itself in its inner correlation. The Father is eternally Father through having a Son, and the Son is eternally Son through being the Son of the Father, and the Holy Spirit is Holy Spirit from everlasting through being breathed out by the Father and by (or through) the Son. None of them has a beginning or an end, since this would make them accidental and not substantial.

To elucidate unity in trinity and trinity in unity, Augustine produced two famous analogies with human beings, who are created in the image and likeness of God: he speaks of mind, knowledge and love (*mens, notitia, amor*),[25] or memory, intelligence and will (*memoria, intelligentia, voluntas*).[26] Each of these terms contains the others: the mind knows and loves, knowledge supposes mind and love, love implies mind and knowledge. The three form the human soul, which is continuous life and action in complete simultaneity of action and being. In the same way, no one remembers without also willing to understand, understands without also willing to remember, or wills without also understanding and remembering. These analogies give us a pale reflection—but perhaps the best of which the human mind is capable—of the unity and distinction that exist in the Trinity.

For Augustine, the three Persons are three respective subjects; that is, they are concerned with one another and related to one another. Being means being-for-itself (*esse ad se dicitur*); person, on the other hand, means being in relation to others or with others (*persona vero relative*).[27] His development of the concept of personhood is brilliant:[28] he realizes the inadequacy of the concept, in that it is a common concept applied to each of the divine Persons, who are each distinct from the others. Each separate reality should really have a name of its own, so why not apply this to the Trinity of Persons? Each divine Person is a Person in a different way, a fact we fail to express when we use the term "person." Yet Augustine keeps the term, despite its inadequacy, out of respect for theological tradition and also—he tells us—because we cannot find any more apt term to describe in words what we understand without words. So Augustine prefers to use the biblical terms Father, Son and Holy Spirit, terms which in themselves are dynamic and relational.

Augustine married the most daring speculation to the deepest reverence. He never lost sight of the aspect of the mystery that is experienced in history, in human endeavours and contemplation: "*Vides Trinitatem si vides caritatem*"—you see the Trinity when you see love.[29] This aphorism underlines all his speculations. In other words, it is the practice of love that opens up true access to the mystery of the Trinity.

(f) On the One and Triune God: St Thomas Aquinas

The theological and speculative genius of St Thomas Aquinas (1224-74) completed the work of St Augustine, creating a highly logical trinitarian system. His starting-point is what is one in the Trinity, that is the divine essence,[30] so guaranteeing from the outset the divine and consubstantial character of the three Persons. Then he studies the "processions," following the route opened up by Augustine, taking the analogy of the mind which, being what it is, knows (Word or Son) and loves (the Gift or Holy Spirit). Having established the distinctions between the Persons on the basis of processions (the different ways in which one "proceeds" from the others), he goes on to analyze the real relationships between them. These relationships are posited by the fact of procession; however, given the type of relationship in question, St Thomas holds it to be self-evident that it is just these relationships that constitute the inner reality of the Trinity.[31]

These relationships are subsistent and permanent because in God, unlike in creatures, there is nothing fortuitous or accidental. Augustine saw the Persons as related subjects, realized that their relationship coincided with their essence, but did not clearly state that the relationships were substantial. Thomas defined the divine Persons precisely as *subsistent relationships*.[32] Just as in human nature, "person" means a distinct subsistent being, so Person in the Trinity means, by analogy, a distinct Subsistent Being in the divine nature. This Subsistent Being always exists in eternal relationship with the other Subsistent Beings. So we have the divine Persons as Subsistent Beings permanently and eternally related, forming one God or one divine nature. In this way, Thomas completed the speculative quest begun by Augustine, and remains the great Western theologian of the mystery of the Trinity. We shall see later how a changed cultural situation has brought additional insights into the concept of personhood, but we shall always relate them to the teachings of these two great masters of Christian thinking.

3. THE STRUGGLE FOR WORDS AND FORMULAS: ONE NATURE AND THREE PERSONS

Every science has its technical terms for expressing exactly what it wants to say. Theology has a mass of key words to express what is thought in faith. Words are more important in theology than in any other science, since no one can see or experience God empirically, as the realities of the world are experienced. Technical terms in theology established the consensus reached after many trials, errors and insights through generation after generation of Christian thinkers.

In the doctrine of the Trinity above all we are tied to a certain number of words and concepts, without which we could not understand tradition or the living language of our faith. These words have to be learned by all those who aspire to a theological view of their faith advancing beyond the simple formulations of everyday life and catechesis. Nor should we forget that there are great controversies embedded in each key word in theology, since each sums up efforts to clarify the contents of the great mysteries of faith. Each word fixes a particular content and determines a certain line of thinking. Yet no content embraces the depth of the mystery, which remains ever fresh, challenging new formulations to come forward.

So, for example, when Tertullian coined the expression "Trinity," and others, he was conscious of the alarm these caused the simple faithful who always make up the great majority of the Christian people. They had been converted from polytheism to belief in a single God. This was a great step for them; now, with the proclamation of the Trinity, they were given the impression of being sent back to what they had abandoned—polytheism. "*Monar-*

chiam, inquiunt, tenemos!," they cried—"They tell us we have monarchy" (i.e. monotheism). As Tertullian himself said: "These simple people are constantly accusing us of preaching two or three gods, and are convinced that they are the ones who adore the only God."[33] And so he made great efforts to show them that the Trinity does not destroy unity, since it derives from unity. The divine unity forms the Trinity by its intrinsic nature, not by a process of subdivision (which would be polytheism) but through a principle of integration which belongs essentially to the divinity.

(a) What To Call What Differentiates in God?

The problem is now this: what to call what differentiates in God, and what to call what in God is always the same? In other words: what common name can be given to Father, Son and Holy Spirit? What do we call their unity, since they form one God? Greek and Latin Fathers evolved different answers. For the sake of clarity, let us stick to essentials, even at the risk of over-simplifying the matter.

The Greeks used the term *prosopon* to describe what in God is three.[34] *Prosopon* designates a specific individual reality: John, Mary, that horse there, this plant here. It does not express whether this reality is sentient or not, a person or a thing, merely that it is something individual and objective. Applied to the Trinity it means: there are three in God—Father, Son and Holy Spirit; these three are different, specific, objective. The Christian God is three *prosopa*. What each *prosopon* (individuality) is like, this term does not tell us.

Tertullian translated *prosopon* into the Latin *persona,* which designated the specific *human* individual—a horse or a plant could not be called *persona*. While his translation is correct, it also adds a connotation the Greek *prosopon* did not have: the dimension of subjectivity, of mind, of personality, even though Tertullian himself approximated *persona* to *res* (thing, object). So when Tertullian said that there are three Persons in God, he meant to say, like the Greeks: in God there are three specific, distinct, objective realities—Father, Son and Holy Spirit; therefore, three objective individualities. Consequently, this matter is not just a question of words, but of objective realities.

So, to sum up, we can say that in God there are three *prosopa* or *personae;* that is, three specific individualities, which the New Testament calls Father, Son and Holy Spirit.

(b) What to Call What Unites in God?

To express the unity of God, what unites the three Persons, the Greeks used the term *hypostasis,* a word whose make-up clearly expresses its meaning: what lies under, basis or constant. *Hypostasis* was also used as a synonym for *ousia,* essence. Essence, as we shall see later, is that by which a thing is what it is. So in God there is one *hypostasis,* one *ousia* or essence, and three Persons.[35]

Hypostasis was translated into Latin as *substantia,* since there is a perfect philological correlation between the two elements of each word: *hypo = sub* (under); *stasis = stantia* (being, standing, from the verb *stare*). So substance means the same as essence, what underlies, is constant, stable. So the Latins said that in God there are one *substantia* and three *personae,* one substance and three Persons.

(c) Confusion and Clarification of Terms

At the end of the third century there was a great confusion of terms. The Greeks found themselves obliged to abandon the term *prosopon* as a designation of the divine Persons, since the word had come to be used by the modalists to spread their heresy. Modalism held that God is one and unique and that no difference could be found in God, but that this one and only God showed himself through three pseudonyms, faces or masks—a Father, Son or Holy Spirit. Now in Greek, "face" or "mask" can be designated by *prosopon,* so to state that in God there were three *prosopa,* in the sense of faces, masks or individualities, could be ambiguous and understood in the heretical sense which destroyed understanding of the Trinity. So for the sake of clarity and to avoid confusion, they replaced *prosopon* with *hypostasis.*

But surely *hypostasis* was reserved for expressing the unity of God, so how could it now be used to designate what differentiates in God? The explanation is that *hypostasis* is not just an abstract expression meaning "substance," what is unchanging in a specific thing, but could also express an objective, "subsistent" reality, as opposed to an "inconsistent" reality, one without content. It was commonly equated with "thing" (*pragma*). There was also the fact that Origen first used the term *hypostaseis* (plural) to designate the Persons of the Trinity, and his authority carried great weight at the time. So it became usual to call Father, Son and Holy Spirit three *hypostases*.[36] *Hypostasis* had become synonymous with *persona*. So the old *hypostasis* expressing unity was replaced with its synonym *ousia,* giving the Greek formula of belief in the Trinity: *treis hypostaseis kai mia ousia,* which became the Latin: *tres personae et una essentia vel substantia,* three persons and one essence or substance.

Confusion arose when the Latins translated the new sense in which *hypostasis* was used when applied to the three Persons. Instead of translating as *persona,* they translated literally as *substantia* (substance, nature, essence). And this was clear heresy, implying that God had three natures or substances, which meant three gods. So they went back to the time-honoured term *prosopon.* This confusion surfaced in Antioch at the end of the fourth century. For some twenty years two bishops had been carrying on a great dispute and created two factions. The first followed Bishop Melecius (d. 381) in conserving the term "three *hypostases*" for the three Persons, and was supported by the three great Cappadocians; this faction ran the risk of being understood as supporting tritheism or subordinationism (Arianism). The other faction followed Bishop Paulinus, was supported by Pope Damasus (d. 384) and St Athanasius of Alexandria (d. 373) and upheld the term "three *prosopa*"; this ran the risk of being understood as modalism. Each group hurled anathemas at the other; the Greeks in particular objected to the term *prosopon* (specific individuality) as highly ambiguous and evocative of modalism; the Latins criticized the term *hypostasis* (in the sense of subsistent individuality, as used by Origen and now generally accepted), fearing that it would be understood literally and so translated into Latin not as *persona* but as *substantia,* thereby leading to tritheism or subordinationism.

Agreement was finally achieved by St Gregory Nazianzen at the Council of Constantinople in 381, through establishing the equivalence, which everyone then accepted, between the Greek *hypostasis* and the Latin *persona.* In 382 the bishops who had been at the Council sent a profession of faith to Pope Damasus explaining this equivalence in the following terms: "we believe in the one divinity and power and substance (*ousia*) of the Father and the Son and the Holy Spirit, the equal dignity and co-eternal rule in three perfect hypostases (*hypostaseis*), that is, in three perfect persons (*prosopa*)." This combines the two classic technical terms: one essence or substance (*ousia*), and three persons (*hypostaseis* or *prosopa*).

(d) Are Hypostasis and Person Real Equivalents?

The Greek and Latin theologians were trying to express the same faith in different words. But the words they used have different connotations and do not always suggest the same reality in Greek as in Latin. We need to be clear about the real intentions of the Council Fathers who used the Greek term *hypostasis* and the Latin *persona*. They were all trying to say that God co-exists in three distinct subsistents, the distinction between which is not something merely verbal or metaphorical, but something real and definite. In a formulation that took christological dogma as its paradigm, this was expressed as follows: what in Christ is one (the divine Person of the Son) is multiple in the Trinity (the three Persons); what in Christ is multiple (the two natures, divine and human) is one in the Trinity (one *ousia,* substance or nature). This was the intention of the Council and became accepted as faith.

But what about the actual make-up of the Three? The Council of Constantinople does not seem to have defined anything about this, leaving the question open to theological speculation. St Augustine expressedly recognizes the difficulty: "When it is asked three what, then the great poverty from which our language suffers becomes apparent. But the formula three persons has been coined, not in order to give a complete explanation by means of it, but in order that we might not be obliged to remain silent."[37]

The words used by the Greeks and the Latins do, both philologically and pragmatically, have different connotations. The Greeks used *hypostasis* to express what differentiates in God. In its normal use, the word *hypostasis* designates just something individual and distinct from another; it could be applied to an animal or a plant as well as to a person, its emphasis being on objectivity, not subjectivity: there is a distinct and identifiable being which is itself and not another. Applied to the Trinity, its implication is: there are three

objective realities co-existing and distinct from one another—
Father, Son and Holy Spirit: the holy Trinity.

Clearly, when applied to God, the word *hypostasis* takes on a
charge of subjectivity, but this is not implied by the word itself,
which stresses that the Christian God involves the existence of three
"things" (*pragmata*) which are real and not merely imagined: the
Father, the Son and the Holy Spirit. It is worth noting that recent
researchers have shown that the term *prosopon* (person) also took
on connotations of subjectivity in the works of theologians such as
Tertullian, Novatian and Irenaeus. Commenting on biblical texts
that might contain possible revelations of the Trinity—such as
Genesis 1:26; 19:24; Isaiah 45:14ff; Psalms 44:1, 8; 109:1—they
used the term *prosopon/persona* to imply dialogue and mutual
relationship, at least between Father and Son, thereby introducing
the subjective and "personal" character of the three divine Persons.[38]

The Latin word *persona,* used to correspond to *hypostasis,*
enshrines the dimension of subjectivity: it implies a conscious
subject, an interlocutor, not merely an objective and definite reality. So, applied to the Trinity, *persona* connotes the idea of three
bearers of the divine attributes in equal measure; this appears from
Pope Damasus' Confession of Faith addressed to Bishop Paulinus:
the Three are equally living, life-giving, creators of all, saving, and
so on (DS 173). The word "person" spontaneously evokes three
divine Beings, as faith has always believed.

The question remains: are hypostasis and person real equivalents? Yes: first, in the sense that both Greeks and Latins sought to
express that God means three "realities" and that therefore God is
Trinity; and, second, in the sense that *prosopon* in some authors
(who helped to formulate trinitarian theology) included a personalist reference. But not in the sense that there are many passages in
which *hypostasis* is used without the dimension of subjectivity
implicit in the Latin *persona: hypostasis,* once again, affirms the
objectivity of the three divine Persons and *persona* their subjectivity. Yet though their connotations are different, they complement
each other, since it makes sense to say that what is objective when
we speak of God is God's nature (*ousia* or *substantia*) and what is
subjective is the three Persons (*personae* or *hypostaseis*).

It was the derivation of the Latin understanding of "person" that, in Western theology, went from Augustine, through Boethius, Thomas Aquinas and Duns Scotus down to modern times, in an original process of deepening the concept of "person" so as to give it orthodox application to the Trinity. This process will be examined in the next chapter.

CHAPTER IV

Dogmatic Understanding of the Trinity

This chapter sets out to give a brief outline of "official" teaching on the Trinity as it evolved in the Councils that dealt with the matter. Christian experience which came to be expressed as faith in God the Father, God the Son and God the Holy Spirit took some 150 years to evolve into a doctrine whose technical terms enable us to *express* an orthodox view of this great mystery. These years span the period from the beginning of the third century to the Council of Constantinople in 381. The formulation of trinitarian doctrine in this period went hand-in-hand with doctrine concerning Christ, the Son of God consubstantial with the Father.

1. OFFICIAL STATEMENTS BY THE MAGISTERIUM

Of the many official statements made by the magisterium (whether papal as in the case of Popes Dionysius and Damasus, or conciliar), I propose to select a few that seem to sum up the substance of dogmatic faith in the Trinity. I use the word "dogmatic" in the positive sense: meaning teaching binding on all the faithful officially expressed by the authentic teaching authority of the church, which is that of the magisterium of the ecumenical Councils or the solemn magisterium of the popes.

(a) The Creed of Nicaea: The Son Consubstantial with the Father

On 19 June 325 the Emperor Constantine summoned 318 bishops to the little town of Nicaea, where they assembled on 25 August
that year. To combat the Arians, who held that Jesus was just like
the Father, but not equal to him in nature, the council fathers
defined most solemnly the following formula, which opens the way
to a trinitarian concept of God:

> We believe in one God, the Father almighty, creator of all
> things both visible and invisible. And in one Lord Jesus
> Christ, the Son of God, the only-begotten born of the Father,
> that is, of the substance (*ousia*) of the Father; God from God,
> Light from Light, true God from true God; begotten, not
> created, consubstantial (*homoousios*) with the Father;
> through him all things were made, those in heaven and those
> on earth as well. For the sake of us men and for our salvation,
> he came down, was made flesh, and became man; he suffered
> and on the third day arose; he ascended into heaven and is
> going to come to judge the living and the dead. And we
> believe in the Holy Spirit.
>
> As for those who say: "There was a time when he did not
> exist"; and, "Before he was begotten, he did not exist"; and,
> "He was made from nothing, or from another hypostasis or
> essence," alleging that the Son of God is mutable or subject
> to change—such persons the Catholic and apostolic Church
> condemns (DS 125, CT).

The following points need to be stressed: first, faith in the
Trinity, Father, Son and Holy Spirit, is expressed; second, the
relation between the Father and the Son is defined: they are one
substance, expressed in the key word *homoousios,* meaning of one
and the same *ousia* (essence or substance), the word that, as we
have seen, came to be accepted as expressing what unites in the
Trinity; third, the word *hypostasis* is used as synonymous with
ousia or substance, as it had been up till Nicaea—later, under the
influence of Origen and the Cappadocians, coming to be synonymous with *prosopon,* "person," to designate what differentiates

in God. Finally, the Holy Spirit is mentioned without any objective description, which was arrived at between Nicaea and Constantinople. But the Spirit was hereby incorporated into the common Creed of the whole church.

Nicaea set the course for later developments in christology and trinitarian doctrine by making clear that the name God implied the co-existence of three, Father, Son and Holy Spirit, who together make up the unity and oneness of God.

(b) The Nicene-Constantinopolitan Creed: The Holy Spirit, God with the Father and the Son

What had been insinuated at Nicaea was made fully explicit at the Council of Constantinople, in which 150 bishops took part from May to the end of June 381: the Spirit is of the same nature as the Father and the Son, and therefore God. Its Creed built on that of Nicaea and completed it:

We believe in one God, the Father almighty, maker of heaven and earth, of all things visible and invisible.

And in one Lord Jesus Christ, the only-begotten Son of God, generated from the Father before all ages, Light from Light, true God from true God, begotten, not made, one in being with the Father, through whom all things were made. For us men and for our salvation He came down from the heavens, and became flesh from the Holy Spirit and the Virgin Mary and was made man. For our sake too He was crucified under Pontius Pilate, suffered and was buried. On the third day He rose again according to the Scriptures, He ascended to the heavens and is seated at the right hand of the Father. He shall come again in glory to judge the living and the dead; to His Kingdom there will be no end.

And in the Holy Spirit, the Lord and Giver of life, who proceeds from the Father, who together with the Father and the Son is worshipped and glorified, who has spoken through the prophets. (And) in one Holy Catholic and apostolic Church. We acknowledge one baptism for the forgiveness of sins. We expect the resurrection of the dead and the life of the world to come. Amen (DS 150, CF).

This Creed clearly indicates what is three in God: Father, Son and Holy Spirit; thanks to Gregory Nazianzen, the Council's text did not use the generally accepted term "three *hypostases*" or "three *persons,*" but still expressed the unity of substance or nature between the Three with equal clarity. Note that this formula merely has the Holy Spirit proceeding from the Father. The form of this procession is left open: whether directly or *through* the Son (as in Greek spirituality) or from the Father *and* the Son (as in Latin spirituality).

(c) The Quicumque *or Pseudo-Athanasian Creed: Unity in Trinity and Trinity in Unity*

The genius of St Augustine produced the first truly systematic treatise on trinitarian doctrine on the basis of the points established at Nicaea and Constantinople: that God is three Persons or *hypostases* and one substance or *ousia.* Augustine typifies the Western approach to the mystery (though not exclusively Western, since Eastern theologians such as Gregory Nazianzen and Epiphanius took the same course), starting from the absolute unity of God. While God in the absolute sense meant the Father to the Greeks, for Augustine God meant the Trinity of Persons, since "The Trinity is the only true God."[1] He moves on from this unity to consider each of the Persons. This differentiation of unity comes from the absolutely substantial relationship proper to God. God's inner relationships are not later or modifying determinations of God's essence; they are that essence in immanent, inherent and eternal correlation. These absolute relationships make up the one true God who is called Father, Son and Holy Spirit. Unity in the Trinity, and the Trinity in unity: this is Augustine's basic formula.

This theological expression of trinitarian faith was embodied in the Creed known as *Quicumque* (its first word in Latin), wrongly attributed to St Athanasius (295-373). In fact it was drawn up by an anonymous author in the South of France between 430 and 500. It acquired enormous authority, to the point of being placed on an equal footing with the Nicene-Constantinopolitan Creed and used in the liturgy. Yet it has internal limitations, in that it repeatedly juxtaposes unity and Trinity without evidencing the connection between the two. The text is given here because it makes use of all the terms that served to comprise theological understanding of the Trinity:

> Whoever wishes to be saved must, above all, keep the Catholic faith; for unless a person keeps this faith whole and entire he will undoubtedly be lost forever.
>
> This is what the Catholic faith teaches. We worship one God in the Trinity and the Trinty in unity; we distinguish among the persons, but we do not divide the substance. For the Father is a distinct person; the Son is a distinct person; and the Holy Spirit is a distinct person. Still, the Father and the Son and the Holy Spirit have one divinity, equal glory, and coeternal majesty. What the Father is, the Son is, and the Holy Spirit is. The Father is uncreated, the Son is uncreated, and the Holy Spirit is uncreated. The Father has immensity, the Son has immensity, and the Holy Spirit has immensity. The Father is eternal, the Son is eternal, and the Holy Spirit is eternal. Nevertheless, there are not three eternal beings, but one eternal being. Thus there are not three uncreated beings, nor three beings having immensity, but one uncreated being and one being that has immensity.
>
> Likewise, the Father is omnipotent, the Son is omnipotent, and the Holy Spirit is omnipotent. Yet there are not three omnipotent beings, but one omnipotent being. Thus the Father is God, the Son is God, and the Holy Spirit is God. But there are not three gods, but one God. The Father is lord, the Son is lord, and the Holy Spirit is lord. There are not three lords, but one Lord. For according to Christian truth, we must profess that each of the persons individually is God; and according to the Christian religion we are forbidden to say that there are three gods or three lords. The Father is not made by anyone, nor created by anyone, nor generated by anyone. The Son is not made nor created, but he is generated by the Father alone. The Holy Spirit is not made nor created nor generated, but proceeds from the Father and the Son.
>
> There is, then, one Father, not three fathers; one Son, not three sons; one Holy Spirit, not three holy spirits. In this Trinity, there is nothing that precedes, nothing subsequent to anything else. There is nothing greater, nothing lesser than

anything else. But the entire three persons are coeternal and coequal with one another, so that, as we have said, we worship complete unity in the Trinity and the Trinity in unity. This, then, is what he who wishes to be saved must believe about the Trinity.

Those who wish to be saved, then, should think thus of the Trinity (DS 75, CF).

As will be seen, this is predominantly a doctrinal statement, with formulations given statutory force. Unlike the earlier symbols with their emphasis on the economic Trinity (its revelation and action in history), this stays on the level of immanent Trinity. It shows that trinitarian doctrine is already established: unity of substance and diversity of persons with equal dignity; so all the divine attributes are given to each.

(d) Creeds of the Councils of Toledo and Florence: The Holy Spirit Proceeds from the Father and the Son (Filioque)

The Nicene-Constantinopolitan Creed, referring to the Holy Spirit, states that the Spirit proceeds from the Father, without mentioning the Son. The Latin church, seeking to strengthen the equality of substance of the Spirit as well as the Son and so refute subordinationism (Arianism), which still persisted in Visigothic Spain, began to state that the Holy Spirit proceeds from the Father and the Son (*Filioque*). The text produced by the first Council of Toledo in the year 400 reads: "There exists also the Spirit Paraclete, who is neither the Father nor the Son, but who proceeds *from the Father and the Son*. So the Father is unoriginate, the Son begotten, the Holy Spirit not begotten but proceeding *from the Father and the Son*" (DS 188).

In the following century, at the third Council of Toledo in 589, King Recaredo, recently converted from Arianism, ordered the new *Filioque* formula to be inserted in the Nicene-Constantinopolitan Creed. The so-called King Recaredo Creed, produced by this Council, clearly states: "The Holy Spirit is equally professed and preached by us as proceeding *from the Father and the Son* and with the Father and the Son possesses the same substance; therefore, the third person of the Trinity is the Holy

Spirit, who with the Father and the Son also possesses the essence of divinity" (DS 470). This formula, designed to combat the Arians, who denied the divinity of the Son and the Holy Spirit, spread through the whole Latin church, and in 1014, at the coronation of Henry II by Pope Benedict VIII in Rome, the Creed with *Filioque* inserted was sung in St Peter's basilica.

In the East, it was considered a schismatic act to modify the sacred text of the common Creed, the more so as the Council of Ephesus (431) had pronounced an anathema on anyone who professed "another faith" differing from that of the Council of Nicaea. The Council of Chalcedon in 451 had repeated the same sanction. But there were also theological considerations. For Eastern theologians, the only source of the divine Persons was the Father (the monarchy of the Father). In the eighth century St John Damascene summed up their position: "The Spirit is the Spirit of the Father . . . but is also the Spirit of the Son, not because he proceeds from the Son, but because he proceeds *by means of* the Son from the Father, since there is but one sole source, the Father."[2] So in the Greek conception, the Father is the originating source of all divinity and of the diversity of the Persons. In another text, St John Damascene stresses: "We do not say that the Son is source, so we do not say that He is Father. . . . We do not say that the Spirit proceeds from the Son, but we do say that he is the Spirit of the Son."[3] The Son and the Spirit come conjointly and together from the Father, in that Word and Breath (spirit) come out together from the mouth of the Father.[4]

I do not intend to go further into this difficult debate here, just to note the Eastern view and the difficulties produced by the interpolation of *Filioque* in the Creed. Together with purely political quarrels between West and East, this *Filioque* question led to the Great Schism of 1054, when the papal legate Humbert placed a document on the altar of St Sophia in Constantinople accusing the Greek church of having suppressed the *Filioque* in the Creed!

The Council of Florence, which lasted from 1431 to 1447, produced, after arduous discussion, a dogmatically conciliatory text, known as the "Decree for the Greeks," designed to reconcile the Western concept of *Filioque* with the classical formulation of the Greek church (from the Father through the Son: *ek Patros dia Hyiou*):

In the name of the Holy Trinity, Father, Son and Holy Spirit, with the approval of this sacred universal Council of Florence, we define that this truth of faith must be believed and received by all and that all must profess: the Holy Spirit is eternally from Father and Son; He has His nature and subsistence at once (*simul*) from Father and Son; He proceeds eternally from both as from one principle and through one spiration.

We declare: When the holy Doctors and Fathers say that the Holy Spirit proceeds from the Father through the Son, this must be understood in the sense that, as the Father, so also the Son is what the Greeks call "cause" and the Latins "principle" of the subsistence of the Holy Spirit. And, since the Father has through generation given to the only-begotten Son everything that belongs to the Father, except being Father, the Son has also eternally from the Father, from whom He is eternally born, that the Holy Spirit proceeds from the Son.

Moreover, we define that the explanatory words "Filioque" have been added in the Symbol legitimately and with good reason for the sake of clarifying the truth and under the impact of a real need at that time (DS 1300-1302, CF).

This declaration is dated 6 July 1439. As can be seen, it makes an effort at conciliation. The basic Greek conception of God made them distinguish between the causality of the Father (*arche*) and that of the Son (*aitia*); for the Greeks, God is basically the Father; everything proceeds from him, since he is the sole source of all things and all persons, including the Son and the Spirit; if the Son is also a source, he is so in a form received from the Father; so they distinguish two types of causality. The Latins, as the conciliar text expresses, embrace both types of causality by the term *principium*. By together breathing out the Holy Spirit, the Father and the Son do not constitute two sources; they are a single source (the Council rightly says "*tanquam ab* uno *principio*") since the Son together with the Father breathes out the Holy Spirit inasmuch as he is the Son of the Father and not just a son. The expressions "the Holy Spirit proceeds from the Father *and* the Son" (Latin), and "the

Holy Spirit proceeds from the Father by [or through] the Son" (Greek) can perfectly well mean one and the same thing.

(e) The Fourth Lateran Council: Harmony between Immanent Trinity and Economic Trinity

Perhaps the clearest use of this terminology and the clearest expression of the balance between an economic and an immanent view of the Trinity come from the fourth Lateran Council, held in 1215 under the presidency of Pope Innocent III. It produced two texts, one designed to confute the Albigensians and other heretics, and the other Abbot Joachim of Fiore who, in the words of the Council, conceived this unity of the Trinity . . . not as true and proper, but, so to say, as collective and by similitude, just as many people are called one nation, and many faithful one church" (DS 803, CF). The first text is as follows:

> We firmly believe and profess without qualification that there is only one true God, eternal, immense, unchangeable, incomprehensible, omnipotent, and indescribable, the Father, the Son, and the Holy Spirit: three persons but one essence and a substance or nature that is wholly simple. The Father is from no one; the Son is from the Father only; and the Holy Spirit is from both the Father and the Son equally. God has no beginning; he always is, and always will be; the Father is the progenitor, the Son is the begotten, the Holy Spirit is proceeding; they are all one substance, equally great, equally all-powerful, equally eternal; they are the one and only principle of all things—Creator of all things visible and invisible, spiritual and corporeal, who, by his almighty power, from the very beginning of time has created both orders of creatures in the same way out of nothing, the spiritual or angelic world and the corporeal or visible universe. And afterwards He formed the creature man, who in a way belongs to both orders, as he is composed of spirit and body. For the devil and the other demons were created by God good according to their nature, but they made themselves evil by their own doing. As for man, his sin was at the prompting of the devil. The Holy Trinity, indivisible accord-

ing to its essence, and distinct according to its personal properties, first gave this teaching of salvation to the human race
through Moses and the prophets and its other servants, according to a well-ordered disposition of time.

Finally, the only-begotten Son of God, Jesus Christ, whose
incarnation is the common work of the whole Trinity, conceived from Mary ever Virgin with the co-operation of the
Holy Spirit, made true man, composed of a rational soul and
a human body, one person in two natures, showed the way of
life more clearly (DS 800-801, CF,CT).

The text designed to refute Joachim of Fiore is no less clear:

But we, with the approval of the holy council, believe and
profess, with Peter Lombard, that there is a certain one
supreme reality, incomprehensible, and beyond description,
which truly is the Father, and the Son, and the Holy Spirit.
That reality is the three persons taken together and each of
them taken singly; and, hence, there is in God only a trinity,
not a quaternity; because each of the persons is that reality,
namely, the divine substance, essence, or nature. That reality
alone is the principle of all things; besides it none other can be
found. And that reality does not beget, nor is it begotten, nor
does it proceed; but it is the Father who begets, the Son who is
begotten, the Holy Spirit who proceeds; thus, there are distinctions between persons, and unity in nature. Although
"the Father is one person, the Son is another person, and the
Holy Spirit yet another person, still none is a different being."
Rather, the very same being which is the Father is also the Son
and Holy Spirit; consequently, according to the orthodox and
Catholic faith they are believed to be consubstantial. For the
Father in eternally generating the Son gave him his own
substance as the Son himself testifies: "What my Father has
given me is greater than all." But it cannot be said that he gave
him part of his substance, and retained part for himself,
because the substance of the Father is indivisible, since it is
altogether simple. Neither can one say that the Father trans-
ferred his own substance in generation to the Son, as though
he gave it to the Son in such a way that he did not retain it for

himself; otherwise he would cease to be a substance. It is clear, therefore, that in being born the Son received the undiminished substance of the Father, and thus the Father and Son have the same substance; and thus the same reality is the Father, and the Son, and the Holy Spirit who proceeds from both (DS 804-5, CT).

These two formulations embody the classic expression of trinitarian dogma: a single nature and three distinct Persons; the distinction between the Persons depends on their origin: the Father unoriginate, the Son originating from the Father and the Holy Spirit from the Father and the Son. The Council's documents strike a marvellous balance between immanent Trinity (the Persons in themselves) and economic Trinity (their actions in history).

(f) The Decree for the Jacobites: Interpenetration of the Three Persons (Perichoresis)

In the three Persons, nothing is anterior, superior, greater, lesser or posterior. They are co-equal, co-eternal, co-almighty. The reason adduced by the magisterium is the unity of nature, substance or essence shared by all three. Because of this one nature, each of the Persons is wholly in the others (circuminsession), penetrates and is penetrated by the others (circumincession or perichoresis). In its 1442 Decree for the Jacobites (Copts and Ethiopians) the Council of Florence expressed the communion between the three Persons, the basic theme of our reflections here. The doctrine it put forward is that of perichoresis, the basis for a personalist and living understanding of the Trinity. This is the Council's text:

On account of this unity the Father is wholly in the Son and wholly in the Holy Spirit; the Son wholly in the Father and wholly in the Holy Spirit; the Holy Spirit wholly in the Father and wholly in the Son. None precedes the other in eternity, none exceeds the other in greatness, nor excels the other in power. For it is from eternity and without beginning that the Son has taken His origin from the Father, and from eternity and without beginning that the Holy Spirit proceeds from the Father and the Son.

All that the Father is or has, He has not from another but from Himself; He is the origin without origin. All that the Son is or has, He has from the Father; He is origin from origin. All that the Holy Spirit is or has, He has at once (*simul*) from the Father and the Son. But the Father and the Son are not two origins of the Holy Spirit but one origin, just as Father, Son and Holy Spirit are not three origins of creation but one origin (DS 1331, CT).

(g) The Declaration "The Mystery of the Son of God": From Economic Trinity to Immanent Trinity

From the earlier consideration of the binding data of faith found in the New Testament, it emerged that God is revealed as Trinity, as Father, Son and Holy Spirit. Starting from the Trinity as revealed in the life and teaching of Jesus Christ and the action of the Holy Spirit, we can begin to see, as in a glass darkly, the mystery of the very communion existing between the three divine Persons. Lately, some theologians, starting from a radical conception of historicity projected into the very Godhead, have maintained that God as Trinity had a beginning, with the establishment of a relationship with creation. This is a denial of the eternity of the Trinity. Such theories provoked a declaration from the Sacred Congregation for the Doctrine of the Faith, dated 27 February 1972. This is important not only for its re-stating of the ontological character of the Trinity (God is eternally triune because this is God's nature), but also for its indication of the order in which we acquire understanding: from experience to theology, from the Trinity manifested in history to the Trinity as it is in itself. This is the text:

The opinion that Revelation has left us uncertain about the eternity of the Trinity, and in particular about the eternal existence of the Holy Spirit as a person in God distinct from the Father and the Son, deviates from the faith. It is true that the mystery of the Most Holy Trinity was revealed to us in the economy of salvation, and most of all in Christ Himself, who was sent into the world by the Father and together with the Father sends the life-giving Spirit to the People of God. But by this Revelation there is also given to believers some knowledge of God's intimate life, in which "the Father who generates, the Son who is generated, and the Holy Spirit who proceeds" are "consubstantial and co-equal, alike omnipotent and co-eternal."[5]

This clarifies the relationship between economic Trinity and immanent Trinity, and also the "certain knowledge" which, through this relationship, we can deduce of the Trinity as it is in itself.

2. THREE TENDENCIES IN TRINITARIAN UNDERSTANDING

Theological doctrine on the Trinity built up a rigorous system of theoretical instruments (terms and concepts) with which to understand and express the truth of the one and triune God. The language of the Trinity is governed by strict rules; these came into being in order to avoid heresies (disfigured formulations of faith) and to speak, as pertinently as possible (given that there is such a possibility), of the unspeakable Mystery.[6] In this interplay of language, each term has its place; emphases, however, vary according to the different ways in which the guiding facts of faith are understood at different times.

There are three main tendencies in the development of trinitarian thought.[7] These have not just arisen spontaneously, but in answer to situations in which the Trinity had to be thought of in a certain way in order to combat errors prevalent at the time. So in the general climate of polytheism prevailing in the Roman Empire and in which the Latin Fathers had to work, it was natural for trinitarian thinking to begin by emphasizing the oneness of God; if they had begun by preaching the Trinity, their hearers might have thought they were hearing a form of polytheism reduced to three gods; the situation favoured reflection based on the unity of God and only following that did it move on to consider the diversity of Persons.

In a different climate, with an insistence on monotheism and the absolute monarchy of God, to the point of rejecting any other aspect of God and so denying the divinity of Jesus (the situation of

the Greek Fathers combatting Arianism or modalism), thinkers
naturally tended to emphasize the diversity in God; they insisted on
the Trinity and the three Persons, and came to unity through
diversity; this was the only way to oppose the errors of a rigid
monarchianism which left no space for acceptance of the Trinity.

In yet another situation, one that lays greatest stress on individu-
alism, the lack of cohesion and of solidarity on the personal and
social levels (as is the case in societies where the majorities are
excluded from the capitalist production process), reflection is
called to set its sights not on monotheism or trinitarianism, but on
the form of relationship existing between the divine Persons; theologians then have to stress communion as the first and fundamental
principle in God and in all beings, which are made in the image and
likeness of the relationship inside the Trinity.

So, different tendencies are defined from the outside in; they all
try to make the truth of faith relevant to human existence where
this is being deformed in ways that can be corrected by the truth of
faith. The doctrine of the Trinity can help individuals and societies
to find their own truth, as willed by the Trinity.

(a) From Unity of Nature to Trinity of Persons

In the Creed we pray: *Credo in unum Deum,* "I believe in one
God. . . ." This formula serves to express a genuine spiritual
experience centered on the oneness of God. The multiplicity of
"gods" is left behind and the faithful address a single principle,
Lord of heaven and earth, God, the beginning of all things and
their end. Praying this formula, the faithful are not addressing a
tri-unity, a Father, Son and Holy Spirit, but simply the supreme
Mystery, intensely personal, spiritual, accessible to human wants.
How do we move from this unity to a Trinity of Persons? Two ways
were found that avoided the historic errors of understanding the
Persons as modes of expression of the one and true God (modalism) or as descending evolutions of the one God (Arianism or
subordinationism).

The first was expressed like this: God is an *absolute* and most
perfect *spirit*. It is proper to all spirits (including created ones) to
think and to love as concretizations of their essence. The most
perfect spirit is *"reflexivus sui,"* that is, it thinks of itself in the most

perfect way, thereby producing an absolutely perfect expression of itself, begetting what faith calls the Son or Word. By begetting this expression, God reveals himself as Father, capable of begetting an eternal and only-begotten Son. Father and Son do not only think each other reciprocally, but also love each other eternally. This love for each other is so perfect that it is called the Holy Spirit. This Trinity of Persons does not multiply the most perfect spirit, but manifests its internal and eternal dynamic. So the Persons are this same spirit in its eternal process, and therefore we can say that the Persons do not have an individual essence but one common essence, the most perfect spirit. In trinitarian theology, this most perfect spirit is called the one Substance or Nature.

The second way was inspired by a long mystical tradition that came from Plato, through St Augustine and St Bonaventure to the medieval Franciscan school and still has many followers today. In this tradition, God is much more than a most perfect spirit: God is *highest Good* or *supreme Love*. The property of Good and Love is to diffuse and communicate themselves, go out from themselves and make of themselves a gift to others. Now revelation teaches that God is love (1 John 4:8, 16). As this infinite loving Principle expands, it reveals itself as Son or Word, of the same nature as itself. The Word is one God with the Father, distinguished from him as Son. The relationship of love and self-giving between Father and Son is so supreme and perfect that it gives rise to the Holy Spirit, the expression of communion between the two, so completing the loving circle of the supreme Lovers in one reality of love.

Unity is thereby assured, since it forms the starting-point, the oneness of either supreme spirit or infinite love; the next step is to see that the inner dynamic of this *summa Res* (supreme Reality) produces an internal differentiation; so the three Persons emerge as three ways of *really* embodying and *truly* possessing the same divine nature. Systematic treatment of this approach begins by speaking of one God (*de Deo uno*) and goes on to speak of the triune God (*de Deo trino*), as we find in St Thomas Aquinas, the main exponent of this approach, following the lines indicated by St Augustine. St Thomas writes: "In the first place we have to consider what concerns the divine *essence* [questions 2-26]; in the second, what pertains to the differentiation of the *Persons* [questions 27-43]; in the third, all that deals with the process of creation of creatures by God [questions 44ff]."

The danger inherent in starting from the unity of the divine essence is modalism, the notion that the Persons appear as simply *modes* of the same Being, not truly three in one God; this leaves us still on the level of monotheism. To face up to this danger and maintain orthodox understanding, theology (mainly, but not exclusively Latin theology) emphasized that the modes of possessing and embodying the same essence are *real* and *distinct* modes; they are not modes of expressing or a progressive revelation made to us—a purely verbal matter. The way in which the Father possesses the essence is really distinct from that of the Son and both in their turn are really distinct from that of the Holy Spirit. The real difference in the modes of possessing and embodying the same and sole essence is based on the different ways in which the Persons relate to each other and to origination. So we say: the Father (the first Person) possesses the essence as unoriginated and uncommunicated essence; the Son (the second Person) receives the essence through being begotten of the Father; the Holy Spirit (the third Person) receives the essence through being breathed out by the Father and the Son together.

The Persons are defined by their relationship one to another; they are never absolute, subsistent in themselves (what characterizes essence), but *relative,* meaning related one to another. So we should understand them in accordance with the teaching of the eleventh Council of Toledo (675): the Father has reference to the Son, the Son to the Father and the Holy Spirit to both the others; even though we speak of three Persons by relationship, yet we believe in one sole essence (DS 528). In other words, the Persons receive their personhood solely from the relationship they sustain one with another.

The distinction between the Persons is real, so that one is not another, even though one is always related to the others. The distinction between Persons and essence cannot be *real,* or we would have a quaternity: one essence *plus* three Persons, making four. Neither is this distinction purely in the mind, or we would have modalism; there would be just one essence and three verbal or mental modes of expressing it. So there has to be some sort of distinction between the one essence and the Persons. Theologians say there is a "formal" ("virtual" in the Thomist school) distinction, which avoids fusing the Trinity into unity and at the same time maintains a differentiation within the divine identity. In this formal distinction, the reality is not multiplied, but it is possible to grasp three distinct modes in which this same reality subsists. These three modes do not originate in our minds but in the reality itself. This is precisely what is meant by "formal" distinction: the same essence, nature or reality is mediated through different "formalizations."[8] Applied to the Trinity, this means: the reality (nature) of God is understood as realized in the formalizations of Father, Son and Holy Spirit; it is an attempt at expressing the inner dynamic and richness of this one and only divine reality.

This explains why the three divine Persons together have the one same nature, why they share the same attributes (the Father is eternal, the Son is eternal, the Holy Spirit is eternal; and the same applies to being infinite, creator, merciful, and so on), and why they act outwardly in union (the three divine Persons act inseparably together in history, redeeming, saving, divinizing, leading everything to the everlasting Kingdom in glory). To sum up: though each Person is truly God, all three Persons are one God. This is the basic argument of this current of thought, which structures the tenets of faith on the basis of the unity and oneness of the divine nature.

(b) From Unity of Substance of the Father to Trinity of Persons

In the Creed we pray: *Credo in unum Deum, Patrem omnipotentem* . . ., "I believe in one God, the Father almighty. . . ." We can start by emphasizing the personal character of God, who then appears as Father. The Father is God by antonomasia; as the Greek theologians said: "He is the source and origin of divinity." Unity is then not so much the equality of divine nature in three Persons as "the unity of the Father, from whom and through whom the other persons are counted."[9] There is only one God because there is only one divine source, the Father almighty. There is only one principle of divinity, the Father, and so the most absolute monarchy holds sway. Therefore, the Father communicates all his divine substance to the Son; alone or through (or together with) the Son, he also hands over all his substance to the Holy Spirit. So in the mystery of the Trinity, everything stems from one begetting and communicating principle: the Father. Unity consists in the communicated substance of the Father. The three Persons are consubstantial because they share absolutely in the substance of the Father.

In this understanding, the relationship between the Persons of the Trinity is not one of opposition or separation, but of differentiation in communion with the Father. The Father communicates all his wisdom, all his love, all his will, all his eternity to the Son and the Holy Spirit. So there are not three eternal beings but one, one Holy One, one Lord. Here, unlike in the previous conception, the nature (or substance or essence) of God is personalized at the outset. The Father establishes the original relationships out of himself, since he is constituted the sole source and origin of all relationships.

The distinction of the Persons with reference to the Father is not summed up or exhausted by saying they are distinct; this would merely clarify that one is not the other—the Father not the Son, and so on. Distinction exists to make communion possible; the three Persons are enveloped in an eternal movement of love, which makes them inseparable from one another. As St John Damascene put it, they are "like three suns fusing together in one light."[10] Each of the Persons is God by reason of consubstantiality. God is the three Persons considered together in complete and eternal communion.

This communion is so complete that the number three transcends all mathematical numbers. St Basil (the Great), the great theologian of the Holy Spirit, says: "We do not count simply from one to many, adding and saying one, two, three, or first, second, third. In confessing the three Persons (hypostases) without dividing their nature into many, we remain with the unity (monarchy) of the Father."[11] In other words, three does not mean a quantity, but a mysterious order of three that are one in communion. A modern Orthodox theologian has expressed it very well: "The triad of hypostases, united by distinction and distinguished by union, designates a difference that does not oppose, but is posed in posing the others."[12]

This way of organizing our thoughts on the Trinity finds its support in the New Testament. There each of the Persons is spoken of as a subsistent reality, each with a character whose purpose is the salvation and divinization of humankind. All essentialist abstraction and formalism is avoided. Its first idea of God is not a divine essence, a mystery without name, but precisely God as Father, Son and Holy Spirit; there is no risk of depersonalizing God. The idea of the unity of God is not of a single nature, the identical basis of each of the Persons, but the concept of the Father communicating his whole substance to the other Persons. The Trinity is one because it stems from the One who is the Father.

While the first conception risked falling into modalism, the danger here is of subordinationism. Both start from unity, whether of nature or of Person (the Father). The monarchy of the Father is so absolute that everything has its being and resolution in him; Son and Spirit form expressions (even if eternal and infinite ones) of the one principle, the Father. The Father is, in the final analysis, everything, with the other Persons being eternal derivations of him. Equality of substance (nature or essence) is of course maintained and emphasized, but nevertheless, by deriving everything from the Father, the theological formulations favour a subordinationist understanding.

The easiest way to avoid this danger is always to bear in mind that the relationships in questions are between divine, supremely loving Persons; we humans can define our relationships as against one another, but theirs are always for, by, with and in one another. As St Gregory Nazianzen put it: "The glory of the Principle [Father] never consists in lessening those who proceed from him. . . . God is the Three considered together; each is God by reason of consubstantiality; the three are God by reason of monarchy [of the Father]."[13]

(c) From Trinity of Persons to Unity of Nature-communion

This conception starts from the specific experience of Christian faith, which puts the Trinity first. What really exists is Father, Son and Holy Spirit. There is one God because there is eternal communion and unity between the three Persons. It is not enough to state that three Persons exist; this can lead to the heresy of tritheism (belief in the existence of three gods). What has to be upheld is the fact that each Person is fully and completely in the others. Tradition, particularly as expressed by the Cappadocian theologians and St John Damascene, insisted on the complete *perichoresis, cir-*

cuminsessio or *circumincessio* of the Trinity.[14] These technical terms are a means of expressing "the intimate and perfect inhabitation of one Person in the other." The three divine Persons are reciprocally inter-penetrating (Greek *perichoresis,* Latin *circumincessio*).

Jesus said clearly, "You must believe me when I say that I am in the Father and the Father is in me" (John 14:11); and, including men and women: "Father, may they be one in us, as you are in me and I am in you, so that the world may believe it was you who sent me" (17:21). The Council of Florence expressed the radical and eternal communion between the three divine Persons: "The Father is wholly in the Son and wholly in the Holy Spirit; the Son wholly in the Father and wholly in the Holy Spirit; the Holy Spirit wholly in the Father and wholly in the Son. None precedes the other in eternity, none exceeds the other in greatness, nor excels the other in power" (DS 1331, CT).

Such an exchange of love obtains between the three Persons: life flows so completely between them, the communion between them is so infinite, with each bestowing on the others all that can be bestowed, that they form a union. The three possess one will, one understanding, one love.

We must not imagine them as three individuals who come together in communion and unite; this would not avoid tritheism. We cannot say that they establish relationships between themselves, but that they exist as Persons precisely because of their mutual bestowal of life and love. So they are distinct in order to unite, and unite not in order to fuse into each other, but so that one may contain the others. Their unity, rather than a unity of substance or origin (the Father), would be a unity of Persons by reason of the reciprocal communion between them. The *Filioque,* therefore, serves to augment the *Spirituque.* This eternal perichoresis of love and life between Father, Son and Holy Spirit forms the original pattern of all love, life and communion in creation, made in the image of the Trinity.

I do not wish to enlarge further on this conception here, as it is the one adopted in this work; later chapters attempt to present a more complete and analytical view of it—its relevance for society and the church as generator of greater participation, communion and symmetry at all levels of human relationships.

Having looked at these three tendencies in trinitarian thought, we now need to go on to consider each of the key words which enables theology to speak with some meaning of this august mystery. In the end, of course, the conscientious theologian and the thinking faithful can only bow down in respectful silence before a mystery that it seems more fitting to contemplate and adore than to reflect on and lay open. But this is only in the end; first we have to make the effort to understand.

3. THE PLAY OF TRINITARIAN LANGUAGE: EXPLANATION OF KEY TERMS

(a) Substance = Nature = Essence: One Sole

To express what is one in God, the teaching tradition of the church has made use of these three technical terms: substance, nature and essence. They are used as synonyms (DS 804), yet each has its own nuances.

Substance (from the Latin *sub-stare,* to be under, to uphold) designates that reality which forms a permanent basis for all the differentiations that arise in it, on it, or from it. So, in the mystery of the Trinity, we say that the divine substance is what permanently sustains and unites the three Persons; the divine substance is in each of them, in a differing manner and an equally real, full and true form, in such a way that the oneness and unity of the divine substance result in the unity of the Persons.

Nature (from the Latin *nasci,* to be born; equivalent to Greek *physis,* from *phyomai,* to be born) designates this same substance in the measure that it constitutes a principle that originates something, a principle of activity. So we can represent the divine nature as such exuberance of inner life, intelligence and love that it differentiates and takes shape in three real modes (not only for us), which are the three Persons; or we can say that this same nature personalized in three distinct manners acts outside the trinitarian circle and creates the universe of beings as manifestations of its glory (see DS 804).

Essence designates the inner rationale of being, that by which something is what it is. The essence of God (God's *divinitas*) is what constitutes God as God, as different from any other being. So the

essence of God is being, goodness, love, truth, and God is these in
an infinite, eternal, omnipotent way. Essence indicates the very
substance or nature in a more abstract way as we enquire into what
is the proper meaning of God as distinct from any other beings we
can imagine.[15]

It is important always to bear in mind that such key words are
theoretical instruments, belonging to Greco-Roman culture,
through which we can utter something—otherwise we would be
totally silent—of the mystery of God. God is not really substance,
or nature, or essence; God is above such categories. So when we
apply these categories to the divine reality we do so by analogy and
approximation, though using the words in an absolute sense which
excludes any shadow of imperfection. Failure to recognize the
limitations of the language we use of God can produce theological
distortions, as we have already seen.

(b) Hypostasis = Subsistence = Person: Three Really Distinct

To express what is three in God, the official theology of the
church has used the words hypostasis (Greek), person (Latin) and
subsistence. Despite the connotations proper to each of these
terms, they are used as equivalents in discourse about the Trinity.
Let us quickly examine the meaning of each.

Hypostasis indicates individuality existing in itself, distinct from
all other individualities. So we say that each divine Person exists in
a singular existence, distinct from that of the other two.[16]

Subsistence is the Latin equivalent of hypostasis. Each divine
Person is a "subsistant," that is, has a real existence, independent
of our appreciation and representation, therefore existence in a
singular mode.

Person designates a thinking individuality or spiritual subject in
possession of itself. The term was originally—as we saw earlier—
used to signify the objective existence of three in God. The words
person and hypostasis did not claim to say more than this, but
since *persona* for the Latins implied a certain subjectivity and
spirituality, the way was opened for deeper theological reflection
on the reality of "person" applied to the Trinity, which reflection
is one of the most significant achievements of Western culture.
The full meaning of what it is to be a "person," one of the most

important concepts in the world today, emerged from the discourse of faith on the Trinity and the incarnation.

Without going too deeply into the different stages of enrichment of the understanding of what it means to be a person, it is worth looking at three decisive steps which led to a better understanding of the incomprehensible mystery of God.

The *first* meaning of "person" is the classical one: an *existing subject* (subsistant) *distinct from others*. This formulation challenged the monotheistic unitarianism which denied a plurality of Persons in God; it also steered clear of modalism (the Persons being just human ways of looking at God). It still, however, contained the danger of tritheism, through over-insistence on the individuality of the three Persons. This danger was avoided through stressing that they are all consubstantial, or that the Son and Spirit proceed from one single principle (the substance of the Father). If the Persons are distinct from each other, this is because each proceeds from the one principle in a different way or because each appropriates the one same divine essence in a different manner.

This understanding helps to show that one Person is not another and that there are, really and truly, three divine Persons. But it does not include reflection on the properties of each Person. When it comes to putting a specific content to each Person, St Augustine expresses his anguish: "When it is asked three what, then the great poverty from which our language suffers becomes apparent. But the formula three persons has been coined, not in order to give a complete explanation by means of it, but in order that we might not be obliged to remain silent."[17] St Augustine also raises the following question: if each of the Persons is really distinct from the others, why do we call them all by a common and generic name—person? Should we not give each of them a specific denomination? From which he concludes: "we cannot find such words; person is a very generic term which can also be applied to human beings, despite the distance existing between God and man."[18] In other words, distinctiveness is only one of the aspects of a person. There are others: in the Middle Ages that of uncommunicability or irreducibility was particularly stressed.

The *second* meaning of "person" was worked out in the process of powerful scholastic reflection on the processions and relationships between the divine Three.[19] In relationship, one term is ordered to another. In God, this ordering is eternal and substantial (not accidental and transitory as with creatures); therefore the relationships are subsistent. "Person" then comes to mean a *subsistent relationship* or the *individual and incommunicable subsistence of a rational nature.* In the Trinity, everything possible is placed in common, enters into the play of relationships and completes the communion.

However complete and eternal the communion, nevertheless, there is always a residue: the fact of being the one who bestows everything on the other. So the Father bestows everything on the Son and the Holy Spirit, except the fact of being Father; the Son bestows everything on the Father and the Holy Spirit except the fact of being the Son begotten by the Father; the Holy Spirit bestows everything on the Father and the Son except the fact of being the Spirit breathed out by the Father and the Son. This incommunicability was seen by the theologians of the Middle Ages as the essence of a person. Duns Scotus, the brilliant Franciscan theologian who speculated deeply on the specificity of each person, defined it as "actual" and "potential" incommunicability. So one person exists in and for himself or herself in complete independence of another precisely in the act of bestowing himself or herself completely on another. This explains the trinitarian axiom that everything in God is one or common to the three Persons except the otherness in the relationship by which one Person proceeds from another and so is distinguished from the other. Put simply: everything in God is one except the fact of the Father being Father, the Son being the Son and the Holy Spirit being the Holy Spirit.

Consciousness of oneself is not an element that distinguishes the Persons: each has it, but it is conferred by the divine substance embodied in each. The reality of this substantial incommunicability could lead to tritheism, but this is avoided through stating that the three Persons are real embodiments of one and the same unique divine substance. The incommunicability of each Person resides in the manner proper to that Person by which each really (not modalistically) embodies that divine substance.

Compared with the first understanding of "person," this step shows an advance: it stresses the *relationship* between the three divine Persons. However, in this relationship, it emphasizes what cannot enter into relationship, being the condition that makes the relationship possible: the incommunicability of each in the act of communicating. Modern thought tries to explore the aspect least considered in medieval thought.

The *third* concept of "person" is that elaborated by modern thought. Here the idea of person is of a *being-for,* a *knot of relationships,* an identity formed and completed on the basis of relationships with others. Persons are, in the first place, conscious beings, with an ontological configuration (or a substantial one, as would have been said in classical times); in the second place, however, they are so structured as always to be oriented toward others. Being-in-itself is enriched in the encounter with the other, which nourishes reciprocity toward the other. Interiority (consciousness in its ontological aspect) and openness to the other (freedom and the ethical dimension) constitute the mode of being proper to a person. Jesus points to this dialectic between himself and the Father: "I am in the Father and the Father is in me" (John 14:11; 17:21).

This concept helps in understanding the relationship between the three divine Persons. It is not a question of applying a strictly modern understanding of "person" to the Trinity, since there are not three consciousnesses there, but only one, just as there is only one freedom and only one happiness. At most we can say that in the Trinity there is one substantial consciousness (nature) which is really expressed by three divine, conscious beings (Persons). What we can say is that, analogically, each divine Person is a centre of interiority and freedom, whose raison d'être (nature) consists in being always in relation to the other Persons, thereby avoiding a purely tritheistic conclusion. Is this the same as the traditional approach, which speaks of three subsistants in one nature? The modern concept is not opposed to the classical one, but develops and completes it, making the mystery of the Trinity more accessible through the mystery of what it is to be a person, and giving a better understanding of why the mystery of being a person is an image and likeness of the three divine Persons of the Trinity.

Again, we need to remember the fragmentary nature of the theoretical instruments we use to try to probe the meaning of the Christian God—Father, Son and Holy Spirit. That there is one and three in God is a matter of faith. That we call what is one in God "nature" (substance or essence) and what is three "persons" is a matter of theology, a human construct whose purpose is better to glimpse the reality of the mystery. St Augustine was right to say that these expressions (nature and person) are "born of necessity" and used more to avoid errors and heresies than to express an adequate appreciation of the Holy Trinity.

(c) Processions: Two—By Begetting and Breathing-out

Our experience of the saving presence of God in history teaches us that besides the Father, the absolute and ultimate mystery, there are the Son and the Holy Spirit, who are also called God. We also know that the Son proceeds and comes from the Father (John 8:42) and that the Holy Spirit is sent by the Son from the Father, since this Spirit of truth proceeds from the Father (John 15:26). There is an order in the three Persons: the Father first, the Son second and the Holy Spirit third. The witnesses of revelation of this mystery further testify that the Persons proceed one from another. "Procession" (*processio* or *emanatio* in Latin, *ekporeusis* or *probolē* in Greek) designates the origin of one Person from another. So there are two processions in the mystery of the Trinity: that of the Son and that of the Holy Spirit. The Father begets the Son from all eternity and with (or through) the Son originates the Holy Spirit.

It is of course understood that there can be no temporal succession in God, since in God everything is eternal (with no temporal before or after) and simultaneous; nor is there anything passive in the acts of begetting, since God is explosion and implosion of life, intelligence and love. The Father proceeds from no one, as the Council of Florence declared: "All that the Father is or has, He has not from another, but from Himself; He is the origin without origin" (DS 1331). His quality is to be not-born, as prime-begetting source from which everything emanates and develops.

Theology after St Augustine, by way of St Thomas Aquinas (whose hermeneutic was taken up by the magisterium), uses an analogy drawn from human spiritual development to explain the procession in the Trinity. This analogy is based on processes specific to and immanent in the human spirit. It is proper to the spirit to be present to itself, to formulate an idea of itself—an operation of the intellect; it also loves itself, with total adherence of itself to itself— an operation of the will; finally, the thinking subject becomes a thought object for itself—setting up a connection between the two terms, which is love.

By analogy with this human process, two immanent operations—understanding and volition—can be attributed to the absolute Spirit, without damaging the infinite oneness of God. The Father knows himself absolutely and the expression of this (Logos, Word) is the Son. This is the first procession, and has the character of a *begetting*. This begetting is described in the same terminology as that used of human cognitive processes (conceiving, concept, reproduction); because it is an eternal and absolutely perfect process, the Father does not cause the Son, but *communicates* his own being to him; this is why the Father is said to be not the cause, but the *origin* of the Son.

God the Father contemplates himself in the Son and loves himself. The love that unites the Father and the Son is called the Holy Spirit. As the Son proceeds from an operation of the intellect, so the Holy Spirit proceeds from an operation of the will of the Father and the Son.

In this way, Son and Spirit proceed from two processes of origination, each in due order: the Son from the Father alone, the Spirit from the Father and the Son (in the Latin understanding). Without beginning, interruption or end, the Father begets, the Son is born and the Holy Spirit proceeds (see DS 804). We shall analyze this type of analogical understanding, which seeks to clarify "processions" in God, in more detail when we look at each of the three Persons in greater depth.

(d) Relationships: Four Real Ones

That fact that the Son proceeds from the Father and the Spirit from the Father and the Son (in Latin theology) as from one beginning, means that there are mutual relationships between the three Persons. "Relationship" means an ordering of one Person to another, a connection between each of the divine Three.

The processions in the Trinity enable us to discern four real relationships within it: (1) the *fatherhood* of the Father to the Son; (2) the *sonship* of the Son to the Father; (3) the *breathing-out* of the Spirit by the Father and the Son; (4) the Spirit's *being breathed out* by the Father and the Son.

As already inferred, the relationships constitute the Persons;[20] in other words, it is through relationship that one Person is situated in relation to the others and differentiated from them, each essentially supposing and requiring the others. So the Father supposes the Son; the Son necessitates the Father; the Holy Spirit can be understood only in the breathing-out by the Father and the Son. The Persons are mutually distinguished (one from another) and required (one situating the others).[21]

Each of the Persons bestows everything (all perfections), except that which is proper and exclusive to that Person and therefore incommunicable: fatherhood in the Father, sonship in the Son, being breathed out in the Spirit. As the Council of Florence put it: "the Father has through generation given to the only-begotten Son everything that belongs to the Father, except being Father" (DS 1301, CF). The same applies to the Holy Spirit. Fatherhood is the personal property of the Father; it is what distinguishes him from the Son. And again the same applies to the Holy Spirit in relation to the source of its procession: the Father and the Son (keeping to the Latin understanding).

Relationship is the key to understanding the idea found originally in St Basil and St Gregory Nazianzen and which received its classic formulation from St Anselm of Canterbury: "In God all is one where there is no opposition of relation."[22] The Persons alone establish difference in God; all the rest is one and shared equally by the three Persons. We have already seen that these relationships are entities in themselves. This means that each relationship is identified with the divine substance: the whole divine substance is in the Father, likewise in the Son and in the Holy Spirit, appropriated in a different way by each.

(e) Notions: Five

By trinitarian "notions" we mean the characteristics or notes (hence "notions") that enable us to know the Persons as themselves, hence different from one another.

There are usually five notions enumerated: *fatherhood* and *unoriginatedness* (origin) for the first Person (the Father); *sonship* (Word, Image, expression, sacrament) for the second (the Son); *breathing-out* for the Son and the Father; *being breathed out* for the Spirit (gift, love, nexus between Father and Son).

(f) Affirmations: Essential and Notional

The designation *essential* is applied to affirmations based on the divine essence, valid both for God (essence) and the Persons, bearers of this divine essence. So we can say: God is merciful, the Trinity is merciful, the Father is merciful.

Notional affirmations are those applied only to the Persons in their distinction from one another. So we might say that begetting and breathing-out are notional realities and allow notional affirmations. And we might say that there are four notional actions in God: *begetting, being begotten, breathing out* and *being breathed out;* also five notional properties: being-without-origin, fatherhood, sonship, breathing-out and being breathed out.

(g) Perichoresis, Circumincession, Circuminsession

The relationships of communion between the three Persons, one totally within the other, the fact of Father, Son and Holy Spirit being consubstantial, allow contemplation of the full interpenetration of one Person by another. This reality is expressed by the Greek word *perichoresis* or the Latin terms *circuminsessio* or *circumincessio.*[23] As the structure of these terms suggests, they mean: cohabitation, co-existence, interpenetration of the divine Persons by one another. There is a complete circulation of life and a perfect co-equality between the Persons, without any anteriority or superiority of one over another. Everything in them is common and communicated one to another, except what cannot be communicated: what distinguishes one from the others. The Father is fully in the Son and the Holy Spirit; the Son is fully in the Father and the Holy Spirit; the Holy Spirit is fully in the Father and the Son. This is the source of the utopia of equality—with due respect for differences—full communion and just relationships in society and in history.

(h) The Trinity as Sole Agent of Action

Perichoresis shows us that the three divine Persons always act together in creation. Such is the communion between them that when they create (the universe, humankind, history), save, judge, intervene in the course of events, they always do so jointly. If this were not the case, we should have three infinite beings, three creators, three eternal beings; the interpenetration between the Three would be lost.

(i) Appropriated and Proper Actions

All actions *ad extra* (directed outside the Trinity, within creation) should be attributed to the three Persons together. Nevertheless, the liturgy and spirituality attribute certain actions which in fact belong to all three Persons to one in particular because of a certain affinity with that Person. So *creation* is attributed to the Father, since within the Trinity he is the begetter and breather-out (along with the Son). *Revelation* is attributed to the Son, since in the Trinity he is the expression and revelation of the Father; likewise, *redemption* is attributed to him, since he became incarnate and set us free. *Sanctification* is attributed to the Holy Spirit, since the Spirit, above all, is called the Holy One. Such actions are therefore "appropriated" by one or another Person, even though they belong to all three. When the Trinity acts as *"suprema causa efficiente"* (DS 3814) in relation to creation, then Father, Son and Holy Spirit will always be acting simultaneously and in perfect *koinōnia*.

Certain actions are, however, "proper" to one Person or another. A Person can establish a personal relationship with a creature, not in creation as such (since this is the work of the Three), but in the self-communication of the Son or the Holy Spirit with a creature. It is as though the Persons, within the Trinity, assimilated the creature on which to bestow themselves personally. So we can say that the incarnation is proper to the Son, since only he became incarnate. Clearly the incarnation also involves a presence of the Father (sending the Son) and of the Holy Spirit (coming down and forming the Son's humanity in Mary's womb), but effectively the Son alone was incarnated. The same can be said of the Holy Spirit: as we put it, the Spirit came upon Mary and bestowed itself on her in such a way that this action is proper to the Spirit; or we can speak of its presence in the lives of the just and as the soul of the church.

(j) The Divine Missions

The idea of proper actions leads to an understanding of divine missions. "Mission" means the presence of a divine Person in a creature, the self-communication of one Person to a created being. The divine Persons do not restrict their self-bestowal to within the circle of the Trinity: the outpouring of divine life and love spreads outward into creation. It is not enough for the Trinity to have given us goodness, beauty, love, strength, and so on: the Trinity sought to insert someone from our history within its own eternal history. So the Father sent his Son into the world so that, in the person of Jesus, he might divinize, teach and "affiliate" all men and women. And with the Son he sent the Holy Spirit so that, through the woman Mary, it could breathe the spirit into humanity and show the maternal face of God.

The scriptures speak explicitly of the sending of the Son and his mission: the Son was sent by the Father—John 3:16; 5:23, 36, 38; the Holy Spirit was likewise sent by the Father through the Son—Luke 24:19; John 14:16, 26; 15:26; 16:7; Galatians 4:6. The personal presence of the Son and the Spirit in the world shows us the unutterable and mysterious visage of the Father. The incarnation and the coming of the Spirit already signify the total coming of God to creation and anticipate enthronement of creation in God and the Kingdom. This makes them eschatological events, definitive and anticipatory of the end eternally willed by God.

(k) Economic Trinity and Immanent Trinity

This quick look at divine missions leads to another expression that needs clarifying. As Karl Rahner put it axiomatically: "The economic Trinity *is* the immanent Trinity and vice-versa";[24] the way God comes to meet human beings is the way in which God subsists. "Economic Trinity" designates the presence of the Trinity or of the Persons of the Trinity within the history of salvation. This history was seen by the early church as an *oeconomia,* that is, a series of phases of a divine plan being progressively both realized and revealed. So we can say that it was through the actual passing of Jesus Christ, the incarnate Son, through history, and by the action of the Holy Spirit in history, that the mystery of the Trinity was revealed to us. In the Christian experience of faith and revelation, God appears as Father, Son and Holy Spirit. The Trinity revealed in this historical-salvific process is called the economic Trinity.

Now, God's revelation to us is of the actual being of God. So if God appears to us as a Trinity, this is because God's actual being is a Trinity. And God is a Trinity (Father, Son, Holy Spirit) not just for us, but in itself. If God appears to us as source mystery and unoriginated origin (so absolute transcendence), and so as Father, this is because God is Father. If God is revealed to us as enlightening Word and Truth, and so as Son or eternal Logos, this is because God is Truth. If God is communicated to us as Love and Power for the purposes of carrying out God's final plan, and so as Holy Spirit, this is because God is Holy Spirit. The reality of the Trinity makes the manifestation of the divine in history be trinitarian, and the truly trinitarian manifestation of God makes us understand that God is in fact a Trinity of Persons: Father, Son, Holy Spirit. The Trinity understood in itself, the internal relationship between the three Persons, the eternal mystery of trinitarian procession—all this is known as the immanent Trinity.

4. SYNTACTICAL RULES FOR CORRECT DISCOURSE ON THE TRINITY

Discourse on the Trinity over the centuries has produced a set of strict syntactical rules governing the way of speaking of God and the divine Persons, the purpose of which is to safeguard faith from inadequate or erroneous expressions. It is not a matter of trying to domesticate the mystery, but of regulating language so as not to divide the divine essence or confuse the divine Persons. So:

(i) Nouns expressing the divine essence should be used in the singular: mercy, goodness, wisdom. So we do not say "three mercies" any more than we speak of three gods; there is one mercy as there is one God.

(ii) Adjectives and adverbs should not be used to designate the nature of God. So we should not speak of the "triple God," or say "the Trinity exists in the only God," but "the one God is the Trinity." Yet it is legitimate to speak of the "triune God" (DS 528).

(iii) Properties of each Person may not be applied to the nature of God. We do not speak of the nature of God begetting, being born, proceeding, but of the Father begetting, the Son being born, the Spirit proceeding (DS 804). But taking God in the sense of

Person (since each Person is God), we can speak of God being Father, God suffering, God dying on the cross, and so on.

(iv) Certain idioms have been coined as better expressing the truth of faith: so we say not that the Persons have *an equal* essence, but *one* essence, since the essence of God is not in common, but *one*, with an absolute numerical oneness. So we can describe the three Persons as "other" than each other, but not as "another thing" than each other, since the three share one and the same nature (DS 805). Nor do we speak of "different" Persons, but of "distinct" Persons; nor of God "alone," since God is always three.

To sum up the grammar of the Trinity in short statements, we can follow St Bonaventure's *Breviloquim* in saying that in God we can discern, in ascending number:

—*One* nature (essence or substance);

—*Two* processions (or emanations): of Son and Holy Spirit;

—*Three* Persons (hypostases or subsistents): Father, Son and Holy Spirit;

—*Four* relationships: fatherhood, sonship, breathing-out, being breathed out;

—*Five* notions: unbegottenness, fatherhood, sonship, breathing-out, being breathed out.

5. CONCLUSION: SEVEN PROPOSITIONS OF TRINITARIAN ORTHODOXY

Having examined all these aspects, we are now in a position to sum up the main tenets of orthodox faith in the Trinity, as worked out by the church over the years, in seven propositions:

1. The first Person of the Trinity is God the Father, almighty creator of heaven and earth, the unoriginated origin, source and generator of the life of the Trinity. He is the Father of the only-begotten Son. He is also the active principle of the breathing-out of the Holy Spirit (DS 1, 10, 19, 21, 25, 27, 36, 40, 44, 46, 48, 50, 55, 60, 64, 71, 125, 139, 150, 441, 470, 485, 490, 525, 572, 683, 1330, 1862, 3326).

2. The second Person of the Trinity is the Son, eternally begotten of the Father, without this making him a creature. He receives the divine nature, essence and substance from the Father, by communi-

cation, not through an arbitrary act of will or any external coercion. Being consubstantial with the Father, he is his Word, image and sacrament both in the intra-trinitarian sphere and in his incarnate mission (DS 2, 11, 25, 40, 60, 71, 125, 150, 178, 258, 266, 300, 683, 3350, 40-51, 250-63, 430, 441).

3. The third Person of the Trinity is the Holy Spirit, who proceeds, as from one source, from the Father and the Son, being consubstantial with them, and together with them adored and glorified. The procession of the Spirit from the Father and from (or through) the Son should not be called begetting, but breathing-out, an eternal expression of the love between the Father and the Son (DS 570, 1300, 1529, 1552, 1561, 1690, 1986, 3330, 3331).

4. This concerns the properties and saving missions of the divine Persons. In the order of immanence (the Trinity in itself), we say that the properties of the Father are unoriginatedness and fatherhood; the property of the Son is to be begotten; that of the Holy Spirit to be breathed out by the Father and the Son (or through the Son). In the order of the history of salvation (the economic Trinity), faith believes and professes that the Father is the origin of saving history and of the missions of the Son and the Holy Spirit. Incarnation is proper to the Son; to the Holy Spirit, the mission of sanctifying and of producing the humanity of Jesus in the womb of the Virgin Mary (DS 71, 188, 284, 367, 470, 532, 800; 101, 145, 527, 538, 1522, 3806; 60, 145, 681, 3325).

5. This deals with the distinction between the divine Persons in the intradivine sphere. The Persons are distinguished from one another by relationships of proceeding and origin. They are distinct in order to unite and the distinction is based on the mutually relative opposition between them: fatherhood, sonship, breathing-out and being breathed out (DS 73, 125, 150, 188, 408, 470, 527, 532, 570, 800, 850, 973, 1330).

6. This has to do with the communion obtaining between the three divine Persons. The distinction between the Persons and the divine nature is merely formal or virtual; otherwise, we would have a foursome: the three Persons plus the divine nature. Their mutual interpenetration—for existing one in, by and for the others—forms the basis of the existence of the divine Persons, an expression of eternal communion (DS 534, 745, 800, 803, 1330, 3814).

7. The revelation of the Trinity retains the character of mystery:

even revealed, the truth of the Trinity remains a mystery ever open to new efforts of human understanding, but finally an absolute mystery handed to us in freedom and love for our divinization (DS 3115, 3814). This mystery is of the essence of the Trinity, and so will remain a mystery for all eternity.

CHAPTER V

The Trinity in Theological Imagery

The rigidity of trinitarian formulas and the exactness of theological expressions serve the purposes of those who are learned in the Christian faith. They do not, it must be said, make for ease of praying, nor do they exactly kindle the hearts of the faithful. They are needed for intellectual understanding of the faith, and this is the limit of their validity. But they are not the only way of approaching the mystery of the Trinity. The language of catechetics, preaching and spirituality makes extensive use of imagery; and it is through symbols and images that we can come to a fuller appreciation of the meaning of this perennial mystery, as the Fathers themselves did in their long and learned treatises on the subject.

1. SIGNIFIER, SIGNIFIED AND SIGNIFICANCE

Before we can go further, we need to clarify three concepts, signifier, signified and significance. The "signifier" consists of the technical terms employed in explanations of this truth of faith, as seen in the previous chapter: nature, person, relationship, processions, missions, and so on. The "signified" is made up of the content of these signifiers: so nature is what unites in God and is one and the same in the three Persons; person is what differentiates the Father, Son and Holy Spirit one from another and at the same time places them in communion with one another; procession is the order that exists between them, and so on. "Significance" is the affective content, the existential vibration set up in our lives by each of these terms (signifier and signified). The images and symbols through which we come to an overall relationship to the Trinity—or rather, to Father, Son and Holy Spirit—belong to this realm of significance. Images are not substitutes for technical terms nor for the defined teachings of the church;[1] we need to know what we want to say and what we should not say of the triune God when we try to think about the mystery. But images can lend definition and embodiment to what we learn from abstract concepts.

Just as words and concepts have their validity and their strict limitations—hiding more than they reveal, as St Augustine said— so images have their own strictly defined sphere of validity. Many of them can even be dangerous, giving us the impression of having caught the immeasurable reality of the mystery of the Trinity in the net of our imagination.

The importance of images lies in their ability to help us take certain attitudes to the Trinity in itself and to each of its Persons. So when we say "Father" or "Mother," the words evoke certain resonances in the depths of our psyche. We are dealing with archetypes charged with values, since they are bound up with the formative experiences of our psychological make-up. When we say "Son," we feel a relationship with Father and Mother, not one of dependence, but one of intimacy because of its source, one that can show itself in terms of recognition, giving, gratitude. In the same way, when we say "Holy Spirit," this evokes all that "spirit" means in terms of life, understanding, communion and loving. And those who allow themselves to be guided by the inspiration of the Spirit accept the Son and those who accept the Son come to see the paternal and maternal face of God. These attitudes form the basis of our living faith in the Trinity. Pedagogically, they also provide another starting-point for reflection. How could it be otherwise? In his great catechism *Oratio catechetica magna,* St Gregory of Nyssa wrote: "So when we learn to know the Word, reaching out of the sphere of our lives to that of the sovereign nature, we also come to know the Spirit, considering it in our own nature which is a shadow and image of the invisible power. . . . Piety requires us to believe in a Spirit (Breath) of God, in the divine nature, since there is also a Word of God. The Word of God cannot be inferior to our words: so just as our words are accompanied by breath, so the Word is accompanied by Breath (Spirit)."[2] This teaching is not deducing the Trinity from our experience; on the contrary, it is discovering likenesses and analogies in human experience in the light of the Trinity; these confirm the faith that we are made in the image and likeness of God who is always three in one.

2. "ECONOMIC" SYMBOLISM

The most accessible way to the Trinity is still the one that God chose: self-revelation through the course taken by Jesus Christ on earth (remember what was said in chapter 2). This shows that the relationship Jesus maintained with his God, whom he called Father, in a context of setting men and women free, reveals the Father and the Son at the same time. Jesus saw himself as the one sent by God, living in such close contact with God that he could express himself as divine. The power that was in him, the enthusiasm that imbued his preaching and the radiance he spread over those who listened to him showed the meaning of the Holy Spirit. We call these three God without thereby multiplying God. The Trinity bestows itself on our understanding through the life and actions of Jesus; not through abstract reflection on the depths of the mystery, but through the relationships, attitudes and actions of Jesus, which show the meaning of what it is to be divine. The "economic" symbolism contained in the expressions Father, Son and Holy Spirit allows us to enter into the reality of God's eternal being, as tri-unity. Access of the Trinity is through the actions of the divine persons: the Father sending the Son and acting as final point of reference for the whole of history; the Son speaking and acting in the Father's name on behalf of men and women, particularly the poor and sinners; the Spirit leading us to accept the Son and encouraging us to adore the Father.

This "economic" language runs right through the theological works of the Fathers. So St Ignatius of Antioch wrote to the Ephesians: "You are stones of the *Father's* temple, worked for the construction of God the Father, raised to the heights through the praise offered by *Jesus Christ,* praise that is the cross, using the *Holy Spirit* as a rope."[3] The three divine Persons appear in their action in human history. The Trinity is not a mystery of pure contemplation; it is a mystery of transformation of human lives, of the inrush of new ways of life, ever more like the life embodied in the divine Three.

3. PIOUS SYMBOLISM

The Holy Trinity is infused into the daily living of Christians who explicitly practise their faith. So all prayers and liturgies, all important acts, begin with the invocation of the Father, Son and Holy Spirit, and end with a form of thanking and glorifying the Father through the Son and Holy Spirit.

This presence of the Trinity is made visible in sacramental rites, particularly those of baptism and the eucharist. In baptism, the triple interrogation on belief in the three Persons with their corresponding attributes runs from the *Apostolic Tradition* of Hippolytus (d. 235) to the current rite. The celebration of the eucharist carries out a sort of universal recapitulation: the history of salvation runs from the Father through the liberating work of the Son and the transforming and unifying power of the Spirit. This is the *sacramentum fidei*![4]

4. ARCHETYPAL SYMBOLISM

The presence of three is more than just a question of numbers. It is a recognized archetype. It expresses a totality; psychologically, it is the symbol of personal individualization to the extent that the unconscious and conscious combine in a creative and harmonious way. The number three appears in endless forms in dreams, in pictorial representations, in conceptual formulas. It is a symbol that responds to human needs in the quest for integration, association and wholeness. On the anthropological level, it demonstrates the religious truth that human beings are the image and likeness of the triune God.

Study of representations of the Trinity shows that a fourth element is often introduced, usually feminine in nature: creation, the Virgin Mary, the eucharist. . . . This does not destroy the nature of the trinitarian symbolism, but shows its inner richness. The fourth element signifies the openness of the whole through inclusion of an extraneous element that thereby shares in integration.

Human integration (expressed in triads) does not rest content with itself, nor does it consist merely of a conjugation of all psychic energies, but reaches out to include other people, the world, history. The same applies to the mystery of the Trinity. In effect, as known to us, the triune God is never alone; God is communicated to us through the creation of the universe, then through self-bestowal in love and communion on intelligent beings. Therefore we say that the mystery of the Trinity is always, for us pilgrims, a historical-salvific mystery and an eternal process of communion overflowing the strictly trinitarian circle. This fact is expressed in the symbol of four: an open totality embracing other elements. So the famous icon by Andrei Rublev (c. 1410) is a wonderful representation of the three divine Persons, equal and at the same time distinct, around a table on which are the eucharistic species. The fourth element is not only the eucharist but also the person looking at the picture, being transported by it and so entering into the process of divinization—a central theme of Eastern spirituality and theology.

At other times the three Persons are seen crowning the Virgin Mary. There is a significant variant in the fresco in the church of Urschalling bei Prien, on the shores of Lake Chiemsee in Lower Bavaria, which shows the Holy Spirit as a woman, between the Father and Son who are resting their hands on the Virgin's breasts, with the lower parts of the Persons united in clear symbols of human generation. Or the Trinity is shown supported on a sphere which represents creation. What is always specifically expressed is the truth of faith that the Trinity is a mystery of communion and love involving and penetrating the whole universe so as to make it swim in the ocean of trinitarian life.

5. ANTHROPOLOGICAL SYMBOLISM

Faith in the Trinity enriches the intuition of faith that human beings are the image and likeness of the divinity, as expressed in Genesis 1:27. If there is a real symbol of this great mystery, this would be found in the vital dynamic of human beings, shown primarily as a living and simultaneous unity of three components, as St Augustine realized and explored in his *Treatise on the Holy Trinity.*[5] First comes the deep feeling that human beings are a mystery; the more they are known, the more there is to know; the exuberance of an individual existence is beyond categorizing. The mystery of human beings shows itself in self-understanding and understanding of the truth of one's own being; it is not intelligence that understands, but persons who are intelligent and bearers of their own truth. This mystery is not just expressed intelligibly; it is also communicated and establishes a communion of love with others; it is not will that loves, but persons who love and bestow themselves on one another. Deep feeling, understanding and will, or mystery, truth and love—these are not just "powers" of the soul; they are human life itself in its dynamic unity, always the same and always differentiated. Such manifestations are seen as figurative of a greater Reality, from which they come and of which they are images: the triune God, Father, Son and Holy Spirit. So by analogy with human life (already created in the image of the Trinity), we can say: the ultimate mystery, as mystery without origin and from which all things come, the source and final reference of all things, represents the Person of the Father. This same mystery, as communicated and seen to be true, symbolizes the Son. Finally, this mystery, inasmuch as it is given in love and brings all things together through the Son with the Father, means the Holy Spirit. There are not three mysteries here, but one, and it is open and living, in an eternal process of being-in-itself, going out from itself and returning to itself, embracing the whole of creation, but human beings in a special way.

The more we live true to our basic nature, in the purity and wholeness of its embodiment, the greater our potential for revealing the Trinity in history, and the further we advance on the road of access to the ultimate mystery that lives in its own existential depth: the Father, Son and Holy Spirit.

6. FAMILY SYMBOLISM

Anthropological symbolism lays special stress on *intra*-subjective relationships (human life as expression of the Trinity), with an emphasis on the unity of the triune God. Family symbolism has the advantage of underlining *inter*-subjective relationships and so emphasizing the tri-personal nature of God.[6]

The Old Testament saw marriage as a symbol of the relationship of love between the chosen people and their God; the New Testament uses the love of husband and wife as a symbol of the love of Christ for faithful humanity (the church: Eph. 5:23), an analogy that was taken up in tradition by great Greek theologians such as Gregory Nazianzen, Methodius and Ephraim. Its essential point is the related entities: father, mother, child (Adam-Eve-Seth). Together they form a single reality we call family. Father and mother love each other, know each other and accept each other. The child is the witness of this love in the eyes of the parents and the outside world. Analogically, relationships of love and knowledge exist in the Trinity: the Holy Spirit is proof that the Father and Son love each other, proclaiming and testifying to this love, and therefore called *condilectus* (co-loved). The Three together form the family of God, within which everything is bound up in the same circle of life, just as in a human family. This analogy is powerfully evocative, being based on the most natural of human experiences, one that has been raised to a sacrament in the Christian faith: married life. There is no need to introduce sexual differences into the analogy; it is enough to consider the personal differences that make up the plurality in unity of every family.

7. ECCLESIAL SYMBOLISM

Tertullian coined a famous phase, of which later theology has made too little use: "Where the Father, Son and Holy Spirit are, there also is the church, which is the body of the three."[7] Where is the mystery of the Trinity most visible today? In that community of faith, hope and love that tries conscientiously to live the ideal of unity put forward by Jesus to his disciples: "May they all be one. Father, may they be one in us, as you are in me and I am in you (John 17:21). The unity of the church does not consist in a bureaucratic uniformity, but in a perichoresis among all the faithful, in the service of others (mission).[8] This unity is built around three main axes: faith; worship; and organization for inner cohesion, mutual love and mission. These three aspects are embodied in the community itself: gathering to proclaim and deepen its faith; coming together to celebrate the presence of the *magnalia Dei* in history past and present; organized for the harmonious building of its own body, so that it can be of service to others, particularly the poor and those who have not heard its message. These axes are not three parts of the church, but the one and only church developing in these three specific aspects of its historical embodiment. This unity is not restricted to the sphere of worship; it shows too in the sharing of goods and life as found in the early community of the Acts (cf 2:44-5; 4:34-6). The community becomes a figure and analogy of the Trinity, making it palpable to humankind, to the extent that it achieves this interpenetration. By following the gospel, the church makes itself the temple of the triune God. The unity of the Trinity, which is always the unity of the three divine Persons, is reflected in the unity of the many who make up one community. This symbolism, like all the others, can be built up organically only in a community that is perpetually renewing itself, overcoming the hardening of its institutional arteries. It becomes "the body of the Three" not by merely existing as a church and calling itself such, but through its continual efforts to become a community of faith, celebration and service.

8. SOCIAL SYMBOLISM

Every human society is built, structured and lasts through history on the basis of the dialectical interaction among three basic structures: economic, political and symbolic. Through the economic structure, organized access to the goods of the earth guarantees production and reproduction; it is a basic structure because it involves everyone without exception, has to be permanently attended to and makes all other manifestations of life possible. The political structure concerns the organization of social relationships, ways of living together and of distributing work for the common good; no one lives outside the complex of social relationships and everyone occupies a particular place in the human whole. The symbolic structure (ideas, philosophies, religions, and so on) deals with the meaning human beings attach to their work, to their living together, to their lives, failings, history, death. No human organization can survive without these three basic structures; they are all necessary for the furtherance of life, for the furtherance of social and community relations and for giving value to human activities and meaning to human hopes.

These three structures are always interwoven, mutually interdependent and inseparable, three embodiments of one and the same society, so that the economic sphere always contains the political and symbolic, the political contains the economic and symbolic and the symbolic contains the economic and political. There is a real perichoresis between these structures. They can take different historical forms, in some of which there will be greater participation and community, in others more segregation and conflict. The more a society develops structures of interaction in which human beings, in private and in society, can find their lives and their hopes promoted and set free, the more it will reflect the Trinity, which is a living-together of diversity in the communion and unity of one life and mystery. As we have seen, the basic reality of the Trinity consists precisely in the interpenetration and harmonious co-existence between the three divine Persons; these find a reflection, even if only a pale one, in the interplay between the three structures that support human society.

9. MATERIAL SYMBOLISM

For teaching purposes, classical trinitarian theology used analogies drawn from the sphere of material creation. So it was said that the sun, its rays and its light made up one reality; or fire, light and heat; or three candles burning with one flame; or the trefoil, which is one leaf with three distinct points, and so on. More recently, the three basic energies of the physical world have been used: gravitational, electro-magnetic and atomic energies forming the single reality of energy.[9] The evocative power of such images is much reduced by their formal nature and slender relation to the processes of life and meaning. Such material symbolism can be useful in explaining doctrines, but cannot lead to an encounter with the triune God.

10. FORMAL SYMBOLISM

Finally, Christian teaching uses purely formal symbols, drawn from mathematics, such as the equilateral triangle, which has one area and three absolutely equal sides. This symbol can be given a halo to express the glory of the Trinity and a brief legend to express the unity of the divine nature as well as the distinction between and equality of the three Persons, as in this diagram:

11. CONCLUSION: THE NECESSARY BUT LIMITED NATURE OF SYMBOLS

Great theologians such as St John Damascene and St Thomas Aquinas[10] have clearly pointed to both the importance and limitation of this way of understanding and interiorizing the mystery of faith. As God is incorporeal, it is both foolish and even impious to attempt to represent God in corporeal figures. Yet the whole of creation, human beings and the incarnation of the Son of God open up possibilities of glimpsing images of God reflected in history. In such images, the fourth Lateran Council said, there is more dissimilarity than similarity between Creator and creature (DS 806). Therefore all human imagery, from whatever source it is drawn, has its limitations. On the level of intellectual understanding, it cannot shed light on the glowing darkness of the mystery of the Trinity.[11]

Nevertheless, as I said at the beginning of this chapter, there is the whole field of human significance which is better expressed in images than in conceptual categories, which fail to satisfy the demands of the human spirit in its endless quest for an expression of the whole. This whole can be expressed only through symbols which spring from the depths of the personal and collective unconscious. No concept, not even the most systematic one possible, can take the place of symbols of the whole with their suggestion of existential significance, unconditional value and unifying of meanings in one final Meaning. This is where symbols of the Trinity have an irreplaceable value. Through them, faith takes on shape, human beings feel themselves to be participants in the life of the Trinity and the Trinity is made present in our daily lives. There is a true perichoresis at work here, whose prototype is the perichoresis of the divine Persons themselves.

CHAPTER VI

The Doctrine of the Trinity in a Changed Cultural Situation

1. CHANGES AFFECTING THE DOCTRINE OF THE TRINITY

The preceding chapters have shown trinitarian theology, in its classic form, as a highly formal business, opening its depths of meaning only to initiates in the grammar and syntax of the Trinity. The great majority of the faithful, including most bishops and priests, hold back suspiciously from such excessively high flights of theological reasoning, which give the impression (not without its repercussions on the practice of faith) that the Trinity seems more of a *mysterium logicum* than a *mysterium salutis*.

Yet the sense of faith tells us that, despite all this, the mystery of the Trinity should be the deepest source, closest inspiration and brightest illumination of the meaning of life that we can imagine. There has to be a way of presenting it that will not hide these riches but bring them out in an adequate manner. There is still the suspicion (in the absence of sufficient evidence to the contrary) that the conceptual and terminological complications surrounding the Trinity owe less to the mystery itself than to our cultural heritage and to an approach that has paid more attention to clarity of concepts and forms than to finding a meaning for our lives.

Our age, too, is marked by a crisis of reason. Since instrumental and analytical reason has shown its destructive power in world wars, the destruction of almost all our eco-systems and the production of totalitarian ideologies, we have come to view it with considerable disquiet. We distrust its flights, its deductions, its capacity to discern truth from error. In the end, we approach reality and truth not only through *logos* (understanding) but mainly through *pathos* (feeling), not just through reason but also through the heart, and that approach is something that religions have both maintained and lived. Because of all this, the classic doctrine of the Trinity—which supposes confidence in reason and enthusiasm for its performance—has, for most if not all of our generation, lost much of its power of persuasion.

We need to remake faith our experience of the Christian God: Father, Son and Holy Spirit. When we speak of the Trinity we need to *see*, in faith, the divine phenomenon expressed in our speech. In other words, there is an urgent need to build a trustworthy bridge between experience and theology. Let me explain: reflection on the divine Persons in themselves, in their eternal process (theology), must keep a close link with the manifestations of the divine Persons in our saving history through the incarnation of the Son in Jesus Christ and the action of the Holy Spirit coming upon Mary and always working through historical processes (experience).

In retelling the mystery of the triune God we cannot leave out the contributions of our modern culture, which directly affect our understanding of the Trinity. The last two centuries have seen the rise of emphasis on subjectivity; perception is highly valued, the human person greatly prized; history is seen as a basic category for understanding life, society and freedom. Sciences of humanity, society and history have sprung up. The category of *person,* so decisive for trinitarian doctrine, has acquired a depth of meaning impossible in earlier centuries. How can we not take account of such contributions in our approach to the mystery of the Father, Son and Holy Spirit?

We are seeing with increasing clarity that God and world are not simply two opposed realities like transcendence and immanence, eternity and time, Creator and creature. This sort of metaphysic of representation belongs to a static vision of things. But if we introduce categories such as history, process, freedom, and so on, then dynamism, interplay of relationships, and dialectics of mutual inclusiveness make their appearance. The world emerges not as a mere otherness from God, but as the receptacle for God's self-communication. The world begins to belong to the history of the triune God.

This truth is confirmed with the incarnation and the coming of the Spirit. Something of creation and history begins to belong definitively to the second Person of the Trinity and something to the third. Through Jesus and Mary, humanity has been irreversibly inserted in the mystery of the Trinity, and this has consequences for our understanding of the Trinity. Reflection on this infinitely happy event has shown that the world and God should be seen as a sort of perichoresis, rather than as categories of simple opposition and distinction.

Such things show the need to rethink the doctrine of the Trinity so as to show the mystery in a more acceptable light. Our teaching needs to point to the reality of the triune God and, as far as possible, lead us into the heart of the mystery.

2. APPROACH ROADS TO THE TRINITY

This section aims to describe some tendencies in theological thought that take the challenges of the changed cultural situation into account. There are more specialized works on this subject,[1] so this is just a broad outline.

Common to all these tendencies is the fundamental view that reflection on the Trinity always has to start from the economic Trinity, that is, from the revelation of the mystery as it appears in the Christian scriptures. The Trinity was not revealed as a "doctrine" but as the story of the Son incarnate in Jesus and of the life-giving power of the Spirit shown in Mary, the church and humanity, with the mystery of the Father as the constant backdrop and final reference. Revelation is made through narrative rather than through formal reflection, though this can be found in John's Gospel. Patristic and liturgical studies have shown that in the church narrative has always been the starting-point for major thought on the Trinity. The economic Trinity, as shown in the documents which are revelations of our salvation in history, enables theology to rise to speculation on the immanent Trinity, what the Persons are in themselves and in their mutual relationship.

The first approach is *doxological:* here theologians are satisfied with what they find in the New Testament and liturgical tradition. For fear of speculation divorced from the history of salvation, they refuse to go beyond what the founding texts relate. They end in doxology, in praise and liturgical celebration of the three divine Persons: *per Filium in Spiritu Sancto ad Patrem* or *a Patre per Filium in Spiritu Sancto.* This is hardly theology; it has more to do with exegesis and spirituality.

The second approach is what might be called *historicist:* theologians confine themselves strictly to the revelation of the Trinity in history, which they see as God's process. For some theologians the one and only God becomes Trinity in the process of penetrating into creation. So in history a process is started whereby there is a "trinification of the one God by reason of his free decision to communicate himself to creatures, as happened in Jesus."[2] Here the Trinity would not be eternal, but would itself demonstrate an evolving history of God. We call this approach "historicist" because it absolutizes history to such an extent that it projects new realities on to the very mystery of God. It seems to break with the tradition of faith (and has been expressedly condemned, as we saw in chapter 4, 1 g), and so will not be adopted here.

In the third—*dialectical*—approach, theologians attempt to find the fundamental meaning of the presence of the Trinity in history and of history in the Trinity. They are dealing with a mystery of salvation, communicated not to satisfy our curiosity but to make us in the image of God.

God's self-revelation is of the real God, and since God is revealed as Father, Son and Holy Spirit, this means that God really is Father, Son and Holy Spirit. We can therefore formulate the basic axiom of trinitarian reflection: *"The economic Trinity is the immanent Trinity and the immanent Trinity is the economic Trinity."*[3]

This identification takes place in the incarnation and the coming of the Spirit. There is a self-communication of the Son and the Spirit in history which is not simply the result of the efficient causality of the one God, but a *personal act* by each of these Persons. The incarnation is the personal self-communication of the Son in such a way that the Son is really, not figuratively or metaphorically, present as Son in the human person of Jesus Christ. We can—following our theologoumenon—speak of the Holy Spirit in a similar way in relation to Mary. Son and Holy Spirit are attested as sent by the Father who makes himself present, in a particular way, in each, and acts in each. So incarnation and coming of the Spirit actualized the unity of the immanent Trinity with the economic Trinity and vice-versa.

On this basis, theology can do what is expected of it: reflect on the triune God not only in relation to history but in itself, as the hidden Mystery which reveals itself yet remains Mystery even in revelation. It can then go on to elaborate systematically on the revealed truth of the Trinity. Christian (Catholic and Protestant) theology, working from the common background of the economic Trinity as starting-point, displays various tendencies, of which the following are the most relevant:

(a) Continuing and Deepening Tradition

A significant number of theologians[4] are concerned with continuing and enriching the classical understanding of *person* (*subsistens distinctum*) in the light of modern contributions to the notion of person, which explore intuitions seminally present in the Cappadocians, St Thomas Aquinas, St Bonaventure and Duns Scotus.[5] The modern notion of person is basically that of being-in-relationship; a person is a subject existing as a centre of autonomy, gifted with consciousness and freedom. To avoid tritheism, stress is laid on *relationship,* the complete openness of one person to another; since what is in question is a spiritual entity, a person is viewed essentially as consciousness, not merely in the psychological sense of the centre of all psychic activity, but in the ontological sense of the permanent presence of the spirit to itself. It is therefore a presence of subject to subject and not just object to subject. The classical expression of this would be that trinitarian consciousness is an *essential act.* Being an essential act, it is performed by each of the Persons; it then appears as a *notional act.* There are then one consciousness and three conscious subjects.

This was given an exact formulation by Bernard Lonergan: "The Father, the Son and the Holy Spirit are, by means of a real consciousness, three subjects conscious as much of themselves as of each of the others, and as much of their notional act as of their essential act."⁶ The Father, the Son and the Holy Spirit are three intelligent and free subjects; but they possess the same intelligence and the same will, like a triangle with three angles but only one area.⁷ All three Persons affirm themselves as an "I," not in order to close in on themselves, but in order to be able to give themselves to the other two. What emerges is a real psychological perichoresis.

This perichoresis of subjectivities can also be expressed in another way, according to the model of a basic ontological analysis of the I-thou-we relationship. Personal existence displays two sorts of relationship, each with its own characteristic. The first consists of the I-thou relationship and produces *dialogue.* The second establishes the communion (common) relationship between the I and the thou and produces the *we.* The personal pronouns I-thou-we denote individuals not as closed in on themselves, but as open to others as their vis-à-vis or interlocutors (cf Gen. 2:18). The Father can be called the "I" in the Trinity who gives rise to the "thou" in the Trinity who is the Son. The Son is not only the Word *of* the Father, but also becomes Word *to* the Father. So, between the "I" and the "thou," a dialogue of knowledge and love, of mutual proposal and response, is established. The Holy Spirit, who proceeds by being breathed out by the Father and the Son, can be considered as the *we* of the Father and the Son, *our* Spirit (of the Father and the Son). The Spirit is also related to the Father and the Son in truth and love, deriving its personality from this relationship. In the Father-Son perichoresis, one is in the other; in the perichoresis involving the Holy Spirit, the Person of the Holy Spirit is in the other two Persons simultaneously.

To quote Heribert Mühlen, who worked out this analysis: "The Holy Spirit *is* as Person one Person in two Persons."⁸ This shows the peculiarity of the Holy Spirit, which classical trinitarian theology failed to clarify.

This line of thought sheds due light on the truth of faith that human beings are created in the image and likeness of the Trinity. The interplay of love, life and interpersonal relations in the bosom of the Trinity is reflected in human interpersonal and social relations, pressing for transformations of the present decadent situation to make it a more faithful reflection of the Reality that is the foundation of all community.

(b) Alternatives to the Concept of "Person"

Other theologians[9] see the concept of person applied to the Trinity as misleading. If we understand "person" as a subjectivity, a spiritual centre of action and freedom, and apply this straight to the Trinity, we fall, they say, into plain tritheism. Consciousness is not triplicated in the Trinity, even though each Person is conscious; each is conscious not in the sense of there being three subjectivities, but in the sense of there being one consciousness consubstantial to the three Persons. Consciousness and freedom are not distinctive in the Three, but common to them.

When classical theology used the term "person," it did not understand it in the same way that we do now. So without explaining this to people every time we use the term, we risk their understanding our words in a heretical sense. Because of these difficulties, Karl Barth proposed utilizing another ancient concept, used in trinitarian discussions in the fourth and fifth centuries: *mode of coming to be* or *manner of being*. These translate the Greek *tropoi hyparxeōs* or the Latin *modus entitativus*.[10] A manner of being is not a new being. So Barth maintains the unity of God while making a diversity in God possible. The Persons would then mean "three modes of coming to be" of one and the same absolute and eternal Subject.[11] Nevertheless, he still suggests keeping the concept of "person" to describe God overall, so as to avoid an impersonal or substantialist representation; God is the absolute Subject, the infinite Spirit, and therefore a centre of consciousness, love and freedom: a divine Person.

Karl Rahner puts forward a brilliant reflection on the Trinity, intentionally seeking to approximate it to Christian experience, on the grounds that the mystery happens in us before we formulate doctrine about it. His basic intuition consists in presenting God as an absolute mystery which communicates itself. This self-communication has a triple aspect: as a communicated reality that remains sovereign, incomprehensible, an unoriginated origin, it is called Father; as a reality that expresses itself, is present and is Truth, it is called Son; as a reality that welcomes this self-communication in love, it is called Holy Spirit. This triple aspect, Rahner warns, should not be seen as a merely *verbal* unfolding of a communication that is in itself undifferentiated; the communication should be seen as having three truly *real* and different aspects.

He advises not abandoning the classical terminology which uses the word "person" to express this triple self-communication: consecrated by long usage, it should be kept. But theologians need to explain it so as to avoid the risks inherent in the modern understanding. Following Barth, but adding a further precision, Rahner defines "person" as a *"distinct mode of subsistence."*[12] The advantage of using this definition to express what is three in God is, he claims, that it brings out the divine unity, whereas "three Persons" on its own says nothing about the unity between them.

While Rahner gains in theological clarity with this alternative to "person" (by dissipating the false tritheist image), he loses in spiritual clarity. No one can adore "a distinct mode of subsistence"; only Father, Son and Holy Spirit can be adored. "Distinct mode of subsistence," or "distinct mode of coming to be," in Barth's terminology, are expressions "situated on a sub-personal plane, somewhat reified, saying nothing to actual Christian life which exists on a personal plane, and above all leaves the *relative* character of the divine Persons in the shade."[13] For this reason, I would attach greater value to approaches that try to deepen the traditional concept of "person" than to those that seek an alternative to it.

(c) A New Starting-point: The Community and Social Aspect of the Trinity

Both the classical approaches to the Trinity and the recent ones sketched above have their serious inherent limitations. They are based either on the category of *substance* (nature or essence) or on that of *person* (subject, subsistant); their dominant tone of thought is either metaphysical or personalist. Social and historical factors are alluded to here and there, almost by chance, but without society, the community or history (of the cosmos and of humanity) forming either a starting-point or the object of sustained reflection; when they appear, they do so as a consequence of reflections on the concepts of "person" and "free subject," realities that find their supreme form of embodiment in the Trinity.

There is a renewal of trinitarian thought taking place now on the basis of reflection, still in its infancy, but very serious, on the links that bind women and men together in community and society—links that also involve the Persons of the Trinity. Society is not just the sum total of the individuals that make it up, but has its own being woven out of the threads of relationships among individuals, functions and institutions, which together make up the social and political community. Cooperation and collaboration among all produce the common good; within a multiplicity of social and political mediations and instruments and manifestations of community life, a unity in the social process can be discerned.

So human society is a pointer on the road to the mystery of the Trinity, while the mystery of the Trinity, as we know it from revelation, is a pointer toward social life and its archetype.[14] Human society holds a *vestigium Trinitatis* since the Trinity is "the divine society."[15] This idea of the Trinity as the supreme society, the model for any society seeking participation and equality, was sketched out by M. J. Scheeben,[16] and later elaborated by the Belgian theologian Taymans d'Eypernon and by Jürgen Moltmann. Taymans stresses the fact that society results from the unity of a multiplicity of individuals and actions. The interaction among all produces social justice and well-being. This serves as an analogy with the one being of God whose divine Persons act in common and on their own behalf to produce eternal communion and infinite equality. Furthermore, the Trinity serves as the model for an integrated society.[17] In God, each Person acts in consonance with its distinctive personality, yet the activity is common to the three. The trinitarian interplay of perfect perichoresis displays co-existence between personal and social, between the happiness of each and the well-being of all. These relationships underlie all community and social life and are enlightened and inspired by the communion of the Trinity.

Moltmann bases his original and stimulating work on the Trinity on a community vision.[18] The basic statement of Christian faith, the one that protects the specifically Christian image of God, is its adherence to the three Persons, Father, Son and Holy Spirit, living in permanent and everlasting reciprocity which is opened out to the whole of creation. God is a community of Persons and not simply the One; God's unity exists in the form of communion (common-union) between the three Persons and with history. There is a trinitarian history; the missions of the Son and the Holy Spirit have brought creation into the trinitarian process. So the Trinity becomes an open mystery; its unity, the fruit of its communion, includes humanity and all creation; eschatologically, everything will be united in the Trinity. "This trinitarian history is nothing other than the eternal perichoresis of Father, Son and Holy Spirit in their dispensation of salvation, which is to say in their opening of themselves for the reception and unification of the whole of creation. The history of salvation is the history of the eternally living, triune God who draws us into and includes us in his eternal triune life with all the fullness of its relationships."[19] This clearly brings out the community and social aspect of the Trinity: unity and diversity shade into communion in God, springing from God's association with what is not-God but what comes through communion and perichoresis to share in the mystery of the Trinity. Such a vision prevents any totalitarianism ostensibly based on divine monotheism and any paternalism based on the monarchy of the Father to whom all must submit and on whom all depend. The domination model is replaced by the communion model: production by invitation, conquest by participation. The Trinity understood in human terms as a communion of Persons lays the foundations for a society of brothers and sisters, of equals, in which dialogue and consensus are the basic constituents of living together in both the world and the church.

This approach will be taken as a stimulus to my own later reflections.

(d) Another New Starting-point: The Trans-sexist Theology of the Maternal Father and the Paternal Mother

The past few decades have seen the development of a deep awareness of the sexist and patriarchal character of Christian theologies.[20] These theologies are not all-embracing since they are produced almost exclusively by men and make use of predominantly masculine symbolism: God is the Father who begets a Son who becomes incarnate in the form of Jesus the man, whose work in history, the church, is controlled and led virtually exclusively by men. Of course, on the level of strict theological understanding, God the Father is trans-sexual, the term Father referring only to the source of life from which everything derives and to which everything tends. But this reality can be presented only in symbols and images. These are produced by particular cultures, and in ours have been controlled by the dominant group, which is made up of men. The image of God the Father, in its prevailing cultural significance, can hardly indicate what lies beyond it—the original, trans-sexual source of life; it is normally identified with a human father-figure, and therefore runs the risk of becoming an idol and legitimizing the domination of fathers and bosses over their children, women and anything seen as feminine in nature. The churches and their theologies have not taken sufficient care over the form in which symbols are used, ignoring the danger incurred in discriminating against the feminine and surreptitiously reinforcing male chauvinist and patriarchal domination. Images play a dominant role in moulding consciousness and compartmentalizing society; the predominance of masculine images in Christianity has prevented women from expressing their religious experience from within their proper feminine condition and with an adequate symbolism to support them.

Certain currents of feminist theology have postulated the creation of concepts that cannot be manipulated in a sexist way (masculine or feminine) and of images that could embrace the whole experience of humanity, of which women are a sign as much as men. So Mary Daly[21] suggests that we should understand God less as substance and more as process, "God" being an active verb rather than a noun. God would mean living, the eternal return including the coming into being of the whole of creation, a creation that, instead of being subject to the supreme Being, would share in the divine living. This God could be expressed by the symbols of either Father or Mother, or by a combination of the properties of each: God as maternal Father and paternal Mother. Christian tradition itself, particularly the Orthodox, has hinted at such formulations. The Council of Toledo (675) spoke of "The Father's womb" in which the Son is conceived and from which he is born (DS 526). The same would apply to the Son, who should not be understood in sexist terms, but inclusively as the final and full revelation of the original source; this can be both masculine and feminine. The humanity taken on in the incarnation is both masculine and feminine, even though Jesus was a man and not a woman; he was not merely masculine but possessed the feminine dimension too, as eternal Word. In the same way, the Holy Spirit can be expressed in trans-sexist language. In biblical descriptions it is allied to the feminine dimensions of life (*Ruah* in Hebrew is feminine): creation, animation, consolation, comforting.

It must be stressed that this is not just a matter of introducing feminine figuration into the Trinity (Mother instead of Father, Daughter instead of Son and emphasizing the feminine attributes of the Spirit), but of working out the feminine dimension of the whole mystery of the Trinity and of each of the divine Persons.[22] Humanity is coming to understand to an ever-increasing degree that feminine symbolism is as apt as masculine to express the triune God. God seen as communion and co-existence can be both masculine and feminine, giving us a more complete and integrating experience of God. This delineation of the feminine features in the revelation of each of the three Persons of the Trinity will be taken up further on in this study.

CHAPTER VII

The Communion of the Trinity as Basis for Social and Integral Liberation

Having so far examined the great theological inheritance we have received from the past and from recent investigations, it is now time to move on to a modest attempt to set out the challenges posed by the situation from which I write, a situation defined by oppression and longing for liberation. This will involve a deeper examination of one of the tendencies from the past: studying the mystery of the Trinity from the basis of the relationship between the divine Persons. This understanding revolves round the terms perichoresis, circuminsession, circumincession, co-inherence and interpenetration.

The starting-point is the conviction that has guided all debates on the Trinity: that the fact that the eternal God is three—Father, Son and Holy Spirit—has to be presented in the most real way possible. This is the primordial and essential question, with that of the unity of the three Persons following later. But affirming the real existence of the Three is not enough; we have to place equal stress on the relationship that obtains between them: the existence of the one God is made up of the most complete communion and the most absolute and eternal participation. The unity of the three Persons expresses the infinite dynamism of communion and interpenetration prevailing in the Holy Trinity.

The task of theological reflection on the Trinity is to present the arguments in such a way as to show the logic of this dynamism and the beauty of this overflowing life of communion in the Trinity. To do this, it has to clarify the three key concepts of this understanding: the concepts of life, communion and perichoresis. The first two are clearly rooted in the Bible; the third is an important theological term, emphasizing what is essential in the concepts of life and communion.

1. GOD IS ETERNAL LIVING

God is purely and simply the living One.[1] Rightly has the concept of life—which humans consider the highest and richest of concepts—been attributed to God. So the supreme goal of human life is represented as sharing in divine life (cf 1 Pet. 1:4).

The Old Testament, in polemics against idolatry (Ps. 115:4-8), presents God as adored as the Lord who lives (Ps. 18:46) and as the source of life (Ps. 36:9). Everything comes to life through God, particularly human beings (Ps. 104:30; Isa. 42:5; Gen. 2:7). Because Yahweh is living, he can present himself as "I Am the one who is there" (Exod. 3:13-15), as the one who establishes an alliance with his people (Exod. 6:7; Deut. 26:12), who hears the cry of the oppressed people and resolves to set them free (Exod. 3:7-10); in a word, the God who builds God's Kingdom in history by promoting life, justice, love and peace.

Because life is the inner nature of God, it is the great promise made by God to humanity and the supreme gift bestowed on God's friends. All those who feel their lives threatened can count on God's support (cf 1 Sam. 17:26, 36; Deut. 6:21; Hos. 2:1). The preferential option for the poor is rooted in the very nature of God. Being drawn to the oppressed and unjustly impoverished comes from the depths of God's being. An offence against them is an offence against the nature and glory of God. There is nothing casual about the frequency with which God takes the side of those whose rights are violated: "Yahweh, forever faithful, gives justice to those denied it, gives food to the hungry, gives liberty to prisoners. Yahweh restores sight to the blind, Yahweh straightens the bent, Yahweh protects the stranger, he keeps the orphan and widow" (Ps. 146:7-9;

cf Prov. 14:31; 17:5; 22:23; Deut. 10:18; Jer. 22:16).

The God of the Old Testament, then, is shown as living, tender to the poor, generating life, defending those whose lives are threatened. When we speak of the Spirit being active in creation, revolutionizing history, empowering human life, we are always dealing with this idea of God as living, vivifying, life-giving (Gen. 1:2; Ps. 104:29-30; Ezek. 37).

In the New Testament, Jesus is shown as clearly understanding himself as life personified (John 11:25; 14:6; 5:26); his mission consists in bringing life and bringing it more abundantly (John 10:10). The resurrection reveals him as "the Living One . . . and I hold the keys of death and the underworld" (Rev. 1:17-19). And anyone who shares in Christ partakes of a "new creation" (2 Cor. 5:17; Rom. 5:18, 21; 6:22; Eph. 2:5-6).

(a) What Comprises Life?

Let us try to analyze what life comprises,[2] without attempting a definition of life itself, except to say that it is a mystery of spontaneity, an inexhaustible and varied process of development from within, manifesting itself in outward relationships. We need a brief schematic exposition to guide our conception of living beings and to provide us with some notion—however minimal—of what eternal life might be: the life of God or God of life. Experiences drawn from various forms of life serve as a basis for a representation of eternal life, and these experiences might yield the following descriptions of characteristics for living beings:

—*Organism*: a conjunction of varied parts, functions or behaviours, which regulates itself from within, constituting an organization or system.

—*Self-functioning:* the organism results from the internal (self-) functioning of various organs, parts and behaviours in a permanent process of emergence, development, maturation, degeneration and dissolution.

—*Architectonic totality:* each functioning organism displays an organic totality and produces evident meaning in itself, since life means the presence and execution of a plan (programme or project); every life contains a *curriculum vitae* which comes from its past, runs through its present and is open to the future; every living being is a universe with an inside and an outside, and a centre from which everything is placed, organized, ordered.

—*Reproduction:* it is a distinctive mark of every living being to possess the faculty to reproduce itself in another living being of the same species, which will carry the same plan of life forward, with a limitless number of individual possibilities.

Perhaps we can sum up the process of life (life itself being impossible to sum up) in a short formula: *life consists in the self-realization of an ex-istent.* Let us try to clarify each of the concepts this includes:

—*Self:* life draws life from its own source and arises from its own being; it does not receive the principle of its spontaneity and activity from outside. The ancients saw life as an *entelechia* (Aristotle [3]), that is, something that has an end and meaning in itself. This is expressed by the particle *self-*, which means a power of realization, expansion and cohesion rooted in itself; for this reason every living being has interiority.

—*Realization:* an action that real-izes, transforms potentiality into reality. Life is a process of emergence, production and expansion, a continual coming-to-be without end, never concluding in an achieved synthesis. It is always an organism, a totality and a level, but always open to new expressions of these. *Presence* is a category proper to living beings; through presence, reality is more intensely real, to the point of being a meaning that spreads out, forcing a position to be taken and giving out a signal that can either be accepted (life-affirming) or rejected (life-denying). Presence is life in process. What is in process cannot be captured in a concept, but can be intuited; life calls to life, summoning everything to adhere to the life-process; we grasp the meaning of life from within, through sharing and living together.

—*Ex-istent:* ex-istent is synonymous with living reasoning. Existence is the property of the being that from within (interiority) relates outward (*ex-*) to other beings, establishing communion and relationships of giving and receiving. So life comprises communion and participation, synthesis with what is different, unfolding of itself in the direction of another.

The life that we live is loaded with ambiguities, since it is always life against death, a process of upholding life against lethal destructive forces. Human hope is set, basically, on a life no longer threatened by death, on a process of self-realization that is continually renewed in line with the future.

(b) God as Eternal Self-realization

When we say God, we seek to express the One who is eternal life and lives eternally (Rev. 4:9; 10:6; 15:7) and therefore is intrinsically immortal (at*anasia:* 1 Tim. 6:16). God is simply the Living One (*zoon:* Rom. 9:26; Matt. 16:16; 26:63; Acts 14:5). Jesus is the Word of life (John 1:4), in whom "life was made visible" (1 John 1:2) because he was the "prince of Life" (Acts 3:15).

Properly speaking, God is more than life, since life represents a state or result of a process of self-realization. God is absolute *living,* as the mystics accurately intuited. Creatures do not live in the complete sense, since they are always dependent on a difficult equilibrium, continually threatened and finally destroyed by death. Creatures pass through life. God remains *in life* in an eternal process of irruption, overflowing, self-communication and pure living. So God is best represented as a *living,* an action eternally "producing" the divine reality, making it manifest, with no need to reply to the question: why live? God lives to live, in absolute spontaneity, in the self-evident meaning of light that shines to shine, clear spring water that gushes to gush, the bird that sings to sing. God *is* in the measure that God is eternally living, that is, in an eternal process of self-realization. Eternal life belongs to God. So, going back to our earlier formula, we can say: "*eternal life consists in the self-realization of the eternal Ex-istent.*" To life, including eternal life, belongs being inwardly and being outwardly, self-communication and self-involvement, being in communion with oneself and with what is outside oneself, though related to oneself.

Christian faith professes that the primary Reality is not undifferentiated eternal Life, but eternal Life gushing out as Father, Son and Holy Spirit. They are three Livings. Because they are living, with the plenitude of eternal living, each one gushes out toward the others, bestows ceaselessly on the others everything except the indestructible fact of being an Ex-istent distinct from the others.

It is not enough to state that the Trinity is the distinction between the three Persons. The essential characteristic of each Person is to be *for* the others, *through* the others, *with* the others and *in* the others. They do not exist in themselves for themselves: the "in themselves" *is* "for the others." The process of self-realization of the Trinity is made up of a dynamism of eternal communion, sharing the life of one with the others, the interpenetration and co-inherence of the Three. So we come back to the traditional formulas: the Father is wholly in the Son and the Holy Spirit, the Son is wholly in the Father and the Holy Spirit, the Holy Spirit is wholly in the Father and the Son. All are equally eternal, infinite and loving in communion.

Diversity-in-communion is the source-reality in God, whose unity can only be the union of this personal diversity. The divine unity is the actualization of the process of one Person communing with the others, of one Living sharing in the lives of the others. To use a pallid metaphor: they are three fountain jets gushing upward and toward each other, mingling and uniting so as to form a single column of water.[4] Logically, it is not the column that comes first, but the jets. The Persons of the Trinity form the beginning without beginning, simultaneous and co-eternal. The process of self-realization in the Trinity is each Person being able to realize the others.

This reality of process, which tradition calls perichoresis, has not generally occupied the centre stage in theological reflection; here it is put at the centre of the mystery. It is therefore the eternal relationships bringing about, realizing, the interpenetration and co-inherence of the divine Three that, properly speaking, constitute the trinity and unity of God: three Persons in one God; three Livings in one Life.

2. GOD IS INFINITE COMMUNING

In the Bible, living implies communing, since living is always living-with, living for and being in the presence of others. Death means the break with all vital links and so absolute solitude. Modern thought understands the concept of person, and also the nature of God, from the starting-point of communion.[5] The idea of communion, which we must now examine more deeply, has been applied in theological thought to the church, to anthropology, to grace.[6] We need to take an analytical approach to the concept, which is generally left without clear semantic definition and coherent application. Having made this analysis, we can then go on to consider how it can be applied to God.

(a) Analytical Perspective

As understood in sociology and anthropology, communion is not a thing, but a relationship between things. It builds up the highest sort of socializing and union, that proper to beings gifted with a spiritual nature. Being a relationship, it exists only in practice, through being performed. So rather than "communion," we should speak of "communing." Let us look at some characteristics of this relationship:

—*Presence one to another:* this means more than physical presence; in order to commune, one being has to face another; it offers the potentiality of being, not just what is; it implies presenting oneself to another and offering a welcome to another. Being present is being open, sending a message to another in the expectation and hope of being heard and accepted while at the same time hearing and receiving a message from the other. The message is the true presence of one person who wishes to enter into dialogue and communion with another.

—*Reciprocity:* communion implies movement of two hands clasping each other. It cannot come from one side alone. By definition, it supposes at least two presences relating to each other, and so reciprocity between two presences. Reciprocity, for its part, presupposes a certain con-naturality between the elements that commune: totally distinct beings, with virtually nothing in common, will find it difficult to form bonds of communion. Reciprocating and con-natural beings feel a certain attraction to one another; the greater this attraction, the more perfect the communion between them. There will never be fusion, since each retains its own identity, but the desire for fusion, to become one with the other, marks the depth of the communing relationship.

—*Immediacy:* in communion, one being wants to be with another, in itself, through its own presence, without intermedaries; wants to be for the other to the point of being *in* the other. Communion implies intimacy, transparency of intention, union of hearts, convergence of interests. Personal and social well-being comes only from bonds of communion between all parts.

—*Community:* the product of relationships of communion is community; this implies living together, valuing the individuality of everyone, accepting differences as the interchange of riches, establishing personal relationships, doing away with formalities. Sociologically speaking, community is a spirit that should inform all forms of human society rather than a specific social grouping. So taken historically, the community spirit implies a utopia: a society that is without conflicts and that consists of an interplay of relationships in which the common good is placed above individual good because the members of such a society feel bound up with each other and completed in each other, through each other and by each other. This utopia, even though never achieved in the conditions of history as we know it, is eminently meaningful in both social and anthropological terms, since it continually unleashes energies directed at bringing about social changes in the direction of more balanced and participatory forms of living together.

(b) Philosophical Perspective

Considered philosophically, communion embraces certain fundamental aspects: these are those considered above, but considered from their ontological perspective, that is by examining what sort of beings these elements presuppose: what sort of being is capable of communion? The answer to this question is a philosophical one:

—*Being-in-openness:* only a being open to others can commune with, relate to, build up a community with other, con-natural beings. Openness is a mark of the spirit; it implies feeling oneself referred outside oneself, not forming a totality of oneself. Without this openness there can be no acceptance or bestowing, nothing new resulting from the meeting of two presences communicating with each other. Being-in-openness is being in freedom, being capable of the love that transfigures the whole universe.

—*Being-in-transcendence:* means that a being effectively goes out of itself, enters into communion with another, creating a history together, establishing bonds of interdependence. This living transcendence is not exhausted in any particular outcome, since it always remains open to other forms of communion. We are here dealing with an ontological mode of being, by which the human spirit is always oriented outwards from itself, seeking rest in an

Absolute. Its greatest achievement is found in communion with this Absolute.

—*Being-us:* the product of the dynamic of communing is the *us,* the actual community, not just in the sense of a social, familial, loving community, but as a mode of being by which we become part of a single whole. We are, we live, we exist as human beings who always find themselves in particular communions with others. The "I" never exists on its own; it is dwelt in by many, since its roots spread out into others, as it is permeated by others. So we can say that it is not so much living that is proper to human beings as living-with, existing-in-communion with even our most distant likes, allowing ourselves to be permeated by others and likewise permeating them. Beings-in-communion live in a permanent state of ex-centricity, since their centre is called by another centre outside them in order jointly to form a community.

(c) Theological Perspective

Theology seeks to discern the presence of God in human and historical processes. If *analytically* one being is present to another, perceives a basic reciprocity with that other, experiences an immediacy of relationship demanding the formation of a community; if *philosophically* this particular mode of being demonstrates an existence characterized principally by oneness, by self-transcendence forming an "us" with whom to relate, then *theologically* this means that these values and this mode of being find their deepest roots and ultimate model in God. As creatures are the image and likeness of God, then God has to be absolute openness, supreme presence, total immediacy, eternal transcendence and infinite communion. If God has to be all this (because the signs of God are visible in creation), then God must also be perceptible in true form in the historical revelation left to us in the scriptures. So let us see how these show us God as communing.[7]

In the Old Testament God is revealed as the God of the Covenant with his people, the God who wishes to assimilate all humanity to himself (Gen. 9). The Covenant with the patriarch Abraham (Gen. 12) is destined to be a sign to the nations, who are all called to be peoples of God (cf Rev. 21:3). The Covenant with the whole people of Israel (Exod. 19, 24) is an anticipation and symbol of what God wishes to do with all nations; the twelve tribes of Israel and the twelve apostles have a symbolic significance: the reunion of the nations of the diaspora to serve God and so become peoples of God, in one united, redeemed humanity made the messianic community. This communion that God seeks with humanity, expressed by the figure of the Covenant, is interiorized in the heart of each individual (cf Jer. 31:33; Ezek. 37:26; Heb. 10:16). God's communion seeks the intimacy and freedom of the human heart and not just a social and political expression.

In the New Testament, St Paul, St John and the Acts of the Apostles best express God as communion. Now communion is made manifest in history in the shape of the reality of Jesus and the sending of the Spirit. Being in Christ and in the Son, living with Christ and with the Spirit—these make up the great communion with the Father (1 John 1:3).

In St Paul there are two channels of communion: faith and the eucharist. Through faith we are united to the risen Lord: living with him, dying with him, being raised with him, seated in glory with him (cf Rom. 6:6; 8:17; 2 Cor. 7:3; Gal. 2:19; Col. 2:12; 3:1; Eph. 2:6; 2 Tim. 2:12); through adhering to Christ we begin a community of life and destiny with him, even to sharing in his sufferings (Phil. 3:10). This communion is deepened through the eucharist; by eating the body of the Lord, the community becomes the body of Christ (cf 1 Cor. 10:16-18; Rom. 12:5). And communion with Christ means communion also with the Spirit of Christ (cf 2 Cor. 13:13).

St John meditates on the communion Christ brought us into, with the Father, so that all might be one (John 17:21). He also expresses communion by the verbs "being-in" and "remaining-in" (cf 14:20; 15:4). Communion with the Father, Son and Holy Spirit is translated into communion between all (cf 1 John 1:1-3). This receives material expression in the holding of all goods in common (Acts 2:42; 4:32) and in care for the poverty of other communities for which collections were made as an expression of communion (cf 2 Cor. 9:13; Rom. 15:26). The Letter to the Hebrews again recalls this sharing of resources as "the sacrifices that please God" (13:16). Acts tells how the community utopia was brought about through faith, the eucharist and the sharing of goods: "the whole group of believers was united, heart and soul" (4:32).

In the early church, the church community was defined as *communio sanctorum*. This described not so much the institution as the attitudes and behaviour that guided relations between the members of one community and between one local church and another. The eucharist celebrated in each community, recognized by the others, was an expression of living in community. Also, the faithful who travelled took with them *litterae communicationis* (letters of commendation), a sort of passport indicating communion between the various local churches. Communion demonstrated openness to one another, reciprocity in relationships, mutual recognition. Moving forward to our own times, the Second Vatican Council (and following it, the Extraordinary Synod of Bishops of 1985) stressed the reality of communion as the basic dimension of anthropology, of ecclesiology and of the political activities of Christians.[8] The Third General Conference of Latin American Bishops held in Puebla in 1979 also made communion and participation the two basic axes of the whole evangelization process and the goal to be achieved through authentic liberation.[9]

These examples provide us with a better idea of what it means to say that God is communion. God is communion precisely because God is a Trinity of Persons. *Three Persons and a single communion and a single trinitarian community:* this is the best formula to represent the Christian God. Speaking of God must always mean the Father, Son and Holy Spirit in the presence of one another, in total reciprocity, in immediacy of loving relationship, being one for another, by another, in another and with another. No divine Person exists alone for its own sake; they are always and eternally in relationship with one another: the Father is Father because he has a Son; the Son is Son only because he has a Father; the Spirit is Spirit only because of the love in which the Father begets the Son and the Son gives back to the Father. In pronouncing the Word (the Son), the Father breathes out the breath that is the Holy Spirit. The fruit of this love, the Spirit, loves the Father and the Son and is loved by them in an exchange of giving and communion that comes from eternity and ends in eternity. The Persons exist as Persons by reason of their eternal relationships with one another. The unity of the Trinity is made up of these relationships; it is a unity peculiar to the Trinity, a tri-unity. This unity is indicated by St John, when he makes Jesus say: "Father, may they be one in us, as you are in me and I am in you . . . that they may be one as we are one . . . may they be so completely one . . ." (17:21-3). The united society that exists in the Trinity is the foundation of human unity; the latter is inserted in the former. Persons are not annulled, but empowered. Unity is composed of actual persons, both in the Trinity and in humanity, inasmuch as persons are essentially related. The union obtaining between persons and in the human community prefigures the union that exists in the Trinity. Despite all ruptures, the Trinity seeks to see itself reflected in history, through people sharing their goods in common, building up egalitarian and just relationships among all, sharing what they are and what they have. Richard of St Victor (d. 1173) best expressed this communing aspect of the Trinity and its incidence on human life.[10] He saw God as essentially love communicating itself and establishing communion. The love of the Father makes the Son rise like fire from the Father's entrails, the Son to whom he gives his whole being. The Son, in turn, gives back to the Father all the love he has received. It is an absolute and eternal meeting, but not the love of shut-away lovers; it expands. Father and Son make a mutual gift of themselves; this is the Holy Spirit. So the Christian God is a process of effusion, of meeting, of communion between distinct beings bound together in life and love.

Christian theology adopted a word to express this life and communion: *perichoresis* in Greek, *circuminsessio* or *circumincessio* in Latin. Let us now look more deeply into what this implies.

3. PERICHORESIS, COMMUNION AND INTERPENETRATION OF THE THREE DIVINE PERSONS

The Greek term *perichoresis*—translated into Latin both by *circuminsessio* and *circumincessio*[11]—is used to sum up the essence of unity in the Trinity and the unity of the natures of God and humankind in Jesus.[12]

(a) What Perichoresis Means

The New Testament witnesses to Jesus' consciousness of his intimate union with the Father: "the Father and I are one" (John

10:30); "the Father is in me and I am in the Father" (10:38; 14:11); "Father, may they be one in us, as you are in me and I am in you" (17:21). Christian tradition, in combatting Arianism, modalism and tritheism, had asserted the consubstantiality of the three Persons of the Trinity. The Council of Florence summed up this tradition by declaring: "The Father is wholly in the Son and wholly in the Holy Spirit; the Son wholly in the Father and wholly in the Holy Spirit; the Holy Spirit wholly in the Father and wholly in the Son" (DS 1331). Earlier, the Council of Toledo had spelt out:

> These three persons are not to be considered separable, since we believe that no one of them existed or at any time effected anything before the other, after the other, or without the other. For in existence and in operation they are found to be inseparable, because we believe that between the Father who generates and the Son who is generated and the Holy Spirit who proceeds, there never was any interval of time in which the one generating would at any time precede the one generated, or in which the one generated would not be present to the one generating, or in which the Spirit who proceeds might appear to come after the Father and the Son (DS 531, CT).

These statements stress the eternal co-existence of the divine Persons and their respectiveness, that is, the relatedness they bear to one another.

Theology came to use the Greek word *perichoresis* to express this interpenetration of one Person by the others. When it was first applied to the Trinity is obscure.[13] It seems to have been Pseudo-Cyril (sixth century) who first used it in this way, but it was St John Damascene who adopted its usage and made it a regular component of trinitarian thought.[14] It was not employed universally; great theologians such as Peter Lombard, Thomas Aquinas, Cajetan and the Salamanca School did not use it; it was, however, taken up by the Franciscan School of Bonaventure, Duns Scotus, William of Ockham and their successors, who extended the usage of the word and deepened its meaning. The Greek word has a double meaning, which explains why two words were used to translate it into Latin. Its first meaning is that of one thing being contained in another, dwelling in, being in another—a situation of fact, a static state.

This understanding was translated by *circuminsessio,* a word derived from *sedere* and *sessio,* being seated, having its seat in, seat. Applied to the mystery of the communion of the Trinity this signified: one Person is in the others, surrounds the others on all sides (*circum-*), occupies the same space as the others, fills them with its presence. Its second meaning is active and signifies the interpenetration or interweaving of one Person with the others and in the others. This understanding seeks to express the living and eternal process of relating intrinsic to the three Persons, so that each is always penetrating the others. This meaning was translated as *circumincessio,* derived from *incedere,* meaning to permeate, com-penetrate and interpenetrate.[15] In this sense, perichoresis is a good term to designate what we have seen to be meant by communion, *koinōnia:* a permanent process of active reciprocity, a clasping of two hands: the Persons interpenetrate one another and this process of communing forms their very nature.

The term perichoresis once was used in two different fields of theology: that having to do with the relationship between God and matter and that having to do with the relationship of the two natures in Christ. God is said to penetrate all the matter of creation; God is in the world; God's presence, actions and providence pervade the world. But there is no reciprocity, since matter is not capable of responding consciously to God and of being in God. This perichoresis is not complete. In Jesus Christ two natures, human and divine, co-exist, united in the Person of the Son. This union is so deep that the properties of one nature are interchangeable with those of the other. So it is correct to say: "God appeared on earth, suffered and died," or "This man is uncreated and eternal." The two natures interpenetrate each other, without fusion or confusion; divine nature takes on human nature, each occupying the totality of the same divine hypostasis and so producing a true perichoresis (also referred to as *communicatio idiomatum*).[16]

Finally, the term perichoresis gained currency in trinitarian theology, though it is only in recent times that it has come to occupy a central position in this field. We need now to look more closely at what it means as applied to the Trinity, since the concept is central to the relevance of the Trinity to our desire for a society that lives together in more open communion, equality and respectful acceptance of differences.

(b) The Interpentration of Persons: Principle of Union in the Trinity

Perichoresis-communion is used in order to express the union in the Trinity, keeping the Christian experience of God as always being Father, Son and Holy Spirit; it expresses that union better than any other formula. The theological traditions of East and West have followed two paths to a balance between unity and trinity. The Greeks started from the monarchy of the Father: he is the principle of all divinity, since he communicates its essence and substance to the Son and the Spirit. Even if its starting-point is personalized (the Person of the Father), this theology is in fact one of essence and of divine unity, centered on the first Person. The Latins started from one divine substance internally differentiated in the three Persons. Both saw the Persons constituted by relationships. This, however, raises a problem: how can the Father be a Person if he is so only in begetting the Son? How can he be a begetting subject, if his personality is only formed by the act of begetting? The Greeks did not devote much attention to this problem; medieval Schoolmen, especially the Franciscans, distinguished between the initial personality of the Father (before begetting the Son) and the complete personality of the Father (on begetting the Son).[17] This is clearly an emergency and unsatisfactory solution.

Modern theological thought starts from God as absolute subject actualized in three distinct modes of existence (Barth) or in three distinct modes of subsistence (Rahner). However ingenious these attempts to combine the unity of the Persons with their trinity, they barely avoid being a Christian version of monotheism.[18] It is hard to reconcile them fully with the binding revelation of salvation history, which speaks of three distinct, inter-related Subjects—Father, Son and Holy Spirit.

In my view, the perichoresis-communion model seems to be the most adequate way of expressing revelation of the Trinity as communicated and witnessed by the scriptures. Seen within the framework of perichoresis, the theories elaborated by theology and the church to signify the Christian God as person, relationship, divine nature and procession, are not invalidated, but become comprehensible.

We have to start from the specific revelation of the Trinity as told in the New Testament (already touched on in chapter 2). Jesus Christ is the centre. He is conscious of being the Son (cf Matt. 11:25-7; Mark 12:1-9; 13:32). He acts as one who stands in God's place (Matt. 12:28ff). He maintains an intimate relationship with his God, expressed in the language of familiarity: Abba, my beloved Father. He feels sent by the Father; the Kingdom he preaches is the Father's, to be brought about for all, starting with the poor (Luke 6:3; 4:17-21). In obedience to the Father, he accepts the conflict brought about by his message of liberation. He prays and beseeches the Father in the Garden of Gethsemane. There is a difference between him and the Father; so he falls to his knees, gives thanks, adores, implores. But at the same time he can say, "The Father and I are one." This union is dynamic and reciprocal, a true indwelling: "I am in the Father and the Father is in me." Between Jesus and the Father there is a genuine, complete perichoresis-communion.

Together with the Father and the Son Jesus, there is also the Holy Spirit. This is the Spirit of Jesus because it produced the sacred humanity of the incarnate Son from Mary's womb (Matt. 1:18; Luke 1:27-35; 2:5). This Spirit, filling Jesus from the moment of his conception, came down on him at his baptism, inspiring his messianic vocation; it pushed him into the desert to confront the principle of the anti-Kingdom (cf Luke 4:1-13), and helped him in his liberating works (Mark 5:30; Matt. 12:28). Where Jesus is, there too is his Spirit. This Spirit "issues from the Father" (John 15:26). Jesus asks the Father to send "another Advocate to be with you for ever" (14:16), the Spirit of truth, whose truth will be "taken from what is mine [Jesus']" (16:14). After the resurrection and ascension of the Son it is the Spirit that carries out Jesus' saving work. The Spirit leads us to the Son, is the "spirit of sons" and makes us cry out "Abba, Father" (Rom. 8:15; cf Gal. 4:6).

Reading the saving actions of the three divine Persons as the scriptures tell them, those Persons emerge as three Subjects who engage in mutual dialogue, love one another and are intimately related. Each Person is *for* the others, *with* the others and *in* the others. The everlasting love that pervades them and forms them unites them in a current of life so infinite and complex as to constitute the unity between them. Unity in the Trinity, as has been remarked before, is always a union of Persons; it is not something that comes after them, but is simultaneous with them, since they are always one *with* the others and *in* the others. The Persons are not the product of the relation of their nature to itself, but are at the origin of the divine nature, being co-eternal and co-equal (DS 616). They are not embodiments of One (nature or substance or absolute Spirit or Subject) but three Subjects in eternal (and therefore essential) communion, always united and interpenetrating one another.

The error of tritheism was in affirming *just* the existence of three divine Persons, without their reciprocal inter-relatedness, the Three being juxtaposed and separated as though they were three natures or substances: "*tres quasdam virtutes ac separatas hypostases tresque deitates dividentes ac discindentes,*" as Pope St Dionysius declared against the tritheists in 259 (DS 112). This was also the error of Roscelinus (d. 1225), who saw the Three Persons as so separate and unrelated that they might have been "three souls or three angels," a position that had been condemned by the Synod of Soissons in 1121. Joachim of Fiore saw the Three as more loosely related, like three friends, their unity merely "collective and apparent," not essential, not derived from a principle intrinsic to three Persons perichoretically bound up in one another, and for this he was condemned by the fourth Lateran Council.

The true unity of the Trinity, made up of the communion-perichoresis of the three divine Persons, reveals the following characteristics:

(i) In the first place, the revelation of scripture, the basis for all our thinking about the Trinity, shows us the existence of Father, Son and Holy Spirit, adored as God in professions of faith, the liturgy and daily spiritual life. This means: Christian understanding integrates distinctions in God without thereby multiplying God and falling into tritheism or polytheism. This profession of faith is laden with consequences for humankind and society, since it supposes that the ultimate basis of reality is not to be found in the solitude of One but in the co-existence and communion of Three. World-views that take Unity and Identity as their goal and all-embracing starting-point find particular difficulty in living with differences. They can generally barely tolerate them, doing everything to reduce them or subject them to the rule of One and of Identity. But New Testament belief in the Trinity forces us to accept differences for what they are and to put forward a vision of God and the universe as open realities engaged in a life-process. Unity does not here mean negation of differences or the reduction of them all to One, but expresses the communion and interpenetration of different strands.

(ii) Father, Son and Holy Spirit are not just different from one another; they are also irreducible one to another. This means that each is unique and non-interchangeable: the Father is not the Son, nor the Holy Spirit, and so on for each Person. The non-interchangeability of the divine Persons is shown in the characteristics and actions attributed to each in the scriptures. The Father is the ultimate mystery, both final refuge and source of everything; he sends the Son into the world, and with the Son the Holy Spirit as Spirit of the Son. The Son acts among human beings as liberator, establishing the Kingdom of life and freedom according to the Father's plan. The Spirit appears as the divine power showing in the works of the Son and as the inspiration leading men and women to accept the Son as Lord and so discover the face of the Father.

(iii) These Three, different and irreducible, exist in eternal communion: the divine names themselves denote relationships. So, the Father is Father in relation to the Son; the Son is always the Father's Son; the Holy Spirit is breathed out by the Father in his Word (Son), since Word (Son) and breath (Spirit) are inseparable. Difference does not mean opposition (one *not* being the other), nor does irreducibility mean pure and simple separation. It is their diversity that enables their communion, reciprocity and mutual revelation to come about.

(iv) According to the scriptures, there is an order in these relationships. The Father is always put first, the Son second, as begotten by the Father, and the Holy Spirit third, as the one who proceeds and who unites in love. We shall discuss later whether this order denotes a causal process, in a strict sense, or whether it is rather a descriptive device to indicate the differences and simultaneous reciprocity between the divine co-eternal Persons.

These four aspects should be understood as logical steps in one real process and as the dynamic of trinitarian life. If we concentrate solely on one of them without maintaining the link between them, we risk falling into false understanding and errors that have been condemned by the church. So if we were to take only the first and second aspects—the existence of three Persons and their irreducibility—we could fall into the error of tritheism. There would then be three gods, each isolated from the others, without communion between them. Against the evidence of philosophical reasoning, we would have to maintain the existence of three Infinites, three Almighties and three Creators. But if we were to concentrate only on the third aspect—the communion relationship between the Three—we could fall into the error of modalism, seeing the relationships in the Trinity as not corresponding to anything actually in God, but merely as a representation of our anthropological constructs. They would exist in ourselves, but not in God who is always single, one, unique. If we dwelt on just the fourth aspect—the order of relationships—we could end in subordinationism, seeing the Father alone as truly God. The Son and Holy Spirit would be God in a minor or subordinate fashion, or the highest form of creature, adopted by the Father (adoptionism).

Reflecting on the Trinity calls all our human concepts into question. We are dealing with the most radical Absolute, the deepest root, in itself, and total reality. What can our words do? They approximate, which does not mean that they are merely relative; they provide pointers to the mystery, images that do not claim to be a definition. So we need to examine the value of such expressions as "cause of all divinity," "begetting," "breathing-out" and "trinitarian processions." Causal metaphysical thought has been used since the days of the early church to explain relationships in the Trinity. The Father was called the final cause of divinity and of the Persons of the Son and the Holy Spirit. But can we legitimately speak of "cause" in a trinitarian perspective? "Origin and cause of the world" is reasonable, but how correct is "divine origin" or the Father as "origin of all divinity"? Causal thinking, so deeply rooted in our anthropological constructs and temporality, is said to come from cosmology and etiology. We can ask: Where did it come from? What is its origin? about everything. So Jesus' contemporaries, astonished at his behaviour, asked where he came from: "Where did the man get this wisdom . . .? This is the carpenter's son, surely?" (Matt. 13:54-6; cf Mark 6:23; Luke 4:22-3; John 6:42). Can we ask the same questions about God, who is by definition eternal, without beginning or end? All three divine

Persons are co-eternal (DS 616-8, 790, 800ff, 853), equally power-ful and immense (DS 325, 529, 680, 790, 800); everything in them is simultaneous (DS 75, 144, 162, 173, 284, 531, 618, 1331); nothing is greater or superior, lesser or inferior, before or after (DS 75, 569, 618). In studying these official pronouncements of the church we are urged to understand traditional theological expressions as anal-ogous and descriptive (and this even though those expressions are enshrined in ecumenical councils). So for example, "cause" ap-plied to trinitarian theology is not a philosophical concept but a linguistic resource for helping us to see the diversity in communion between the three Persons. It is a descriptive figure of speech. In the Trinity, the "cause" (the Father) is not anterior to the "effects" (the Son and Holy Spirit). The "effects" possess the same eternity and dignity as the "cause." So what is cause and what is effect here? In the same way, what does "begotten Son" or "procession of the Holy Spirit" mean? It is not surprising that the Fathers, particu-larly the Greeks, approached such questions with the greatest reverence and ended with an apophatic response (no longer using words, which are totally inadequate).

Instead of using causal terminology, we could use the biblical terminology of revelation and recognition: the three Persons reveal themselves to themselves and to each other. One is the condition for the revelation of the others, always in eternal love and reciprocal communion. This implies accepting—and this is my basic thesis—that the three divine Persons are simultaneous in origin and co-exist eternally in communion and interpenetration. Each is distinct from the others in personal characteristics and in the communion estab-lished by that Person in everlasting relationship with the others, each revealing that Person's self to itself and the self of the others to them.

In the first centuries of the church, Christian theologians ex-pressed their faith in the Trinity within the category of thought prevailing in both West and East: the metaphysics of unity and identity. In both the East and the West they started from unity: the Greeks from the monarchy of the Father and the Latins from the unity of the divine nature. Both made the other Persons *derive* (the term preferred by the Latins) or *proceed* from a source—the Greeks naming the Father, the Latins divine nature.

The exposition of this trinitarian derivation/progression, as found in the manuals of theology, often gives the impression that the Persons of the Son and the Holy Spirit are the products of theogonic representations, mere expressions of the principle of causality. St Augustine never lost sight of the artificial nature of our concepts of the Trinity. In his *De Trinitate* he clearly says:

> In order that we might have some words for the ineffable, and so might be able to speak in some way about that which we cannot fully express in any way, the phrase was employed by our Greeks, one essence, three substances. But the Latins said instead, one essence or substance, three persons. As we have already said, in our language, that is, in the Latin language, essence usually means nothing else than substance. And during the time in which it was given us to understand what is said, at least in an enigma, this formula was decided upon, in order that we might be able to give some kind of an answer when we were asked, what are the three. The true faith proclaims that they are three, when it teaches that the Father is not the Son, and that the Holy Spirit, who is the Gift of God, is neither the Father nor the Son.
>
> When it is, therefore, asked what the three or who the three are, we seek to find a generic or a specific name which may include the three together. But we come across none, because the supereminent excellence of the divinity transcends all the limits of our wonted manner of speaking.[19]

Elsewhere, he completes this: "When it is asked three what, then the great poverty from which our language suffers becomes apparent. But the formula three persons was coined, not in order to give a complete explanation by means of it, but in order that we might not be obliged to remain silent."[20]

This text clearly shows what is of faith—acceptance of the Father, the Son and the Holy Spirit as really distinct—and what belongs to the realm of human endeavour to find formulas in which to express trinity and unity in God. In its solemn pronouncements, the magisterium of the church took up the language that came down from Greek and Latin tradition, and within the bounds of this approach, and dealing with the questions it raised, succeeded in reformulating orthodox faith. But while it spoke of "processions," it also insisted on the perichoresis of the divine Persons and their co-eternity and co-equality. So the Father's "begetting" of the true Son is outside time, with no beginning. Talk of "processions" should not be understood as a genesis in God or as a theogonic process, as though God were subject to the principle of causality. The idea of the different processions is used to emphasize at once the difference between the Persons and their reciprocal respectiveness or communion. If the Persons are distinct, it is so that they can commune and be in union. The Orthodox theologian Paul Evdokimov puts it perceptively: "The Trinity is not the result of a process, a theogony, but a primordial fact of divine existence. It is not the work of hypostatic will nor of natural necessity: God is eternally, without beginning, Father, Son and Holy Spirit, the inner reciprocity of their love."[21] It would be hard to find a better expression of what we are trying to say: that God is, originally and without beginning, Father, Son and Holy Spirit in such absolute and eternal communion that they are always united; hence they are one Trinity or triune Unity.

In his sermons and homilies, St Augustine developed a more open conception of trinitarian unity—one based on a metaphysics of the spirit—than that found in his great treatise.[22] He starts from God as *perpetua caritas,* eternal love.[23] An intercommunion so sublime operates between the Persons that it makes for *trina unitas* or *una trinitas.*[24] For him, "person" always means a relationship to another; in the Trinity the Persons are always *relativae* (related one to the others), *vicissim* and *ad invicem* (turned to face each other) or *pluraliter relativae* (multiply related). Yet they are "respective Subjects," that is, subjects who are involved with each other.[25] In his treatise on the Trinity he summed it up: "Each [of the divine Persons] is in each, all are in each, each is in all, all are in all, and all are one."[26]

The basis of perichoresis has traditionally been seen as lying in the unity of the divine nature appropriated by each of the Persons, or in the reciprocity of their relationships of origin with reference to the Father. I would add yet another basis to these: the perichoresis of the divine Persons, without beginning, simultaneous and co-eternal, in infinite reciprocal communion, so that they, without confusion, uni-ficate (become one) and are one God. St Thomas Aquinas confirms this view in his commentary on St John's Gospel: "There is a double unity of Father and Son, of essence and of love (*duplex unitas essentiae et amoris*), and through both unities the Father is in the Son and the Son in the Father."[27] Love is the highest form of union, making the different Persons into a union of life, self-bestowal and communion.

The concepts analyzed at the beginning of this chapter, such as life, communion and perichoresis, are all expressions of the term the New Testament reserves for God: God is love (1 John 4:8, 16). They all intrinsically imply overflowing, differentiation as an expression of inner riches and proper essence. If theological tradition tells us that God's essence (nature or substance) is what constitutes God, then we have to say that God is the love and communion between the three divine Persons. God is Three in a communion of love, and this eternal communion of love makes these Three one God.

This understanding excludes the monarchy of One (the substance of the Father or the unity of the divine nature) in favour of the eternal communion of a simultaneous Three who are always one in, by, with, through and for the others, interpenetrating one another in love, one containing the others, in St John Damascene's felicitous expression, "like three suns, each one contained in the others so that they would be but one light by reason of their intimate compenetration."[28]

(c) The Always Triadic Relationship between Father, Son and Holy Spirit

If we recognize the descriptive and analogous character of classical expressions such as "cause," "begetting," "processions," etc., we also have to admit that they possess a high degree of suggestiveness. They also have an internal relational logic, since to say Father, Son and Holy Breath (Spirit) is to mean difference and relationship. So it is always valid to say that the Father is fecund and originates the Son and that both Father and Son exist in an ecstasy of love and communion and allow the revelation of their Gift and Love that is the Holy Spirit. I propose to go on using the terms "begetting" and "breathing-out," as the church does in its worship and theology, but to do so with an appreciation of their specifically trinitarian application; they do not indicate any theogony, any result of an intra-divine production process, any causal dependence. Each one of the Persons is "without beginning" and is therefore revealed simultaneously and at the outset, each breaking out, as it were, in the direction of the others. This, the co-existence of Father, Son and Holy Spirit in communion, or, in more formal language, of the Three Uniques in perichoresis, being one single God, is the primary reality. This formulation avoids the danger of subordinationist hierarchization in God (first the Father, then the Son, then the Holy Spirit) or of unequal subordination: the Father has everything, receiving nothing from the others; the Son receives only from the Father, while the Holy Spirit receives from the Father and the Son, or only from the Father through the Son. It also avoids theogonism or modalism—deriving the Persons from a divine nature appropriated, in distinct ways, by each of the Persons, or a divine nature multiplying, through its intrinsic power, into three hypostatic embodiments.

We must start with the Trinity: with Father, Son, and Holy Spirit in eternal perichoresis. God is a Trinity of Persons intertwined in love and communion. The Three have their origin from all eternity, none being anterior to the others. Their relationship is one of reciprocal participation rather than hypostatic derivation, of correlation and communion rather than production and procession. What is produced and proceeds is intra-trinitarian and interpersonal revelation. One Person is the condition for the revelation of the others, in an infinite dynamism like a series of mirrors endlessly reflecting the image of the Three. This emphasis on communion and perichoresis, the always triadic relationship operating between the Persons, avoids the risk of tritheism. This perichoretic communion does not result from the Persons, but is simultaneous with them, originates with them. They are what they are because of their intrinsic, essential communion. If this is so, it follows that everything in God is triadic, everything is *Patreque, Filioque* and *Spirituque*. The coordinate conjunction "and" applies absolutely to the three Persons: "and" is always and everywhere.

Consequently, we should say that the Father reveals himself through the Son and the Holy Spirit as the inviting, utterly mysterious depth, a mystery both paternal and maternal. The Father reveals the Son as his Word with the participation of the Spirit, who is always the Spirit of the Son and the Father. The Son is "begotten" by the Father in the Holy Spirit. Put figuratively: the Father "begets" the Son virginally in the maternal-virginal womb of the Holy Spirit. In trinitarian terms: the Father "begets" the Son *Spirituque,* that is, in communion with the Holy Spirit. In turn, the Son reveals the Father in the light of the Holy Spirit, who "reaches the depths of everything, even the depths of God" (1 Cor. 2:10). The Son is also revealed to the Holy Spirit as co-related to the Father, since the Father will be eternally the Father of the Son. He also reveals to the Spirit the unfathomable mystery of the Father in his overflowing outpouring of love and self-bestowal. The Spirit, finally, "proceeds" from the Father and rests on the Son, being thus *ex Patre Filioque.* The Spirit reveals the power of the Father, manifest as Wisdom in the Son. The Spirit is an infinite power of love and union through communion. The Spirit and the Son share in the unborn quality of the Father and together witness to the diversity and communion in the Trinity. It is the Holy Spirit who permits the Father and the Son to love one another infinitely, who is ever innovating and renewing, since love is never repetition and the exuberance of life is never exhausted.

Finally, each Person receives everything from the others and at the same time gives everything to the others. As they are Three Uniques, there are in fact never binary relations of opposites between them (Father to Son, or Father-Son to Holy Spirit) but only triadic ones of communication and communion. Eternally existing as three, they are also eternally interwoven and convergent in the supreme communion that is the unity of the same and only trinitarian God. By their own inner dynamic, the three divine Persons spill over outwards, creating other different things and beings (the cosmos and humankind) for them to be receptacles of the transfusion of communicative love and the boundless ocean of trinitarian life.

(d) The Inclusiveness of the Trinity: All in All

Trinitarian unity is that of perichoresis and communion. This appears not only from the New Testament revelation concerning Father, Son and Holy Spirit, but also from universal salvific history and its condensation in the church. Here, in the church, are those whom the Spirit has raised to accept Jesus as saviour and Son and who are guided by the Spirit, to discover the Father as Abba. This Spirit and the risen Christ act together on the level of all creation, inspiring transformations in the world, advancing the Father's plan: the progressive inauguration of the Kingdom till its eschatological culmination. The Father emerges as the omega-point of history through the expansion of the lordship of the Son, made Lord of the universe through his resurrection from the dead (cf Rom. 1:5), in the empowering and transforming power of the Spirit.

St Paul and St John summon us to include all people and history in the perichoretic unity of the Trinity. In his priestly prayer Jesus says this clearly: "May they all be one. Father, *may they be one in us,* as you are in me and I am in you, so that the world may believe it was you who sent me" (John 17:21). This trinitarian unity is integrating and inclusive; its end is the full glorification of all creation in the triune God, healing what is sick, freeing what is captive, forgiving what offends divine communion. This integration in the Trinity has to make its appearance in history, as ruptures in community are healed—between Jews and pagans, Greeks and barbarians, slaves and masters, men and women (Gal. 3:28; cf Rom. 10:12)—and an economy of giving is brought in, in which needs are met, a community "united heart and soul" (Acts 4:32; cf 31-5). St Paul refers to the steps towards the Kingdom of the risen Christ, taken through the power of the life-giving Spirit, till "God may be all in all" (1 Cor. 15:28). In a way we can say that the Trinity still has a future to the extent that creation, which belongs to it, is still not fully taken up and integrated into the communion of the three divine Persons. Only when this has happened will the three Persons be one single, complete communion.

4. TRINITARIAN COMMUNION AS CRITIC OF AND INSPIRATION FOR HUMAN SOCIETY

Consideration of the communion of the three distinct beings of the Trinity produces a critical attitude to personhood, community, society and the church. On the personal level, our dominant culture stresses the predominance of the individual, of isolated personal development, of the rights of individuals divorced from any consideration of their relation to society. The a-trinitarian monotheism of the churches, their ideology of subjectivity, of unity/identity, serve both to reinforce and reflect this distortion. Seeing people as image and likeness of the Trinity implies always setting them in open relationship with others; it is only through being with others, understanding themselves as others see them, being through others, that they can build their own identities. Personal incommunicability exists only so as to allow communion with other people. In the light of the Trinity, being a person in the image and likeness of the divine Persons means acting as a permanently active web of relationships: relating backwards and upwards to one's origin in the unfathomable mystery of the Father, relating outwards to one's fellow human beings by revealing oneself to them and welcoming the revelation of them in the mystery of the Son, relating inwards to the depths of one's own personality in the mystery of the Spirit.

The Trinity forms an open communion going beyond the existence of the three Persons by including creation. So in the same way human beings cannot concentrate on their own interpersonal relations to the exclusion of a sense of their wider, trans-personal and structural relationships, with society and history. Personalization through communion must not lead to a personalism alienated from the conflicts and processes of social change, but must seek to establish new, more participatory and humanizing relationships. The same criticism applies to the community, with its network of close relationships integrating individuals with their work, life and common interest; the community has to place itself within a greater whole, since it cannot exist as a closed and reconciled little world of its own. "Communitarianism" is close to anarchy.

When set against the ideal of trinitarian communion, modern society in its two principal current embodiments—socialism and capitalism—shows considerable aberrations. Liberal-capitalist society in fact means the dictatorship of the property-owning classes with their individualistic and business interests always shored up by mechanisms of state control. Such regimes have produced the greatest divisions in history between rich and poor, between the races and between the sexes. Most of the misery of the world's poor, particularly those of the Third World, is the result of the unchecked hunger for personal or business gain that is reinforced by the capitalist system, which today operates on a world-wide scale. Alongside the economic thrust aimed at making all markets the same, there is a simultaneous imposition of one political model, based on concentration of power in the hands of an elite, with the consequent marginalization of the great majority of the people, encouraged to maintain the system by voting within it rather than stimulated to be creative and seek forms of society better suited to advancing the cause of the majority. With these goes an ideological thrust reducing everything to the values of mass consumption; that thrust is indifferent to real values and merchandises the culture of the elites who hold power. Capitalism, with the profanization it embodies, promotes domination based on the One: one all-embracing capital, one market, one world of consumers, one legitimate view of the world, one way of relating to nature, one way of meeting the Absolute. Differences are regarded as pathological and deviations from the norm; they are either eradicated or at best barely tolerated.

The greatness of trinitarian communion, however, consists precisely in its being a communion of three different beings; in it, mutual acceptance of differences is the vehicle for the plural unity of the three divine Persons. So by their practice and theory, capitalist regimes contradict the challenges and invitations of trinitarian communion. They are not (except through negation) a vehicle for people in general and Christians in particular to experience the Trinity in history.

Societies with a socialist regime are founded on a right principle, that of communion between all and the involvement of all in the means of production; they have grasped the basic relevance of the social element for society. But this social element is understood and put to work collectivistically, that is, without going through the essential process of accepting differences between persons and between communities. Socialism has to be seen as the imposition of the social element from above, through the Party, which sees itself as the vanguard of social revolution and the interpreter of the meaning of history. There is no full realization of the social dimension, starting at the base, involving personal relationships, building a network of communities which in turn become the basis for the organization of civil society, leading up to the apparatus of linking and leading we call the State. Bureaucratic imposition of the social dimension does not produce a society of equality within the bounds of respect for differences, but one of collectivization with elements of massification.

In the light of trinitarian communion, the type of community that emerges from socialist practice seems to annul individuals; it subsumes them into a homogenizing and egalitarian whole; it does not recognize individuals as different-in-relationship, a recognition that would safeguard their differences.

Trinitarian communion is a source of inspiration rather than of criticism in the social sphere. Christians committed to social change based on the needs of majorities, above all, see tri-unity as their permanent utopia. The three "Differents" uphold their difference one from another; by upholding the other and giving themselves totally to the other, they become "Differents" in communion. In the Trinity there is no domination by one side, but convergence of the Three in mutual acceptance and giving. They are different but none is greater or lesser, before or after. Therefore a society that takes its inspiration from trinitarian communion cannot tolerate class differences, dominations based on power (economic, sexual or ideological) that subjects those who are different to those who exercise that power and marginalizes the former from the latter.

The sort of society that would emerge from inspiration by the trinitarian model would be one of fellowship, equality of opportunity, generosity in the space available for personal and group expression. Only a society of sisters and brothers whose social fabric is woven out of participation and communion of all in everything can justifiably claim to be an image and likeness (albeit pale) of the Trinity, the foundation and final resting-place of the universe. As Jürgen Moltmann writes: "Only a Christian community that is whole, united and unifying, free of dominion and oppression, and only a humanity that is whole, united and unifying, free of class domination and dictatorial oppression, can claim to respect the trinitarian God. This is a world in which human beings are characterized by their social relationships and not by their power or possessions. This is a world in which human beings hold everything in common and share everything, except their personal characteristics."[29] It is not the theologian's task to devise social models that best approximate to the Trinity. Nevertheless, if we take basic democracy in the sense that the ancient Greeks (Plato,

Aristotle and others) took it, as not so much a definite social structure as the principle underlying and providing inspiration for social models, then we should say that the values implied in this constitute the best pointers to how to respect and accept trinitarian communion. Basic democracy seeks the greatest possible equality between persons, achieved by means of progressive development of processes of participation in everything that concerns human personal and social existence. And beyond equality and participation, it seeks communion with transcendent values, those that define the highest meaning of life and history. The more such ideas are put into practice, the more will divine communion be mirrored among men and women.

As this communion, participation and equality are at present denied to a majority of men and women, who remain oppressed and permanently marginalized, it has become urgent that a process of liberation should start from the oppressed themselves. Oppressed Christians find an incomparable inspiration for the liberation struggle in the God of their faith. This liberation aims to bring about participation and communion, the realities that most closely mirror the very mystery of trinitarian communion in human history.

Trinitarian communion can also be a critical aid to appreciating the organization of the church. Before all else, we should see the church as belonging to the realm of mystery,[30] since in its bosom dwell the incarnate Son and the Holy Spirit as its animating, sanctifying principle, its principle of communion. It is the great sacrament of the risen Christ and of his Spirit, both sent by the Father to build the messianic community—the forerunner of the community in the kingship of the Trinity—around themselves. Nevertheless, this basic and strictly theological reality takes shape in history, moulded to particular conceptions of the world and power, as well as to elements that undeniably belong to the tradition that comes from Jesus and the Apostles.

So the representation of church unity, in the Western church, lends itself, as eminent ecclesiologists have pointed out,[31] to a vision that comes from pre-trinitarian or a-trinitarian monotheism. The monarchical structure of the institutional church is similarly based on this: a single church body, a single head (the pope), a single Christ, a single God. The roots of this understanding go back to St

Ignatius of Antioch at the beginning of the second century: the celestial monarchy is the foundation for earthly monarchy—the concentration of all power in one person, sole representative of the sole God. This sacred power then comes down through descending orders of hierarchy, allowing inequality within the community to appear. In this pre-trinitarian vision, authority adopts a paternalistic attitude; it is imbued with goodwill and caring, but fails to recognize and appreciate the capacity of subordinates to think intelligently and creatively. It does everything *for* the faithful of the People of God, but little or nothing *with* the faithful of the People of God. Within this scheme of things, it is difficult to speak realistically of a church-community of the baptized and of charisms. When there is a crisis of acceptance, the solution usually lies with the authorities; the rest have no choice other than to submit or to revolt, with attendant excommunication or other canonical penalties. This is not to question the primacy that belongs to Peter, but to situate it in its proper place, within the church-community of the faithful and not above or outside it.

The solar mystery of perichoretic communion in the Trinity sheds light on the lunar mystery of the church. This is a "derived mystery" (*mysterium derivatum,* an expression used by the Fathers), derived from other more basic mysteries and in particular that of love and communion between the three divine Persons. Just as there is trinitarian *koinōnia,* so there is ecclesial *koinōnia.* The main definition of the church is this: the community of the faithful in communion with the Father, through the incarnate Son, in the Holy Spirit, and in communion with each other and with their leaders. The Spirit and the risen Christ have lavished many gifts and charisms on the faithful (cf 1 Cor. 12). But the Spirit who gives is the same as the Lord (1 Cor. 12:4). Episcopal collegiality finds its best theological basis in the communion of the Trinity.[32] There are many bishops, but they form one episcopal body. Just as the three Uniques are one God in communion, so the twelve Apostles form one single episcopal college. In the same way, there are many local churches, but all together make up the one church of God. The catholicity of the church resides in the respect and welcome it affords to the gifts and specialities the Spirit gives to each local church. All the local churches are united through the risen Christ, in the Spirit. Ecclesial communion expresses trinitarian communion: each Person is distinct, but accepts the others and surrenders fully to the others. The text from St John quoted earlier (17:20-21) demonstrates the perichoretic relationship between the Son and the Father. It is put forward as a model for the community of those who follow Christ: "may they be one in us." The trinitarian vision produces a vision of a church that is more communion than hierarchy, more service than power, more circular than pyramidal, more loving embrace than bending the knee before authority.

Such a perichoretic model of the church would submit all ecclesial functions (episcopate, presbyterate, lay ministries, and so on) to the imperative of communion and participation by all in everything that concerns the good of all. Then the church would in fact be "a people made one with the unity of the Father, the Son, and the Holy Spirit" (LG 4).

CHAPTER VIII

Glory Be to the Father, and to the Son and to the Holy Spirit

So far, we have been reflecting on the mystery of the Trinity in the light of the teaching of the church and the pronouncements of theologians, a process that has more to do with reason and understanding than with devotion and praise. We now turn to the same themes in the light of another concern that has never been really absent from the foregoing: that of doxology.[1] By "doxology" (from the Greek *doxa* meaning "glory"), we mean experience of the divine realities expressed in praise and thanksgiving; these are expressions of respect for and joyful acceptance of the deeds done by God for men and women. Doxology—celebration of God's self-revelation—lies at the root of all theology—reflection on and from revelation. This is especially true when dealing with the truth of the Trinity. Before theologians discussed and the magisterium pronounced, there were the prayers of the faithful, liturgical celebration and peaceful, unreflecting daily experience of the presence of the Father through the Son in union with the Holy Spirit in the midst of humanity, in the bosom of the church, in the hearts of the faithful.

Jesus revealed the secret of his Sonship and his intimate relationship with the Father in a prayer (cf Matt. 11:25-7; Luke 10:21-2) full of joy in the Spirit: "I bless you, Father, Lord of heaven and of earth. . . . No one knows who the Son is except the Father, and who the Father is except the Son and those to whom the Son chooses to reveal him." So it seems proper to approach the mystery of the Trinity through a prayer: the daily prayer of the "Glory be. . . ." In commenting on this prayer we shall use theological reflection as well as doxological and mystagogical (Christian initiation into the mystery of the Trinity) service.

1. THE HOLY TRINITY AS GOOD NEWS TO MEN AND WOMEN, ESPECIALLY TO THE POOR

In what sense can the Trinity be called "gospel," good news, to people, especially to the poor and oppressed? For many Christians it is simply a mystery in logic: how can the one God exist in three Persons? How can a Trinity of Persons form the unity of the one God? Any Christian coming into contact with debates on the Trinity for the first time might well form this impression: the Christian faith developed intellectually in the Hellenic world; Christians had to translate their doxology into a theology appropriate to that world in order to assert the truth of their faith. So they used expressions accessible to the critical reasoning of that time, such as substance, person, relation, perichoresis, procession. This was a most difficult path to follow, as we saw in earlier chapters; it has left its mark even today, even though the mystery defies all human categories and calls for new approaches, springing from an encounter between biblical revelation and dominant cultures. We should never forget that the New Testament never uses the expressions "trinity of persons" and "unity of nature." To say that God is Father, Son and Holy Spirit is revelation; to say that God is "one substance and three Persons" is theology, a human endeavour to fit the revelation of God within the limitations of reason.

The same thing happens when Christians read the pronouncements of the magisterium. These are statements of great pithiness and logical coherence, designed to curb the speculative exuberance of theologians. Dogmatic progress virtually came to an end with the Council of Florence (1439-45); from then to the present (with some noted exceptions, as we have seen) theological works have generally confined themselves to commenting on the terms defined and investigating historical questions of detail of the system already constructed.[2]

It is not easy to explain to Christians caught up in the "logical mystery" of the Trinity that the number "three" in the Trinity (*trias* and *trinitas,* words established by Theophilus of Antioch and Tertullian at the end of the second century) does not signify anything that can be counted and has nothing to do with arithmetical processes of addition and subtraction. The scriptures count nothing in God; they know only one divine number—the number "one": one God, one Lord, one Spirit. This "one" is not a number, not the number "one" in the sense of first in a series; it is rather the negation of all numbers, simply "the only." The Father is "an only," as are the Son and the Holy Spirit; these "onlies" cannot be added together. As we have tried to explain earlier, it is the eternal communion between these Onlies that forms the divine oneness in the power of life and love (the divine nature). Nevertheless, by reason of the communion and relationship revealed to us between the Father, Son and Holy Spirit, there is an order to the divine names. Though each Person is co-eternal with the others and, therefore, none can exist before the others, we must, nevertheless, affirm that the Father who begets is logically "before" the Son who is begotten, as is the Son "before" the Spirit, breathed out by the Father with and through the Son. This is the explanation for the order of the divine names, and from this comes the human convention of speaking of three "Persons."[3] But theology has never been satisfied with the expression "three Persons," as the continuous debates have shown.

We need to go beyond the understanding of Trinity as logical mystery and see it as saving mystery. The Trinity has to do with the lives of each of us, our daily experiences, our struggles to follow our conscience, our love and joy, our bearing the sufferings of the world and the tragedies of human existence; it also has to do with the struggle against social injustice, with efforts at building a more human form of society, with the sacrifices and martyrdoms that these endeavours so often bring. If we fail to include the Trinity in our personal and social odyssey, we shall have failed to show the saving mystery, failed in evangelization. If oppressed believers come to appreciate the fact that their struggles for life and liberty are also those of Father, Son and Holy Spirit, working for the Kingdom of glory and eternal life, then they will have further motives for struggling and resisting; the meaning of their efforts will break out of the restricting framework of history and be inscribed in eternity, in the heart of the absolute Mystery itself. We are not condemned to live alone, cut off from one another; we are called to live together and to enter into the communion of the Trinity. Society is not ultimately set in its unjust and unequal relationships, but summoned to transform itself in the light of the open and egalitarian relationships that obtain in the communion of the Trinity, the goal of social and historical progress. If the Trinity is good news, then it is so particularly for the oppressed and those condemned to solitude.

2. REVERENCE IN THE FACE OF THE MYSTERY

Doxology is an attitude of adoration, thanksgiving and respect in the face of the mystery of the Trinity. If we are to know how to approach the mystery, we first need to know in what sense the Trinity is a mystery. The official teaching of the church presents it as a mystery "in the strict sense" (*stricte dictum*), by which it means a truth that surpasses the possibilities of human understanding, a truth guaranteed solely by divine communication and which, even having been communicated, cannot be positively apprehended. This understanding of mystery was worked out against rationalism, especially the idealist sort which attempted to turn revealed truths into mere products of human reason. In this sense, mystery is something expressed in language and considered by reason; it is something transient, valid for the time our reason is obscured in history; in eternity it will come to an end, since we shall then see God face to face.

Understood like this, the Trinity is certainly a strict mystery, since it is beyond reason to understand how three distinct Persons can be in one another in such a way as to form a single God; the absolute equality of these Persons, given that the Son "proceeds" from the Father and the Holy Spirit from the Father and from/through the Son, is also inaccessible to reason; nor can human reason encompass the combination of the radical oneness of God with the trinity of Persons.

Approaching mystery in this way is scarcely conducive to an attitude of veneration. If we are faced with something that sets a limit to reason, a block to its sphere of understanding, the result—despite the validity of the concept, in the sense just expressed—will be to provoke a response of anxiety and a feeling of mental strangulation. We need to face the fact that this concept of mystery fails to encompass the breadth and depth of mystery as understood in the early church. God and the Trinity were then seen as a mystery, certainly, but as a *revealed* mystery. It was the property of Christian mystery to have been revealed and communicated by the witnesses of faith (cf Rom. 15:25; 1 Cor. 2:1-6; Eph. 1:9; 3:9; Col. 1:26; 1 Tim. 3:9-16; Mark 4:11; Matt. 13:11; Luke 8:10). But it is also the property of mystery to remain mystery in revelation. As such it does not represent the limit of reason, but the unlimited sphere of reason. It is con-natural with human existence, since this is also ultimate mystery, indwelt by the Infinite, which makes it feel the desire to love God and to live in absolute communion with God and with everything in the universe.[4] In the case of the mystery of the Trinity, this has been revealed in the actions of Jesus Christ in history and in the manifestations of the Spirit. For this reason, it can rightly be called a sacramental mystery—that is, a mystery communicated in the incarnation and in the coming of the Spirit on Mary and on the Apostles at Pentecost. It is possible to tell the story of its course and of how it was, gradually, understood by the first witnesses to the Christian mystery.

Seeing mystery in this perspective enables us to understand how it provokes reverence, the only possible attitude to what is supreme and final in our lives. Instead of strangling reason, it invites expansion of the mind and heart. It is not a mystery that leaves us dumb and terrified, but one that leaves us happy, singing and giving thanks. It is not a wall placed in front of us, but a doorway through which we go to the infinity of God. Mystery is like a cliff: we may not be able to scale it, but we can stand at the foot of it, touch it, praise its beauty. So it is with the mystery of the Trinity. It is not outside us; it wraps us round on all sides, dwells within us and invites us to make ours the eternal communion between the divine Persons.

Respect and veneration are a proper response to the mystery of the human person; these plus faith are the proper response to the mystery of God. Believing is much more than accepting the existence of the Holy Trinity (*credere Trinitatem*); it is even more than accepting the pronouncements made by Jesus and the Apostles in the name of the Trinity (*credere Trinitati, Christo*) and about the Trinity. Believing ultimately means entrusting ourselves to the Father, Son and Holy Spirit, entrusting the course of our life and our death to the mystery of communion which is our final resting-place and supreme consummation. In this all-embracing sense, believing implies a mode of being; it is not so much reflecting on the mystery as letting oneself be carried away by it, involving oneself in the dynamic of its revelation, entering into the communion with the divine life in the Trinity. As we need hearing to understand music, aesthetic sense to understand art, so with mystery: we need faith to put us in a position from which it makes sense to talk of the mystery of the communion of the Father, Son and Holy Spirit as making one God. Once this space is granted to faith from the heart, then reason can perform its task, which consists in scrutinizing the elegant logic of mystery, not emptying it of content, but appropriating it to human existence. And the more reason plumbs the depths of God, the wider the horizon of mystery that opens up. God is then not a transient mystery for while we are on earth, ceasing to be one in eternity. God (like human beings and human societies in history) is an intrinsic mystery and will remain so in the eternity to come. God's mystery is more than a revealed truth; it is God the Father, Son and Holy Spirit entering into creation, sharing its dark side, ransoming it from the rebellion of sin and integrating it in eternal communion. God, then, is always the Transcendent pervading the immanent and rendering it transparent.[5]

If reason laden with faith cannot grasp even the fundamentals of God, this is not a motive for resignation or despair. Reason itself recognizes calmly that "God can be what we cannot understand."[6]

3. WE SAW HIS GLORY!

Revealed mystery manifests the glory of the triune God. What does "glory" mean in this context? Glory consists of the manifestation of the true reality of the triune God. Glory implies more than revealing the existence of the Trinity; it is showing the *presence* of the Trinity. Presence is existence potentialized, handed over, communicated; so other realities are connected to presence and glory: splendour and benevolent love, "divine philanthropy" as the Fathers called it. The human response to this perceived presence is joy, fascination and the feeling of being saved and full of grace. Karl Barth was right to say: "The Trinity of God is the mystery of his beauty. To deny it is to have a God without splendour, without joy (and without humour!), a God without beauty."[7]

The beauty of God has appeared; God's glory has been made manifest. Nothing better illustrates the consciousness of this gracious presence of the triune God than the Letter to Titus: "But when the kindness and love of God our saviour for mankind were revealed, it was not because he was concerned with any righteous actions we might have done ourselves; it was for no reason except his own compassion that he saved us, by means of the cleansing water of rebirth and by renewing us with the Holy Spirit which he has so generously poured over us through Jesus Christ our saviour" (3:4-6). The glory of God is humankind living, redeemed, and the poor brought back to God's justice and righteousness.

The glory of the Trinity appears in the wonder felt by people, who are "God's beloved" (Rom. 1:7), the "beloved of the Lord" (2 Thess. 2:13). That glory and that wonder appear in the exclamation "Think of the love that the Father has lavished on us" (1 John 3:1); or in: "Nothing can come between us and the love of Christ. . . . Nothing still to come . . . can ever come between us and the love of God made visible in Christ Jesus our Lord" (Rom. 8:35-9); or in this: "the Son of God who loved me and who sacrificed himself for my sake" (Gal. 2:20). St John sums up the whole process of divine self-giving: "Yes, God loved the world so much that he gave his only Son" (3:16).

The response to this communicated glory can only be to give glory, give back love, sing praises to the mystery (cf Rom. 11:33): "We are to love, then, because God loved us first" (1 John 4:19). When Christians pray the Gloria, they adopt this tone of response. They thank the Trinity for its revelation and communication: the Father who sent his Son to save us and sent the Spirit whose love is poured into our hearts (Rom. 5:5); the Son because he showed us the merciful face of the Father; the Spirit which makes us welcome the Son and cry: Abba, my beloved Father! They can say of the Trinity what John said of Jesus Christ: "We saw his glory!" (1:14). It is not surprising that the greatest theologians who have helped to provide insights into the depths of the mystery, such as Gregory

Nazianzen, Pseudo-Dionysius and Augustine, ended their treaties with fervent prayers of praise and thanksgiving, in recognition of their limitations.[8] In the end, reason is silent so as to give the heart room to express its admiration. As St Thomas said of the Trinity: "We honour God with silence, not because there is nothing to say . . . but because we realize that we always fall short of an adequate understanding."[9] This reverent silence is the proper response of the faithful to the mystery of the Trinity.

4. REASONS FOR GIVING GLORY

Giving glory comes from contemplating the mystery of the Trinity in its economic expression (as it has been revealed to us in history), or in its immanent dimension (as God truly is from all eternity), or in its saving-liberating significance. Let us look once more at each of these aspects.

The New Testament shows us the process of revelation of the Trinity through the words and deeds of Christ and through the coming of the Spirit on the early communities. Jesus reveals the Father as merciful, as the father of the prodigal son or the shepherd of the lost sheep. He feels himself to have been sent by the Father. His actions are aimed at bringing about the kingship of the Father through setting people free from what oppresses them. He frees people with a power and enthusiasm that amaze those present. This is the Holy Spirit working through Jesus, the Spirit that continues to work with Jesus in history. Jesus' particular revelation is the union and communion between himself, the Father and the Spirit. He is never alone, but always in relationship. Even on the cross, when he feels abandoned by the Father, he still continues to call on him as "my God"; it is into the Father's hands that he commends his spirit.

This revelation is given through the various expressions of Jesus' human life: his prayers of thanksgiving, his proclamation of the good news, his dealings with the poor, his encounters with the Pharisees, his acts of healing and exorcism, his sharing with the Apostles. His words, deeds and attitudes all provide revelation. For our part, contemplating the "mysteries/sacraments of Jesus in the flesh" forms the doxological way leading us to give thanks, to adore and make the trinitarian mystery our own.

The economic Trinity is the gateway to the immanent Trinity, in which God is revealed in essence, as Father, Son and Holy Spirit. The deeds of the incarnate Son and the Holy Spirit acting in history, starting with the annunciation to Mary, provide glimpses of life inside the Trinity. The Father is eternally life in its deepest, darkest mystery; the Son is life in its shining mystery, because received from the Father and given back to him in filial love; the Spirit is forever the mystery of life that unites source to channel and channel (the Son) to source (the Father). The unity of the three "Uniques," three Persons forming a single communion, a single triune God, appears by virtue of the life communicated from one to another and the love that flows between them.

All this mystery has meaning for us in itself; contemplation of it is alone motive for joy and lifting of our spirit. God is glorified in the mystery itself, since the glory of the diversity of Persons and unity in communion is so absorbing that our only attitude to it must be one of praise, adoration and thanksgiving. This glorification is increased when we realize that we too are involved in this trinitarian communion: the three Persons want to introduce all of us and the world we live in to their overflowing life of community. This communion is not a promise for the future; it is happening amongst us now, in persons and communities. It is experienced whenever we know true communion of being and having. The Trinity communicates itself whenever communion is established on earth. It is also experienced as hope and anticipated in this hope whenever the oppressed and their allies fight against tyranny and oppression. The communion of the Trinity is then their source of inspiration, plays a part in their protest, is a paradigm of what they are building.

CHAPTER IX

Glory Be to the Father: Origin and Goal of All Liberation

There are many ways of seeing God as Father.[1] In cosmology, God is seen as Father for having created the universe: this is a common appellation in world religions. In the *political* sense, in which it is used in the Old Testament, God is Father for having created, chosen and freed his people (cf Exod. 4:22; Isa. 63:16; Jer. 31:9). In a *spiritual* sense, God is Father because he shows pity and mercy, because he is the refuge and protection of the pious, the sinners and the abandoned (cf Pss. 27:10; 103:13; Isa. 63:15; 64:7). In a *psychological* sense, God is experienced as Father as the final consolation in human loneliness, the utopic realization of our thirst for immortality and omnipotence.

All these senses have their value, even theological value, but theirs is not the approach taken in this chapter, where we look at the Father from a *trinitarian* viewpoint,[2] as the first Person of the Trinity, the Father who begets the Son and who together with (and through) the Son breathes out the Spirit—in the analogous sense of such words. We reflect first on the economic dimension: on the Father as revealed in the history of salvation by the incarnate Son; then on the immanent aspect: on the Father in his perichoretic relationship with the Son and the Holy Spirit in the bosom of the Trinity. Our conviction is that the Father reveals himself as he is in himself; that what we see of him from time is a revelation of what he is in eternity—always bearing in mind that it is impossible to speak of the Father without including the communion between him and the other Persons and vice-versa.

1. THE INVISIBLE FATHER, UNFATHOMABLE MYSTERY

Christian faith has no image of God the Father. The Son appeared in human form in the person of Jesus of Nazareth; the Spirit is described as appearing in the form of a dove. The Father is invisible, as the New Testament makes clear: "No one has ever seen God; it is the only Son, who is nearest to the Father's heart, who has made him known" (John 1:18; cf 6:46; 1 Tim. 6:16; 1 John 4:12). He is unfathomable mystery; the deeper we plunge into this mystery, the more our knowledge grows and the farther off the shores of the ocean of divine life appear. The Father is he who always was, before any creature. God the Father is more the beginning than God the creator: even if there had been no creation (which does not come from necessity, but as the fruit of trinitarian communion expanded outwards, freely), God would be Father because he is eternally begetting the Son and entering into communion with him. As St John rightly makes Jesus say: "Father . . . you loved me before the creation of the world" (17:24).[3]

This Father, unfathomable mystery, was revealed to us by Jesus Christ, his only-begotten Son. Jesus is undoubtedly the Son of God, but in a trinitarian perspective, he is more properly Son of the Father. The Father is always Father of our Lord Jesus Christ (Rom. 15:6; 1 Cor. 1:3; 2 Cor. 11:31; Eph. 3:14; etc.), with an everlasting fatherhood belonging to the essence of God. If the Father is invisible, then our only access to him is through the Son and the Spirit who come from him. Outside the unique revelation bestowed by the Son and the Spirit, God the Father is no more than synonymous with God the creator. It is through Jesus that we discover the reality of the one, true God as Father, Son and Holy Spirit: the Holy Trinity.

2. "NO ONE KNOWS THE FATHER EXCEPT THE SON"

In a context of prayer and spiritual exaltation ("filled with joy by the Spirit," Luke says), Jesus presents himself as the one who reveals the Father: "Everything has been entrusted to me by my

Father; and no one knows the Son except the Father, just as no one knows the Father except the Son and those to whom the Son chooses to reveal him" (Matt. 11:27; Luke 10:22). Jesus has an extremely intimate experience of his God: gospel evidence points to Jesus' consistent use of the baby's word "Abba" in speaking of God. What does "my beloved *Abba*" mean? Just that God the Father is the creator of the holy and prophetic man Jesus of Nazareth? Jesus' consciousness as portrayed in the synoptic Gospels and the insights that John adds from his knowledge of Jesus lead to a mystery. The Father is not the creator of, but the begetter of a Son. Jesus calls God Father because he feels himself to be his Son. The relationship of fatherhood and sonship comes from begetting. Jesus' phrase "everything has been entrusted to me by my Father" holds the true secret: the Son received his whole being from the Father. Since this is so, the Jesus of St John's Gospel can say: "all I have is yours, and all you have is mine" (17:10), a statement completed with "The Father and I are one" (10:30). This understanding was not lost on his adversaries, who sought to have him killed because, "he spoke of God as his Father, and so made himself God's equal" (John 5:18). Because the Father begets the Son, there is a priority of the Father, expressed by Jesus in the phrase "the Father is greater than I," which can properly be understood only in a trinitarian reading of God. He receives everything from the Father, so the Father is the original source, but he possesses all that the Father possesses and so is equal to him. So: "To have seen me is to have seen the Father" (John 14:9).

The very appellation *Abba* shows the deep intimacy existing between Jesus and his Father. He calls him "my Father." He says "I am not alone, because the Father is with me" (John 16:32); later, this is deepened into interpenetration of one with the other: the Father in him and he in the Father (17:21).

3. IN THE NAME OF THE FATHER, JESUS THE SON LIBERATES THE OPPRESSED

Jesus feels himself sent by the Father. The Father is the power behind his actions: "The Son can do nothing by himself; he can do only what he sees the Father doing" (John 5:19). The Father is the prototype of mercy, welcoming the prodigal son, loving the "little ones." If Jesus himself made a personal commitment to the poor and outcasts of his time, it was surely not from any mere humanistic impulse, but a direct outcome of his relationship to the Father: "As the Father raises the dead and gives them life, so the Son gives life to anyone he chooses" (5:21). So Jesus, in the name of the Father, healed, contested the legalistic image of God held by the Jews of the time, put himself above the sacred day of the Sabbath (cf Mark 3:1-6). He called on God as Father while performing his liberating actions.[4] He elaborated no teaching on the Father, but lived his experience of the Father in drawing close to the fallen, in offering forgiveness to sinners seeking conversion, by frequenting people drawn from bad company. His acts were always to set people free of what oppressed them, and those actions sprang from his meeting with the Father. His justification of performing a cure on the Sabbath shows his basic attitude in relation to the Father: "My Father goes on working and so do I" (John 5:17).

The Father's great purpose is the establishment of the Kingdom. "Kingdom" here does not mean God ruling in the style of the powerful of the world; it means the inauguration of goodness and mercy, the renunciation of privilege in favour of service; it implies the exaltation of the humble and the restoration of violated rights. "Kingdom" supposes a great and global liberation; this is why its coming is "good news." It began with the presence of Jesus the Son, but is still open to a process of fulfillment, to be brought about by people clinging to it. So it is continually the object of hope and supplication: "thy kingdom come" (Matt. 6:10; Luke 11:2).

The Kingdom of the Father begins to be brought about in history and in human society. This is why Jesus, in his tender relationship with the Father, revealed the Father also in creation, in the birds of the air that neither sow nor reap, but are fed by his Father in heaven (Matt. 6:26). He also sees the Father as Providence, a Father who knows the needs of his children (6:32). This is not a perception of the creator, but of the Father whose fatherhood spreads through creation and is understood by Jesus in his sonship.

4. FATHERHOOD AS THE BASIS OF UNIVERSAL FELLOWSHIP

The universal fatherhood of God needs to be understood correctly. It is usually seen as stemming from the mystery of creation: the Father created all beings; therefore all are his sons and daugh-

ters. Such a view belongs to monotheistic religion, whether Old
Testament or more recent a-trinitarian: it is attributing a metaphorical fatherhood to God because God created all things. The trinitarian view assigns fatherhood to the Person of the Father: the Father
begets the only-begotten Son. With the very same love which is
responsible for begetting the Son, he gives origin to all other beings
in the Son, by the Son, with the Son and for the Son. All are
therefore the image and likeness of the Father and the Son in whom
they are made (cf John 1:3; Col. 1:15-17). All beings share the
sonship of the only-begotten Son; they are sons and daughters in
the Son (cf Rom. 8:29). Because all are sons and daughters, they are
also all brothers and sisters through their sharing in the sonship of
the Son, Jesus Christ, "the eldest of many brothers" (Rom. 8:29)
and sisters. This paternity is more than the result of creation; it
derives from the eternal begetting of the Son in which all of us,
companions in love, are held in mind and loved; in which we too are
made sons and daughters of the eternal Father by sharing and
adoption. So human beings are not mere creatures, existing outside
the Trinity; they find the roots of their being in the superabundance
of life, love and communion that comes from the Father, is filtered
through the Son and poured out in the Holy Spirit. If we want to
hold on to the word "creation," then we have to say: the Father
creates through the Son in the power of the Holy Spirit. Starting
with the only-begotten Son, all are sisters and brothers. Theology
introduced the distinction between the only-begotten Son and
adoptive sons/daughters to point out the difference between the
divine source and its images and likenesses outside the circle of the
Trinity, in creation. The Son was not created out of nothing, but
begotten from the substance of the Father; other beings are made
from nothing, but created in the Son and in the same movement by
which the Son was begotten and born. Our adoption should not be
understood legalistically, but ontologically: that is, in a true sense,
not as a figure of speech. We are in fact sons and daughters in the
Son Jesus (cf 1 John 3:1).

After his resurrection, Jesus showed how this fatherhood was to
be understood in terms of universal brother- and sisterhood. He
called his disciples "my brothers" when he said: "I am ascending to
my Father and your Father" (John 20:17). The Father of Jesus has
become our Father. This is why we can call on "Our Father, who art

in heaven." In trinitarian language: the Father begets divine life in human beings, who become really and truly daughters and sons in the Son who is eternally being begotten. The distinction between "my Father" and "your Father" points to the distinction between eternal, natural begetting and temporal, adoptive (but real) begetting. Some mystics, such as Meister Eckhart, went so far as to describe the Son being eternally begotten by the Father in the hearts of God's sons and daughters.[5] In other words: the Father is eternally begetting the Son and simultaneously, with the Son, creating the Son's brothers and sisters in the Father's own image and likeness. By loving human beings as his daughters and sons, the Father is begetting, as in one single act, his own eternal Son, the first-born fruit of his love.

This trinitarian understanding of the fatherhood of God is important if we are to avoid a unilateral religion of the Father, as outlined in the first chapter. In this, God is presented as Great Father because he created heaven and earth. As such he is the supreme authority of the universe, from whom all other religious and civil authorities derive, in descending orders of hierarchy. As there is only one eternal authority, so the tendency to have only one authority in each sphere of the world is confirmed: a single political leader, a single military chief, a single social leader, a single religious head, a single guardian of truth, and so on. God is presented as the great universal Superego, alone and unique. Much of the atheism of developed societies today is no more than a denial of this sort of authoritarian God and of the patriarchal sort of religion that follows from it and obstructs the development of human freedoms.[6]

Seeing the divine fatherhood in its true shape, as the Father-Son relationship augmented by the daughter- and sonship of all other adoptive sons and daughters, shows us universal communion, fellowship. Because we are all sons and daughters in the Son, because the eternal Son became the temporal son of Mary through the incarnation, we are all truly brothers and sisters. The Father is never without the Son and these sons and daughters. If we deprive him of this link, then we let in the patriarchal Father, creator of all but himself, solitary and unique, a conception open to political manipulation so as to provide an ideological support for authoritarianism or for the "king, lord or leader by the grace of God." The patriarchalism and paternalism that have so humiliated the poor throughout history are in fact most strongly criticized and most firmly rejected on the basis of the Father of Jesus Christ, who clearly said: "You must call no one on earth your father, since you have only one Father, and he is in heaven" (Matt. 23:9). Universal daughter- and sonship is the basis for bringing in a society of brothers and sisters, all sons and daughters, united with the only-begotten Son in a communion of love with the Father.

The true religion of the Father always includes the Son and the sons and daughters in the Son thereby preventing authoritarian distortions and oppressive images of God as absolute Lord, supreme Judge and solitary Father.

5. THE MATERNAL FATHER AND PATERNAL MOTHER

Calling God "Father" is not using sexist language. Properly understood, it includes calling God "Mother" too, as "Father" is used as a single source of procreation, for which either "father" or "mother" would be possible, just as we can speak of "fatherhood" or "motherhood" in human terms. The actual terminology used in tradition suggests a trans-sexist representation of the Father: so the Father is said to "beget" (not "create") the Son; the Son is "born of" the Father, not "made by" the Father. Being begotten and born can just as well refer to motherhood. So the Council of Toledo, for example, typically stated that "we must believe that the Son is begotten or born (*genitus vel natus*) from *the womb of the Father,* that is, from his very substance and not from nothing or from some other substance" (DS 526, CT). The Father is here given maternal attributes. We need both the figures of earthly father and mother to express the riches of divine fatherhood. So we can say—without claiming this as a dogmatic understanding—that the Father, in his begetting of the Son and breathing-out (with the Son) of the Holy Spirit, can also be called Mother. But it would be better to say, in faithfulness to the suggestions provided by the language of the Bible, which shows God with both paternal and maternal attributes, that the Father is maternal and the Mother paternal.[7]

In fact, the Old Testament portrays the love of God for God's people through the figure of a mother in several places: "Does a woman forget her baby at the breast, or fail to cherish the son of her womb?" (Isa. 49:15). Tenderness and comfort are expressions of motherly love. The prophetic oracle says: "Like a son comforted by his mother will I comfort you" (Isa. 66:13). One of the foremost characteristics of the God of revelation is mercy—see Exodus 33:19; 34:6-7. This mercy is presented in the figure of the bowels of a mother (*rahamim*).[8] The prodigal son returns to be greeted by his father with maternal tenderness: "While he was still a long way off, his father saw him and was moved with pity. He ran to the boy, clasped him in his arms and kissed him tenderly" (Luke 15:20). Compassion is the great perfection of the maternal Father whom Jesus asks us to imitate: "Be compassionate as your Father is compassionate" (Luke 6:36). In a word, if we want to describe the Father, the characteristics of an earthly father are not enough. The perfections of an earthly mother have to be added to them. Jesus' Father is a Father only through being also a Mother, uniting the strength of paternal love with the tenderness of maternal love. Only by postulating the two figures of an eternal Father and an eternal Mother can we express what we believe in faith: there is an ultimate mystery, our final resting-place, the source and origin of everything, that invites us to communion, from which everything comes and to which everything tends, and it is the heavenly Father and Mother. In communion with the heavenly Father and Mother, all divisions and slaveries are surpassed; the Kingdom that the sons and daughters trust in is installed, the sons and daughters being free, equal members of the divine family. Jesus taught us to cry "Abba"; the Son revealed our sonship. The most absolute mystery (the Father) becomes close and intimate (in his sons and daughters and in the incarnate Son).

6. THE FATHER IN THE IMMANENT TRINITY: THE UNORIGINATED ORIGIN

What can we say about the Father in himself in his eternity? We can begin to glimpse something of the mystery of the Father, in the immanent dimension of the Trinity, from what Jesus told us of his Father. When theology speaks of God the Father, it refers to the absolute and unfathomable mystery underlying all reality, divine and created. This is always a mystery of life, of communion, of bursting out in all directions. Everything else has to be enlightened and understood from the basis of this loving mystery. The texts of the magisterium speak of this God as the unoriginated origin (DS 1331); everything he has, he has of himself from all eternity (ibid.), being the source and origin of all divinity (DS 490, 525, 3326). The Greeks said the Father was the original cause (*archē*) and primordial source (*pēgē*) of everything in the spheres of the Trinity and creation. The Latins translated these two concepts as *principium*—source. In the belief of the Orthodox Church, the Father is properly God; without losing anything of himself, he transfers the fullness of his divinity to the Son and the Holy Spirit. Focussing divinity on the Father in this way has not always steered clear of subordinationism. The liturgical formulations of the early church still have a certain ambiguity with regard to the identity of substance of the three Persons. The doxology originally went: "Glory be to the Father through the Son"; St Basil modified it to "Glory be to the Father with the Son and with the Holy Spirit" in order to stress that the Son and the Spirit were also divine.[9] But the equality of their nature-communion was still not clear from this, and it was modified again to its final form: "Glory be to the Father, and to the Son and to the Holy Spirit," which gives full expression to the simultaneity of the divine nature-communion of the divine Three.

This impenetrable mystery was bestowed as intelligibility, as the light that illumines everything, as the supreme sense: as the Son begotten by the Father. The Son is other than the Father, but not something other than the Father. So the Son possesses all that the Father possesses, in communion and mutual interpenetration, except the fact of the Father being the Father. The Father also transmits to the Son the power jointly to breathe out the Holy Spirit. The distinction—Father and Son—makes possible a relationship of communion, understanding, love, mutual bestowal. What emerges from this is their union and reciprocal giving: the Holy Spirit. The Father, therefore, is determined by two original relationships, with the Son and the Holy Spirit.

As we have already stated, this causality-oriented thought is deeply analogical. It should not give the impression of derivation, as though we were in the field of cosmology, which always asks about origins: where does the world come from? This type of thought can give the impression of reducing everything to an infinite chain of causes, so that we fall back on a final and transcendent cause of everything. We cannot do this in the realm of the Trinity. Here everything is eternal and simultaneous, Father, Son and Holy Spirit emerging simultaneously and originally. As the Council of Toledo rightly taught: "the Son was born . . . from the substance of the Father, without beginning, before all ages" (DS 526). As the Lateran Council declared in 1215, the same is true of the Holy Spirit: it is without beginning, forever and without end, being consubstantial, co-omnipotent and co-eternal (DS 800; cf 850, 1331, 1986). Processions and derivations belong to a thought-pattern that starts from the unity and oneness of God. If we start directly from trinitarian faith in the Christian God as Father, Son and Holy Spirit, all equally original and originating realities, unity emerges as the expression of the eternal communion and essential interpenetration of life and love between the three divine Persons. This, it seems to me, better expresses the Christian novelty of the primacy of love and communion in our access to God and in our understanding of what God actually is, an eternal communion of the eternal Persons.

The thought expressed in terms of "processions" is still meaningful, however, since it follows the language of the New Testament and the official teaching of the church; it also expresses the idea of a Trinity of Persons in a form acceptable to the human mind, without multiplying God, keeping God's unity and oneness intact. Besides, how can we speak of the ineffable without appealing to the limit-concepts, the most sacred images in our language, those of generation of life and communion in love? This thought-form shows both the distinction in God and the reciprocity of the Persons: one is not the others, but is bound in essence to the others. The Father will always be Father of the Son; the Son will always be of the same nature as the Father and in infinite communion with him. The Spirit is from always and for always the gift of the Father and the Son. This circle of love is not closed in on itself, but opens out to the universe of creation as the expression of the superabundance of intra-trinitarian life extending beyond the face-to-face encounter between the Persons; it gives rise to other differences in which God can also be in communion and love.

The great theologians who created trinitarian terminology and buried themselves in the depths of the mystery were conscious of the obscurity of what we call "processions." St Hilary of Poitiers, author of a major treatise on the Trinity, wrote:

> Begetting is the secret of the Father and the Son. If anyone is convinced of the weakness of his intelligence through failing to understand this mystery, even though he knows what the separate words Father and Son mean, he will undoubtedly be even more downcast to learn that I am in the same state of ignorance. Yes, I don't know either, and I am only consoled by the fact that the archangels are ignorant of this mystery, the angels cannot understand it, nor can the ages, nor the prophet; the Apostle failed to clarify it and the Son himself told us nothing about it. So let us stop lamenting.[10]

St Gregory of Nyssa said much the same, somewhat nervously replying to those who showed little sensitivity to mystery:

> How is the Son begotten? I reply with the disdain the question deserves: God's begetting receives the honour of silence. It is more than enough for you that the Son was begotten. As to how, not even the angels are allowed to know this, and far less you. You want me to explain how? It is as the Father who begets and the Son who is begotten know. The rest is hidden in cloud, hidden from your short-sighted eyes.[11]

If we speak of begetting without knowing exactly what this means, this is because, as St Gregory of Nyssa says, the notion of Father and Son does not suggest it. When we say that God is Father, unoriginated origin and source of all things, we mean that God is never alone. Though he exists independently of creation, the Father is inconceivable without the Son; just as they have fatherhood and sonship, so there is an eternal inter-relationship between them.

7. THE MISSION OF THE FATHER:
THE MYSTERIOUSNESS OF CREATION

The phrase "the mission of the Father" refers to how the Father appears, as Father, in creation. Mission here means the way or process in which the Father acts in creation and in human salvation. Investigation into this aspect is, one has to repeat, shrouded in mystery. The Father is invisible and ineffable of himself, as the ultimate source from which everything else takes its existence and is understood. Understanding is always understanding of something already begun; the origin is, by definition, incomprehensible. Yet despite these insuperable limitations, it is possible to discern some traces of the Father in the order of creation.

Creation, we have seen, is the fruit of the eternal love between the Father and the Son. In begetting the Son, the Father at the same time projects imitable possible beings, the sons and daughters in the Son. Within the Trinity, creation is seen as eternally thought and loved in the very act of the Father thinking and loving the Son. This means that we can say that the creation of the universe (things and people) is basically the Father's work. It is the work of the whole Trinity, but starts with the eternal fecundity of the Father— begetting the Son, with the Son breathing out the Spirit. So creation is not merely the result of a later act of will external to the Trinity, but is an expression of the intimate, perichoretic life of God, a life that expands outwards, creating different beings with whom God can communicate and enter into communion.

Everything to do with creating and originating expresses the ineffable presence of the Father. The production of human life is a mystery of tenderness, a sacrament referring us back to the eternal fecundity of the Father. The appearance of a new being, even in orders lower than human, commands the respect due to mystery: it is a sign of the Father's presence in his creation.

Everything relating to mystery, to what constantly and yet again challenges our capacity for understanding; everything that escapes us, dazzles us with blinding light and is therefore indecipherable, has to do with the Father. The mysteriousness of the origins of the world, the impenetrable meaning of the course of men and women through history, the unfathomable depths of each person's heart: these too refer back to the mystery of the Father.

The age of ignorance of the trinitarian nature of God also belongs to the mission of the Father. The God discovered and loved as an intimate and at the same time transcendent, cosmic force, as a mystery infusing the existence of the world and of life, still without a name: this is the emergence of the Father in history. The "*ignotus deus*" of world religions, the Yahweh of Judaism, are in reality none other than the Father revealing himself and hiding himself among us under a thousand different names. Being experienced without being consciously named, as absolute mystery: this is part of the mission of the Father. He is the hidden spring from which all channels flow; these channels lead back to the source, but this is hidden and invisible in them.

A final aspect of the mission of the Father is the recognition that we receive our being from another, from God. Jesus makes a fundamental point of this, as we have seen. Accepting ourselves as being derived from and intimately bound to the mystery that dwells in us makes it possible to call God Father. This process is loaded with tension, since our desire is for immortality and omnipotence; infantilism can lead us to see the Father as a refuge from the terrors of life and a utopic realization of our frustrated and repressed longings,[12] a father-figure that can never be the Father of Christian experience. Once we accept our dependence and limitations (we are neither immortal nor omnipotent), once we welcome our daughter-and sonship, we can then freely call God Father and call on God as Father; then the Father comes to be the mystery of our origin, which is neither forgotten nor repressed but respected and accepted as source of our being, of our life, of the meaning that sustains our limited existence.[13] We feel God as Father when we feel ourselves to be brothers and sisters in faith of our brother Jesus, the only-begotten Son. Being sons and daughters, our origin is not reduced to an act of love by the Father who creates, but is an eternal act of begetting the Son which resounds in us, his younger brothers and sisters. Our origin is lost in the mystery of the Father.

The Father does not appear only in this ontological dimension of sustaining our existence and being the final answer to the question of our origin. He is also Father in the process of liberating the oppressed. It was in the context of liberation from slavery that Israel discovered Yahweh as Father: "For Abraham does not own us and Israel does not acknowledge us; you, Yahweh, yourself are our Father; Our Redeemer is your ancient name" (Isa. 63:16). Yahweh is first felt to be Father as he forms his people, and then when he frees his people from oppression. The Father hears the cry of his downtrodden children; intervening in history to redeem them from their slavery and lead them back to their freedom as his sons and daughters, the Father demonstrates his creativity. He is the God of liberation, *goel,* the avenger of those unjustly impoverished. This God-Father, far from being paternalistic, sends his children, as he sent his Son Jesus, to shake off their fetters and take their proper task in hand, building up the Kingdom of freedom of his sons and daughters.

Finally, the Father appears as protector and defender of the "least," of those who are completely unprotected—orphans, widows, strangers and those who have been stripped of their rights. The Father of all becomes their intimate; as source of all good—the principal of which is life—he defends them and protects them and makes the cause of these "wretched of the earth" his cause. His only-begotten Son made them the first to receive the good news, the blessed of his Kingdom, and finally identified himself with them. The Father is most present in those whose daughter- and sonship is most denied and downtrodden. Only women and men freed from their oppressions can be signs of universal fatherhood and kinship.

CHAPTER X

Glory Be to the Son: Mediator of Integral Liberation

Beside the Father stands the Son, whom we glorify in the words of the first Councils of Nicaea and Constantinople: "the only-begotten Son, born of the Father before all time; light from light, true God from true God; begotten, not created, consubstantial with the Father" (DS 150, CT). This makes two fundamental statements: the Son is begotten by the Father, so is God like the Father, but is distinct, as Son, from the Father—not the Father, though he comes from the Father; secondly, that this only-begotten Son is consubstantial with the Father. This expression "consubstantial" (*homoousios*) is aimed at safeguarding the oneness of God. The Son is not a second God, but through communion in one and the same nature is the one God. Consubstantiality goes still further: it stresses the interdependence of Father and Son. The Father cannot exist without the Son, just as the Son cannot exist without the Father. Father and Son do not add to one another in divinity, but through mutual dependence form one God.

When speaking of the Son, we use the word "Son" in a strictly trinitarian sense; any comparison with human sonship is purely by way of analogy. So the Credo states that the Son is not created, but begotten and born of the substance (essence or nature) of the

Father. Because of this, the Son possesses everything in common with the Father, except fatherhood (otherwise, the Son would be a second Father). The world, as we saw in the preceding chapter, is projected in the Son, but as repeatable and created companion for the glory of the whole Trinity. We profess that this Son became incarnate and suffered under Pontius Pilate. Let us rapidly see how the incarnate Son, Jesus of Nazareth, showed himself as Son— never forgetting that all the credal statements about the only-begotten Son of the Father refer to Jesus of Nazareth. How did Jesus, in his humanity, show his relationship of Son to the Father, and how did he show us that we too are sons and daughters in the Son?

1. HOW JESUS SHOWED HIMSELF THE SON

Without repeating what was said in chapter 2, let us look at some relevant aspects. There is a general consensus among scholars that the titles used to identify Jesus (Messiah, Son of God, Lord and so on) originated after the resurrection.[1] This makes it exegetically difficult to establish how Jesus of Nazareth actually showed his understanding of being the only-begotten Son of the Father. In general we can say that what was important for him was not to present himself either as liberating Messiah or as eternal Son (both of which claims, formulated like that, would have scandalized his audience), but to act as one imbued with liberating power and as one who possessed the freedom proper to one speaking in God's name and feeling himself to have come from God. So the overall impression of Jesus derived from the New Testament is one that can only be fully understood by making use of the category "divine."[2] In this sense, the resurrection is the flash that lights up the mystery of Jesus; this unique, eschatological event justifies the statement that he was of divine nature (Phil. 2:6) and the eternal Son sent into the world (Gal. 4:4; Rom. 8:3; John 3:16).

Jesus opened himself to the Father in deep intimacy: anyone who can call God "Abba" certainly feels himself to be God's Son. Yet the synoptic Gospels never put the expression "Son of God" into Jesus' mouth. It is only the demons (Mark 3:11; 5:7), the voices from heaven heard at his baptism and transfiguration (Mark 1:11; 9:7) and Peter in his profession of faith—taken as divine revelation

(Matt. 27:43)—who state that Jesus is the Son of God. The taunting crowds at the foot of the cross attribute the words "I am the Son of God" to him (Matt. 27:43), but exegesis has shown this to be a later accretion.

There are two occasions when Jesus uses the term "Son" on its own: "But as for that day or hour, nobody knows it, neither the angels of heaven, nor the Son; no one but the Father" (Mark 13:32), and "Everything has been entrusted to me by my Father; and . . . no one knows the Father except the Son and those to whom the Son chooses to reveal him" (Matt. 11:27). This last passage in particular shows how Jesus thought of himself, even if the term "son" did not at the time have any messianic significance. St John then took the title of Son and made it the main theological basis for identifying Jesus. Jesus himself did not so much communicate a doctrine of the Father or a reflection on the Son as demonstrate a practice: he behaved in the manner of a son and in this revealed the Son.[3]

2. HOW JESUS BEHAVED AS A SON

Jesus' behaviour as Son is revealed in his prayer.[4] The evangelists—especially Luke—report quite frequently how Jesus withdrew into the wilderness or the mountains to pray. We are not told what the content of these prayers was, but from the few prayers of Jesus that have been preserved, we can deduce that they would have been extremely intimate. He calls on God as his "beloved Father," feeling himself God's Son and sent by God into the world. He takes up God's cause: the Kingdom. "Kingdom" is not a territory, but a way of God acting in the world, setting creation free from all that disfigures it and filling it with divine glory. God's action, as the Old Testament foreshadowed, begins with the outcast and the poor, giving them back life and dignity. When God intervenes in creation, justice flourishes, rights are upheld and life smiles. Jesus in his actions sees himself as producing these goods. He does not act as one accomplishing a personal programme, but as one carrying out a mission, the Father's mission. He is the Son in his obedience, which is not submission, but free adherence to the Father's will. No one has ever been as free as Jesus. Because he felt himself to be the Father's Son, he took the liberty of eating with sinners so as to give them trust in divine mercy, to flout oppressive laws and to reinterpret tradition.

Jesus showed he was the Son not just through his intimacy with the Father, which hinted at his eternal begetting, but through demonstrating the freedom of sonship. In the New Testament, "son" is opposed to "slave." Jesus sees himself as Son through having received the freedom of the Father, a freedom he passes on to the men and women around him; so he frees them from their infirmities, from the various oppressions that stigmatize life, from sin and from death. St John makes Jesus say emphatically: "I tell you most solemnly, everyone who commits sin is a slave. Now the slave's place in the house is not assured, but the son's place is assured. So if the Son makes you free, you will be free indeed" (8:34-6). One of the most fundamental ways in which Jesus acts is this: as Son, he forgives sins in the Father's name, freeing people from the injustice that holds truth captive and prevents access to God, blurring the features of the Father and disfiguring the faces of other people, no longer recognized as brothers and sisters. Jesus is the great liberator from this major oppression. The freedom brought by his forgiveness is that of sons and daughters who can rediscover God as Father. St Paul saw this clearly when he wrote: "The spirit you received is not the spirit of slaves bringing fear into your lives again; it is the spirit of sons, and it makes us cry out, 'Abba, Father!' " (Rom. 8:15). To be able to call God "Abba" is the proof that we are no longer slaves but sons and daughters, free and set free to receive the promises of the Kingdom (cf Gal. 4:6-7).

Jesus also showed himself Son in obedience and resistance.[5] His message, his actions and the new image of God he communicated, provoked conflict with the Judaism of his time. Threatened with death, he clung to his course, obedient to the Father's cause and resisting all temptations. This obedience even to death on a cross expressed his radical faithfulness as Son to the Father. His decision to give his life over to torture and crucifixion was the supreme proof of this. The resurrection revealed the Father's glory and also the hidden glory of the Son. While he lived amongst us, he appeared as servant, as wandering prophet, as master of the inspired word, as healer who worked miracles to free the oppressed. Then through his resurrection, being raised high, we saw the glory of the eternal Son, full of grace and truth (cf John 1:14).

The Son does not relate only to the Father, but also to the Holy Spirit, the power of the Son. They are together from the beginning and both are sent by the Father. It is the Son who is incarnate, but the Holy Spirit who creates the humanity taken on by the Son. It is always in the power of the Spirit that Jesus acts, reveals the Father, transforms deformed reality. It is in the joy of the Spirit that Jesus invokes his "Abba" (cf Luke 10:21).

In a word, Jesus as Son first reveals who God is: the Father of the Son and of all beings created in God and for God; then he is Son through becoming the mediator and executor of the Father's plan: he proclaims the Kingdom and anticipates it through his liberating acts; finally, Jesus is Son because he communicates the Father's love to all men and women, particularly to sinners and outcasts; this love is merciful because it frees us from the slavery of sin and gives us back the freedom of sons and daughters of God.

3.THE FEMININE DIMENSION OF JESUS THE SON

Femininity is a basic constituent of every human being, male or female. It involves a number of characteristics: tenderness, care, self-acceptance, mercy, sensitivity to the mystery of life and of God, cultivation of the interiority that does and must exist in any human life that has reached a minimum level of maturity. The gospel accounts present Jesus as a free and integrated person; compared to the general attitude toward women of his time, his is a liberating stance. The movement he started contained both men and women. He had no truck with the social discrimination suffered by women in his age. On the contrary: he professed attitudes which scandalized even the disciples (as with the Samaritan woman—John 4:27), let alone the Pharisees (by letting himself be touched, kissed and anointed by a public sinner—Luke 7:36-50). Women took an active part in the general activity surrounding his life as a preacher (as in Luke 10:38-42, the story of Martha and Mary); many women were healed and consoled by Jesus (e.g. Mark 1:29-31; 5:25-34; 7:24-30; Luke 8:2; John 11:23-38).

Jesus did not suppress his femininity but gave it free rein.[6] The suffering and death of others never left him indifferent. He took pity on the crowd who were "like sheep without a shepherd" (Mark 6:34) and on the innumerable sufferers who were brought to him to be healed, to the point where he had no time to eat (Mark 3:20); he put his arms round small children (Mark 9:36), rejoiced when "mere children" could understand the mysteries of the Father (Matt. 11:25-7); he did not hide his tears on hearing of the death of his friend Lazarus (John 11:35); he wept in disappointment at Jerusalem's refusal of his message (Luke 19:41) and lamented at the unbelief of Chorazin and Bethsaida (Luke 10:13-15); in a very feminine way he declared how he had longed to gather up the children of Jerusalem as a mother hen gathers her chicks under her wings, but they refused (Luke 13:34).

This feminine dimension belongs to the humanity of Jesus, hypostatically taken on by the eternal Son. Femininity thereby strikes roots into the very heart of the mystery of God. Though Jesus was a man and not a woman, the feminine dimension in him is equally divinized, revealing the maternal face of God.

4. "THE ONLY-BEGOTTEN SON WHO IS IN THE FATHER'S BOSOM"

The trinitarian axiom that "the economic Trinity is the immanent Trinity and vice-versa" is especially useful for understanding the Son in his immanent expression in the bosom of the Trinity. The analogy with human generation allows us to see that the Son has the same nature as the Father. The Son receives everything from the Father: nature-communion, eternity, glory and infinity. He does not derive from an act of will or from any coercion on the Father's part (DS 71, 526). Nor should he be understood as an extension of the Father, since he would then not be distinct from the Father. As Son, he is distinct from the Father, but united to him by the same nature-communion. He is called the Only-begotten (DS 2, 11, 125, 150, 350, 3352); the Father has handed all things over to him, so that there cannot be another beside the Son (*solus Filius de solo Patre:* DS 75, 800, 1330). How this generation comes about, we have no idea. It is an unrevealed absolute mystery, contemplation of which is promised to the just in the Kingdom of the Trinity. What we can say is that it is not a matter of causality in the technical and logical sense. The Son is not the product of a process of causation. The reciprocal Father-Son relationship is shrouded in mystery, and is supra-causal.[7] This realization is expressed dogmatically by saying that the Son "is begotten without beginning" (DS 357, 470, 617, 1331), that "from the beginning he is with the Father" (DS 61) and that "he subsists in him from all eternity and for all eternity" (DS 126, 147). As we have already seen, instead of using a dialectic of causality (trinitarian processions), we should perhaps use one of revelation: the Persons mutually reveal themselves to one another; the Son is the full and complete revelation of the Father.

This revelation of the Father in the eternal Son is well expressed in another analogy found in tradition and rooted in the Old Testament and the Prologue to St John's Gospel. The Son is the Logos or Word of the Father. St Augustine and St Thomas in particular developed this understanding of the Trinity through a theology of the Logos.[8] This has the advantage of avoiding certain anthropomorphisms present in the analogy of generation. As it is drawn from the world of the spirit, it allows approaches to the mystery of the Trinity that hint at certain likenesses between God and human beings, made in God's image and likeness.

"Word" in its full sense (best caught by the Greek *Logos* and Hebrew *Dabar*) is more than an instrument of communication. It represents the whole structure of meaning of reality and of the spirit; it is reality itself as shown to itself and to others, the revelation of being to thought and speech, and the unity that links thought, speech and being. Applied to the Son as the Word of God, it means that in the Son the Father expresses himself completely by knowing himself and representing himself in the totality of his being. Through this image of himself, the Father expresses himself so substantially that this image has the same living nature as he does himself. This expression is the Word that communicates the complete truth and intelligibility of the Father. This Word is born of the Father, but distinct from the Father. The invisible mystery of the Father becomes visible in the Word.

This same idea is also portrayed by another statement found in the New Testament. This is that Christ is "the image of the unseen God" (Col. 1:15). "Image" is here used in its Semitic sense: it is the presence of the Prototype itself in its actuality; not a more or less faithful copy of a model, but the model itself revealed and present in all its force. By this, the Son is the nature of the Father, his glory and omnipotence communicated in loving self-bestowal. This is why we say that the Son is like the Father in everything, save for the fact of not being the Father, the source and origin of all communion. The Son does not become another source and origin (which is what makes the paternity of the Father); so when Latin theology says that the Spirit is breathed out by the Father and the Son (*Filioque*), it adds "as from one single origin" (Council of Florence, DS 1331). The Spirit is breathed out by the Father through the Son and with the Son (since it is the Father of the Son who breathes the Spirit out). From the perichoretic viewpoint expressed earlier we could say: on being "begotten" by the Father, the Son simultaneously receives the Spirit, which comes down upon him and is eternally inseparable from him. So we would say that the Son is born of the Father and of the Spirit (*ex Patre Spirituque*).[9] These relationships belong less to the order of "production" than of mutual revelation, given the fact that the Three Unique Ones share the Father's property of being unborn.

The Son, Word or Image also shows, in himself, traces of the eternal paternal Mother or eternal maternal Father, traces received from his source of generation or revelation. It is difficult for us to identify what is feminine in the eternal sisterly Son or brotherly Daughter, without falling into cultural clichés or mere arbitrary statements. What we can see as the feminine dimension in the incarnate Son is ultimately based on the nature of the immanent Son/Daughter. All that is tenderness in persons and creatures, all that is respect for the processes of life (everything that lives deserves to live), all that is care and acceptance, expresses the divine femininity in the eternal Father/Mother, communicated to the Son/Daughter from the beginning. As everything is a sacrament of the Son, everything contains and reveals this deep feminine dimension as well as his masculine dimension. God the Son is beyond the sexes, but both masculine and feminine created perfections—in that all creation is made in, for, by and with the Son—find their ultimate rationale and infinite exemplar in the eternal masculinity and femininity of the Son.

5. THE MISSION OF THE SON: THE UNIVERSE REFLECTS BACK ON THE WORD

The Son is not just the supreme revelation of the Father, his Word and perfect Image within the circle of the Trinity. He is all these within creation too. He was sent by the Father to the world (cf John 3:16ff; 5:23, 36, 38; Gal. 4:4, etc.). We can therefore speak of the mission of the Son. By "mission" in the context of the Trinity, we mean God's self-communication to creatures. This concept of mission is different from the meaning commonly found in scripture: the missions given to the prophets, wise men, kings, to act in God's name. God was with them, but not in the sense of complete self-giving, of personal (hypostatic) communication to the point of God being absolutely in them so that there was no longer any distance between them and God. In the case of the Son, mission means this incarnation; the man Jesus of Nazareth was taken on by the Son in such a way that his humanity became the humanity of the Son.

What is the ultimate purpose of the incarnation? From earliest times, there have been two opposing schools of thought.[10] The first, basing itself on the formula of the Creed, said that the Son "for our salvation, came down from heaven and was conceived by the Holy Spirit." So the incarnation would be due to the sinfulness of the human race; the Father, in his infinite mercy, sent his only Son to set us free in our own situation. The second, drawn from texts in the Prologue to St John's Gospel and the Letters to the Ephesians, Colossians and Hebrews, would say rather: the Son became incarnate, irrespective of sin, because everything was made by him, with him, in him and for him by reason of the very intrinsic love of the Trinity, overflowing beyond itself and creating companions in love for the glory of the Father, Son and Holy Spirit. So the incarnation is not an emergency solution thought up by the Father to bring creation back from its going astray. It shows the Trinity's eternal design: to bring all beings into its communion through the mediating of the Son and the driving force of the Holy Spirit.

This second school of thought seems to accord better with the lines we have so far been pursuing. Duns Scotus and the Franciscan school that followed him have set out the various steps in this incarnational mission of the Son.[11] The whole of creation is involved in the begetting and revelation of the Son; creation should not be thought of as coming later than the revelation of the Son but rather as an aspect of his complete revelation. Briefly: the Father bestows himself completely and begets and reveals the Son, and in the Son the infinite images and likenesses of the Father and the Son. As the Father's projection in the Son, creation possesses an infinite and eternal dimension. It contains an infinite number of possible creatures that could be made out of nothing. As projections of the Father, they are begotten in the same act of begetting as the Son; as they are actively produced by the Father in the Son, they reflect the Father and the Son at once; they are the image and likeness of both. All these possible creatures, once created, form the glory of the Trinity, and among them is the holy humanity of Jesus of Nazareth. He is the best image and likeness of the Father and the Son, and the true visible image of the invisible Father. So that he should really be the most perfect and supreme created expression of the Father and the Son, the Father wanted him— really and not metaphorically—to be united to the Person of the Son. He would give supreme glory to the Father, Son and Holy Spirit, greater than any possible in the order of creation we know. In other words: the Father wanted the individual Jesus of Nazareth, hypostatically united to the Son, to give supreme glory to the Father through his life, his works and his passion, and to root the Trinity in the midst of the human race and all of creation. If all things were created in the Son and this Son became incarnate, then this means that all things reflect the incarnate Son. All beings, from the simplest to the most complex, contain traces of the Son; they are, in their manner, sons and daughters in the Son.

This filial dimension has a trinitarian aspect; if all beings are sons and daughters, they show trinitarian communion opening outwards, giving itself, revealing itself. No created being is opaque and closed in on itself; each participates in a structure of meaning: it gives and receives. So the eternal Son is at work within creation from its earliest moment, making creatures express their nature as sons and daughters. This Son is supremely at work in taking on the humanity of Jesus of Nazareth, in whom he communicates himself completely. The filial structure that pervades the whole of creation took on its most definite and supreme form in Jesus of Nazareth, because from all eternity he was planned and willed to be the vehicle for the full coming of the Son to his creation; this is the mystery of the incarnation.

The mission of the Son is to make the universe reflect back on the Word, to transform it into the glory of the Father from whom he came.[12] The actual historical form the incarnation took, in an aspect of humiliation rather than of glory, as a servant rather than a lord, is due to human sinfulness. The Son chose to follow this dark path so as to share in the suffering of the world; he sets free from within this situation so as to give full glory to the Trinity. This glory was seen in its fullness only in the resurrection. It still belongs to the future. As long as the incarnate Word has not set all creation free through the cross, God still cannot be "all in all" (l Cor. 15:28). The lordship of the incarnate, crucified and risen Word consists in this immense process of liberation from the sin that hides the glory of the Father. So, as the Word goes on bringing in the Kingdom of life, liberty, reconciliation and peace, he redeems the sonship of all created beings, particularly of human beings in the position of captivity in which they now find themselves. Only through that redemption will we see the triumph of the Kingdom of the Trinity, of the Father, Son and Holy Spirit, and of creation as part of the communion of the Trinity.

CHAPTER XI

Glory Be to the Holy Spirit: Driving Force of Integral Liberation

The Christian God is always trinitarian. This means that the face-to-face relationship of Father and Son is complemented by the third Person, the Holy Spirit. The Spirit is the Different One, enabling us to understand the perichoretic communion of the life of the Trinity and how other differences arise which produce an open and dynamic communion extending beyond the circle of the Trinity.

We can produce representations of the Father and the Son; the very names given to them suggest a logic of relationships in the line of fecundity and generation. We have no images of the Holy Spirit. It has been represented by sub-human symbols such as wind, hurricane, breath, fire, anointing, chrism, salt, water, dove. This symbolism shows the difference between the third Person and the Son and the Father. Because we lack human names to give the Spirit, it has been relegated in Christian thought, particularly Latin thought, to a certain anonymity. Also, by calling the third Person "Spirit" we are referring to something common to all three: each of them is Spirit, since as St John's Gospel says, "God is spirit" (John 4:24). But the third Person is Spirit in a special way, being, as the Latin Fathers interpreted, the one that unites Father and Son as the link of love between them. In this formulation the Spirit appears to surpass the separation of Father from Son to overcome the dyad (the two poles, Father and Son) and to form the Trinity of Persons. But what exactly is the Holy Spirit? Is it more than the unifying connection between the divine Two?[1] The church's most important dogmatic declaration on the Holy Spirit was made at the Council of Constantinople in 381.[2] There it was said in the Creed: "We believe in the Holy Spirit, the Lord, the giver of life; he proceeds from the Father, is adored and honoured together with the Father and the Son; he spoke through the prophets" (DS 150, CT). Calling the Spirit "Lord" (the Septuagint used the word Lord [*Kyrios*] to designate God) means that the Spirit is of the same nature as the Son, Jesus Christ, who is called Lord and God. The expression "giver of life" emphasizes the action of the Spirit, making it more than the gift of life—it is the very giver of life. The giver of life can only be God: therefore the Spirit is God. This affirmation is made still more explicit in the phrase "he proceeds from the Father"; this clearly implies that the Spirit is of the same nature as the Father and the Son, who, in turn, also proceeds from the Father and is of the same substance as the Father. This credal formulation of Constantinople says nothing about the relationship between the Son and the Holy Spirit. It simply recognizes that being of the divine nature the Spirit is equally adored and honoured with the Father and the Son. The expression "he spoke through the prophets" underlines the presence of the Holy Spirit in the history of the human race. This presence appears most obviously in the prophets' strength and creativity, but it also appears in thousands of other personal and historical agents in the sense of sanctifying (the Spirit is holy because its function is, above all, to sanctify) and introducing humanity to communion in the Trinity. The prophets represent all these.

This short dogmatic statement was amplified at the Third Synod of Toledo in 589: the famous *Filioque,* which means that the Spirit proceeds from the Father and the Son (*Filioque*). This is not the place to examine the (contradictory) reasons that motivated this addition.[3] But it wounded the theological mentality and political-ecclesial sensibilities of the Orthodox Church, which rejected the addition. Later the Council of Lyon in 1284 made clear that the proceeding of the Spirit from the Father and the Son did not constitute two origins or two breathings-out but a single origin and a single breathing-out (DS 850 and 853). The Council of Florence (1439), searching for a formula that would facilitate union with the Orthodox, also used the expression "The Holy Spirit proceeds from the Father *through* the Son (*per Filium*)" (DS 1301). The debates produced by the "filioquism" (of the Latins) and the "monopatrism" (of the Greeks) prevented any deepening of theological thinking about the Holy Spirit till recent times. The last few years have seen a new concentration on examining the specificity of the Person of the Holy Spirit, to an extent that has never been known before in trinitarian theology.[4]

Starting from our basic thesis—the complete perichoresis between the three divine Persons—we shall try to bring out the qualities proper to the Person of the Holy Spirit, following the same plan as the preceding chapters: first showing the action of the Holy Spirit in history (economic Trinity), then pointing out some characteristics of the Holy Spirit in the bosom of the Trinity (immanent Trinity) and finally reflecting on the mission corresponding to the third Person of the Trinity.

1. THE INFLUENCE OF THE HOLY SPIRIT ON PROCESSES OF CHANGE

The Hebrew for "spirit" is *ruah,* the Greek *pneuma.* Both terms are tied to living processes, meaning breath, wind, storm or hurricane.[5] Initially, the Spirit was not thought of as a Person, but as an original, divine power acting on creation, moving in living things and influencing human beings, especially the prophets. These were seized by the Spirit and spoke so much under the influence of the Spirit as sometimes to be transported in ecstasy (cf 1 Sam. 10:1; Num. 11:24-30). The Spirit also came upon certain political leaders in times of crisis. They became charismatic leaders, carrying the people to victory over their enemies (cf Judg. 3:10; 6:33; 11:29; 13:25; 14:6, 9; 1 Sam. 11:6). The Spirit even became institutionalized in the figure of the king (cf 1 Sam. 16:13) who was imbued with charismatic power so as to govern his people, defend the poor and guarantee peace in justice. But when the kings themselves fell victim to the seductions of excessive power, the Spirit raised up prophets who denounced their authoritarian excesses, and gave these prophets strength to bear persecution and martyrdom. Para-doxically, the Spirit was conferred on a figure standing in marked contrast to the king: the Suffering Servant, stripped of all pomp and grandiloquence, who is anointed to set his people free from injustice and oppression through his sufferings, and to redeem the rights of the poor (Isa. 61:1ff; cf 11:2; 42:1ff). The Messiah, as a servant who suffers, was to receive the fullness of the Spirit. Jesus himself, launching his programme of liberation in the synagogue of Nazareth, based himself on a prophetic text from Isaiah (61:1). Finally, the Spirit is promised to all, to give them a new heart and enable them to bring in a new humanity (Ezek. 36:26-7; Joel 3:1ff).

Later, the Spirit in Judaic understanding became not merely a transforming power of God in history, but the presence of God himself (cf Ps. 139:7; Isa. 63:10-11, etc.). In the inter-testamentary period, the conviction grew that the Spirit was God in person leading creation, inspiring the people, consoling the just, judging the wicked, renewing the face of the earth.

In chapter 2, we saw how the Spirit was revealed in the New Testament. The Synoptics, and John and Paul above all, are immensely rich in insights into the influence and life of the Holy Spirit. Without attempting to plumb the depths of what they say, we can pick out the salient points.

In the first place, the Spirit is seen as the *power of the new* and of a *renewal* in all things. So it was present at the first creation (Gen. 1:2) and in the definitive creation brought about by Jesus. Matthew and Luke attribute the origin of the incarnation of the Son to the Spirit: "She was found to be with child through the Holy Spirit," since "she has conceived what is in her by the Holy Spirit" (Matt. 1:18-20). Luke talks of the Holy Spirit "coming upon" Mary, so that the child she is to bear "will be holy and will be called Son of God" (Luke 1:35).[6] Jesus has the "power of the Spirit" in him when he begins to preach in the synagogue in Nazareth (Luke 4:14). The Spirit comes upon the Messiah in the hour of his baptism, when he becomes conscious of his messianic, liberating mission (Mark 1:9-11). The Spirit raises Jesus up from among the dead (Rom. 1:4; 1 Tim. 3:16). The Spirit is there at the beginning of the church community at Pentecost (Heb. 2:32). The influence of the Spirit is above all creative, looking to the future. All creation implies a break with what had gone before, a crisis of the established modes, an opening out to what is not yet known, has not yet been tried. The Spirit sets humankind free from an obsession with its origins, its desire to return to the original paradise, access to which has been finally closed (cf Gen. 3:23). The Spirit moves us on toward the promised land, the destiny that has to be built and revealed in the future.

In the second place—and this seems to contradict the first point—the Spirit in the New Testament is the *memory* of Jesus' deeds and words. Looking closer at this function, it is complementary to the first—being the power of the new—not contradictory. St John makes Jesus say explicitly: "the Advocate, the Holy Spirit, whom the Father will send in my name, will teach you everything and remind you of all I have said to you" (14:26); the Spirit will be Jesus' witness (15:26-7), will lead the disciples to complete truth, tell them of things to come, but always within the perspective of what Jesus himself has said, "since all he tells you will be taken from what is mine" (16:13-15).

It would seem as though the Spirit follows the logic of imagination and its wonderful constructs, against the power of established facts. The great new fact established by the Father is the presence of his Son in the flesh so that we may be sons and daughters in the Son (cf Rom. 8:29). This incarnation is the work of the Spirit. Therefore, "everyone moved by the Spirit is a son of God" (Rom. 8:14) in the Son. The Spirit makes us welcome the Son in the flesh (1 John 4:2). This means that we have to accept the form of servant and prophet-martyr taken on by the Son. It would be a betrayal of the Son and a rejection of the Spirit to make Jesus a prop for any sort of greatness or domination that destroys the aspect of sons and daughters by establishing and legitimizing relationships of oppression of some of us by others. The Spirit makes us live as sons and daughters in our following of the incarnate Son, preventing us from forgetting the simplicity, humility, prophetic courage, will to serve others and intimate relationship with the Father that characterized the Son. The mission of the Spirit consists in permanently actualizing the significance of the incarnation as a process through which God the Son takes on history with all its changes and makes it holy history, the history of the blessed Trinity. The Spirit preserves continuity between "that time" when the Son took flesh and the "today" of history. The full meaning of divine sonship and of our insertion in the mystery of the Trinity has yet to be explained fully. It is the task of the Spirit to develop and realize the divine and human significance of this unique event as it affects different cultures (such as those of India, of China, of the Amerindian tribes). This is why the Spirit will take what is Christ's and tell it to us (cf John 16:14). What is new in the incarnation of the Son will be shown only in the newness of what comes from the extension of the incarnation of the memory of Christ into the depths of human history.

The Spirit's third mission is to *liberate* from the oppressions brought into being by our sinful state. The Bible uses the word "flesh" to express this state. The flesh and the Spirit are opposed to one another (Gal. 5:17). The flesh produces lives turned inward on themselves, passionately devoted to the furtherance of their own interests. The law often legitimates such interests and so becomes oppressive in its turn. It inclines people to discriminate against others; it upholds religious traditions that prevent free access to the God of mercy; it traps life in nets that hold creativity back from being able to face up to new situations. It is the Spirit that sets us free to face new situations creatively, since "where the Spirit of the Lord is, there is freedom" (2 Cor. 3:17). The poor in particular are defenceless in the face of oppression by the most powerful. The Spirit is the father of the poor (*pater pauperum*), giving them strength to resist, courage to rise up, creativity to find new ways. In order to build up a world founded on truth, justice, and love, the social order must be changed on a deep level, and "God's Spirit, who with a marvelous providence directs the unfolding of time and renews the face of the earth, is not absent from this development."[7] It is the Spirit who opens up horizons that block the human spirit, who breaks the bonds holding back the process of liberation of the oppressed, who keeps alive hope and the utopic vision of a world free from dominations and ruled by justice and a spirit of community.[8] Paul saw the Spirit as the power setting human beings free from the legalism of the old Judaic regime and establishing the freedom brought by Christ (cf Gal. 4:6-7; 5:22-5).

Finally, the Spirit is the *principle that creates differences and communion*. The community of those who follow Jesus is built on two columns: the risen Lord and the Spirit.[9] The column of Christ represents the dimension of continuity and permanence, linked to the mystery of the incarnation. The column of the Spirit represents the emergence of newness, which brings discontinuity. Institution and charism march together and make up the living, taut dynamic of Christian life. Christ is never alone and the Spirit never works except in communion with Christ. So Paul rightly says that the Spirit is always the Spirit of Christ (Rom. 8:9; Phil. 1:19), the Spirit of the Lord (2 Cor. 3:17), the Spirit of the Son (Gal. 4:6). The Spirit always leads us to Christ, since "no one can say 'Jesus is Lord,' unless he is under the influence of the Spirit" (1 Cor. 12:3). To say that Jesus is Lord is to affirm everything great about him: his divinity, his lordship over the cosmos, his redeeming presence among men and women. The Spirit is the one who makes us cling to this Jesus, our Lord. This coordination between the Spirit and Christ is expressed by St Paul, for example, as being *in* Christ and being *in* the Spirit (cf Col. 2:10; Eph. 5:18; 1 Cor. 1:2, 30; Rom. 15:16, etc.), using Christ and the Spirit as interchangeable realities.

The presence of the Spirit is indicated by the diversity of gifts and services that appears in the community, as the Spirit chooses (1 Cor. 12:11). Paul lists some of these in verses 7-11; in effect, every local church, however small it may be, has someone who can organize prayer, lead the celebration, instruct children, prepare engaged couples for marriage, teach the brothers and sisters their rights, articulate a Christian presence in the process of liberation in society, consolidate union among all. In Paul's language we should say: "There is a variety of gifts but always the same Spirit" (1 Cor. 12:4), since each of these tasks represents a different form of the presence and activity of the Holy Spirit itself. The various services are to be used for the good of the community, since "the particular way in which the Spirit is given to each person is for a good purpose" (12:7).

The Spirit is creativity and the spirit of innovation in a group, but never in an individualistic sense or for self-advancement, always for strengthening the community in working to fulfill its needs. Therefore, the Spirit is the originator of differences, on one hand, and, on the other, the instigator of communion: "For by one Spirit were all baptized into one body" (12:13), however different we may be—"Jews as well as Greeks, slaves as well as citizens" (12:13). People are not reduced to a single category, nor are their differences suppressed; on the contrary, these differences make up the riches of the community. At Pentecost, the Spirit did not make all those present speak the same language, but made them all hear the good news of salvation in their own language. The multiformity of expressions of vitality and of services in the community is not a threat to unity, but an opportunity for all to be enriched. Communion does not suppress or reduce differences, but integrates them into the purpose of the common good. This unity is the work of the Spirit. What is opposed to charisms is not the institution itself, but egoism, the preponderance of some over others, the will to power that usurps the charisms of the rest. Such actions constitute an attack on the building of the community, precisely because they represent the rupture of communion. As St Paul advisedly warns: "Never try to suppress the Spirit" (1 Thess. 5:19).

All these works of the Spirit show that we are not talking about just the power of God in history, but about an active agent, a divine Person. According to St Paul, this is the one "sent into our hearts" (Gal. 4:6), the one who enables us to find God as Father (Rom. 8:16), who reaches "even the depths of God" (1 Cor. 2:10), the one who "has been given to us" (Rom. 5:5), God present to us giving us God's self: this is not some*thing* given to us, but some*one* self-giving and life-giving (1 Thess. 4:8). St John makes this even clearer: the Spirit is the Advocate (one who defends and intercedes for us—John 17:14-16), who bears witness to Jesus (15:26-7), who teaches us, guides our memory, leads us to the fullness of truth; asked for by the Son, the Spirit comes from the Father, and will be with the disciples forever (14:13-16; 26-7; cf 15:26). All these actions enable us to see the Spirit as a Person, on the same level as the Father and the Son. How theology views the communion of the Spirit with the Father and the Son will be examined in a later section.

2. THE FEMININE DIMENSION OF THE HOLY SPIRIT

What the New Testament and some theological traditions tell us about the Holy Spirit indicates the presence of feminine, especially maternal, traits in the Spirit.[10] The first thing to note is that, in Hebrew and Syriac, the word for *spirit* is feminine. As we have seen, the Spirit is always concerned with processes that have to do with life and the protection of life. St John presents Jesus as depicting the Spirit in terms that suggest typically, though not exclusively, feminine characteristics: consoling, teaching, reminding, not leaving us orphans (14:18, 26; 16:31). In St Paul, the Spirit takes on a mother's role, teaching us the true name of God ("Abba"), teaching us the secret name of Jesus, who is the Lord, teaching us to pray and expressing our plea in a way that could never be put into words (Rom. 8:26; cf 8:15; 1 Cor. 12:3).

In the Old Testament, the Spirit performed feminine functions. Some interpretations would see the Spirit of God hovering over the primeval void (Gen. 1:2), acting to incubate and fructify the whole of creation and so enable every kind of life to come from it.[11] Wisdom, loved and pursued as a woman (Ecclus. 14:22ff), presented as bride and mother (15:2ff), is sometimes identified with the Spirit (Wisd. 9:17), commonly so in the early Fathers. In Syrian and Jewish cultures, for which "spirit" is feminine, the Spirit is often interpreted as a mother. In the *Odes of Solomon,* a text dating from the origins of Christianity in Syria, the dove at Jesus' baptism is compared to the mother of Christ giving milk from the breasts of God.[12] The Fathers, as we saw earlier, also use the human family as an analogy of the mystery of the Trinity, using feminine expressions to denote the Holy Spirit, which appears analogically as the eternal mother, who later, at the virginal conception of Jesus through the power of the Spirit, somehow becomes the divine mother, without conflicting with Mary, who is rightly called *Theotokos,* mother of God incarnate.[13] Macarius of Jerusalem says: "The Spirit is our mother because it is the paraclete, the consoler, ready to console us as a mother does her child (Isa. 61:13), and because the faithful are reborn in the Spirit and are thus the children of the mysterious mother, the Spirit (John 3:3-5)."[14] Furthermore, the special relationship between the Spirit and Mary cannot be gainsaid, as we shall see later (cf Luke 1:35). The Spirit has a special mission relating to the giving of life: it gives origin to the world at the first creation (Gen. 1:2); in the new creation, it is responsible for Jesus' conception (Matt. 1:18) and gives rise to his messianic mission (in the female figure of a dove) and to his new birth through the resurrection (Rom. 1:4; cf Heb. 13:33; Phil. 2:6-11; Heb. 5:5). The Spirit also exercises a maternal function in the body of Christ, the church community, conceiving new brothers and sisters of Jesus, sons and daughters in the Son, giving rise to charisms and inspiring the whole life of grace. In the well-found words of Lémonnyer: "The divine person [of the Holy Spirit] is the one who *gives* itself in a special way. It is God's gift above all, and so bears that name. In the Trinity it is love, which is also one of the names given to it. Now, these qualities fit a mother rather than any other human figure, and in a way define her. On earth we have no other person *given* to us in the same way as our mother; she personifies love in its most disinterested, most generous, most purely given form."[15]

We need to remind ourselves that God is beyond sex; as St Gregory Nazianzen said: God is neither masculine nor feminine.[16] Yet masculinity and femininity both find their prototypes in God; the roots of these basic determinants of human nature lie in the mystery of the Trinity itself; we all, in our own ways, men and women, bear within us the source of these central values of humanity. In thinking of the Holy Spirit, we need to remember what St Jerome wrote—not without a touch of humour: "The Spirit is feminine in Hebrew, neuter in Greek and masculine in Latin."[17] In other words, by saying that each of the Persons contains masculine and feminine dimensions, we are not conferring sexual characteristics on the mystery of the Trinity, or trying to find them in it.[18] What we are trying to do is discern the ultimate source of the values the Trinity itself has conferred on human beings in their masculine and feminine embodiments. Through being beyond human sexes, the Trinity embraces the dimensions of the feminine and the masculine in all their mystery insofar as those dimensions are image and likeness of the source of all existence, the most Holy Trinity itself.

3. THE HOLY SPIRIT CO-ETERNAL WITH THE FATHER AND THE SON

We have looked at the Holy Spirit present in the history of salvation. The Spirit shows itself in time as it is in eternity, to the degree that this is possible in time. What is the Holy Spirit like in the bosom of the Trinity? This question may seem like impertinent curiosity. Or it may mean that we are searching for illumination so as to increase our praise and make our adoration perpetual. Any answer must be made in a spirit of reverence for the mystery; respectful silence is more appropriate than exuberant speech. The history of theology is full of polemics on the procession of the Holy Spirit, leading up to the schism between the Orthodox and Roman churches in 1054. The background to these was a series of political-religious struggles between the old Rome (in Italy) and the new Rome (Constantinople), between what remained of the old Roman Empire in the Middle East and its new form in the Holy Roman Empire (based in Aachen) under the Franks of Charlemagne. This is not the place to examine the history of these debates, which revolved round the term *Filioque* (the Holy Spirit proceeding from the Father *and the Son*) and occupied the Councils of Toledo in 589 and 633, the Synods of Gentilly in 767, Frankfurt in 794, Friuli in 796, Aachen in 809, and the Councils of Lyon in 1274 and Florence from 1438-9. Let us just examine the basic theses of the Eastern approach (summed up in the Patriarch of Byzantium) and the Western (based on St Augustine), the efforts at mediation between them, and finally, the new endeavours to find a way round the historical polemic to a deeper and specifically trinitarian understanding.[19]

(a) The Biblical Sources for the Procession of the Spirit

All reflection on the Trinity starts from its "economy." We have already examined the main texts dealing with the Holy Spirit. Here we need to concern ourselves with the three basic passages in John's Gospel—16:14-15; 15:26; and 20:21-2—which are worth setting out in full: "He [the Spirit] will glorify me, since all he tells you will be taken from what is mine. Everything the Father has is mine; that is why I said: all he tells you will be taken from what is mine." "When the Advocate comes, whom I shall send you from the Father, the Spirit of truth who issues from the Father, he will be my witness." " 'As the Father sent me, so I am sending you.' After saying this he breathed on them and said: 'Receive the Holy Spirit.' "

These texts refer as much to the mission of the Holy Spirit as to the relationship of the Spirit to the Father and the Son. According to these texts, the Spirit somehow depends on others. How do the Father and the Son figure in the procession or breathing-out of the Spirit? History shows us two different answers, each closely tied to different mentalities and styles of theology, which complement rather than contradict one another. These are the Greek and Latin answers.[20]

(b) Does the Holy Spirit Proceed from the Father Alone or from the Father and the Son?

The Greeks saw God as first and foremost the Father, as being the sole and supreme cause, principle and source of all divinity. The Councils of Nicaea and Constantinople state that the Son is begotten "from" (*ek*) the Father, and go on to say the same of the Spirit: the Spirit proceeds "from" (*ek*) the Father. The Father is the source of the begetting of the Son and the procession of the Holy Spirit. Therefore they are consubstantial with the Father and form one sole God, possessing the same eternity, glory and omnipotence as the Father. Yet the three Persons are distinguished by possessing different properties: the unbornness of the Father, begottenness of the Son and procession of the Spirit. These properties are incommunicable and exclusive to each Person. Everything else they share in common. They are in everlasting communion and belong one to another. The Son and the Spirit derive from the same Father, but in different ways; this means they are also different from one another. The Son derives by begetting (*gennēsis*), the Spirit by procession (*ekporeusis*). In figurative language, this can be expressed—and often was by the Greek Fathers—as the Father pronouncing his word which is the Son (Word), the breath that accompanies this word, makes it audible and receivable, being the Spirit. Though distinct from one another, word and breath come from the same Father and are always together.

The Latins saw God not primarily as Father, but as Trinity, one nature in three divine Persons. In begetting the Son, the Father bestows everything on him—John 16:15: "Everything the Father has is mine." He gives him the same nature. So the Son receives the capacity to make the Holy Spirit proceed and has that capacity together with the Father. Through their same, common and unique nature, the Father and the Son are one and the same (John 10:30). Therefore, in proceeding from the Father, the Holy Spirit proceeds from the Son also, not as from two sources (which would suppose two Fathers), but from a single source. St Augustine coined the classic expression of this: the Holy Spirit proceeds principally (*principaliter*)[21] from the Father, but also from the Son (*Filioque*). This avoids one difficulty arising from an extrinsic reading of the Greek conception: that the Father would have two Sons, since the Son and the Holy Spirit both proceed from the Father.[22] On the other hand, if it is the single, common nature of the Father and the Son that gives rise to the Holy Spirit, then we have to see the Spirit as at one and the same time cause and effect of itself, since it shares this single, common nature. To overcome this obstacle, it was argued, we have to speak in a differentiated way of the third Person's proceeding and participation in the same, single and common nature. So, for example, St Cyril of Alexandria claimed that the Holy Spirit as Person derived its existence *solely* from the Father, but in its substantial mode of existence proceeded from the Father *and* the Son. As Persons, the Son and the Spirit have a single relationship with the Father, and only with the Father, since the Father is the origin of the specific incommunicability of the Persons of the Son and the Holy Spirit. But in accordance with the specific manner in which each of the divine Persons appropriates the divine essence, an order is established in which the Persons are, one for the others, the condition of their consubstantial communion.[23]

For Greek thinking, admitting the *Filioque,* the Son's sharing in the procession of the Spirit would mean confusing the individual properties of the Persons of the Trinity. Then, it could not be said absolutely that the Father is the sole origin and source of all divinity, that the Son alone is begotten and the Spirit alone breathed out. The Son would share in the Father's exclusive property (which would thereby cease to be exclusive), that of being the source of all divinity.

Latin theology, in its turn, explained the procession of the Spirit in the way we have examined in chapter 4. The Father knows himself absolutely and projects a substantial image of himself, which is the Son. Father and Son recognize one another and love one another. Love seeks union; the Spirit is this love and union between the Father and the Son. In a vivid phrase of Marius Victorinus, a contemporary of St Augustine, the Holy Spirit is "the copulation of the Father and the Son."[24] Such a representation gives a clear image of the dyad Father-Son; the Holy Spirit performs a unitive function to complete the Trinity, but what exactly *is* the

Holy Spirit? There is no indication of the Spirit's original qualities as a Person. The model of the process of loving was also used by the Latins, and is still the model in commonest use today. There are the lover, the beloved and their love. Love, which is God (cf John 14:18), gives itself. The Father in his love gives everything to the Son. The Son, in turn, receives everything from the Father and gives it to the Holy Spirit. The Father and the Son love the Holy Spirit, who is the *condilectus,* the co-loved. The Spirit, finally, loves the Father and the Son, and so an absolute communion and interpenetration between the three divine Persons is revealed.

Finally, one has to understand the intentions behind these two theological currents:

—The Greek intention was to assure the divinity of the Son and the Holy Spirit through the fact that both proceed from the Father, who is the only source and ultimate origin of all divinity, God first and foremost.

—The Latin intention was to assure the divinity of the three divine Persons by showing them as consubstantial; the Holy Spirit possesses the same nature that the Son received from the Father; as the Son received it from the Father, he bestows it with the Father on the Holy Spirit. Therefore the Spirit proceeds from the Father and the Son.

(c) Attempts to Mediate between the Greek and Latin Approaches

Various formulas were produced by both camps in efforts to move beyond polemic. So Greek texts from St Epiphanius and St Cyril of Alexandria, speaking of the Holy Spirit proceeding from the Father *and* the Son (*ek tou hyiou*), were quoted in a non-polemical context.[25] St Leo the Great and St Gregory the Great used similar phrases in the fifth and seventh centuries. Others were: the Holy Spirit proceeds from the Father *through* the Son (*per Filium*), or *in the presence of* the Son. The Council of Lyon in 1274 attempted to explain the *ab utroque* (from both Father and Son) by stating that this was not duplicating causality: "The Holy Spirit proceeds eternally from the Father and the Son, not as from *two principles,* but as from *one;* not by two spirations [breathings-out] but by one" (DS 850, CT); it also insisted that the breathing-out by the Father and the Son did not imply this taking place later than the begetting of the Son; since all in God is co-eternal, it is also simultaneous (DS 853). The Council of Florence in 1439 explained the general sense of *per Filium:* "When the holy Doctors and Fathers say that the Holy Spirit proceeds from the Father *through* the Son, this must be understood in the sense that, as the Father, so also the Son is what the Greeks call 'cause' and the Latins 'principle' of the subsistence of the Holy Spirit" (DS 1301, CF). Then it clarified that the Son received being, cause or origin of the Holy Spirit from the Father, and that therefore, as the Greeks wanted, the Father is principally (*principaliter*) the breather-out of the Holy Spirit. It sought to equate *Filioque* with *per Filium.*

But its efforts were still not generally accepted. The Greeks saw other overtones in the terms that had been thrashed out through long struggles against subordinationism (Arianism) and modalism (Sabellianism): they could never say that the Son could also be the source (*archē*) of the Spirit; for them being the source was the exclusive property of the Father. When the Latins used the term *principium* to translate *archē,* they meant something generic, a supreme or mediated principle. The Greeks also found it difficult to accept the application of the term *ekporeusis* (procession) to the Son (the Holy Spirit proceeding from the Father and the Son), since they reserved this word solely for the relationship of the Spirit to the Father, as absolutely first cause of the Spirit. Nor could they accept that *ex Filio* meant exactly the same as *per Filium: ex* meant equality of substance, and not the order of the Persons, whereas *per* indicated the order of the Persons and not the equality of the same substance.

The Latins, for their part, always mistrusted *per Filium* as suggesting an inferiority of the Son, that the Son might be merely an instrumental cause, not a completely equal principle with the Father. The Council of Florence made an enormous effort to overcome differences of expression and find a way to unite East and West. But it could not overcome the idiosyncracies of the two languages, so deeply embedded in the flesh and bones of each way of thinking. And so the debates continue to this day.

It also needs to be said that neither *Filioque* nor *per Filium,* though endorsed by the Councils of the Lateran, Lyon and Florence, really expresses the ever-trinitarian relationship between the Father, Son and Holy Spirit, and so both hinder understanding of true perichoresis. The Latin understanding really produces two dyads: Father-Son and Father/Son-Holy Spirit. The significance and implications of relationships that are eternally and absolutely trinitarian will be examined in later chapters.

(d) Steps toward Trinitarian Balance

The ecumenical dialogue (among Orthodox, Roman Catholics, Old Catholics and Anglicans) has in recent years sought new approaches to the mystery of the Trinity, reaching beyond the horizons defined by historical differences.[26] The Orthodox Paul Evdokimov and the Lutheran Jürgen Moltmann both refer to the Russian Orthodox historian Boris Bolotov (who died in 1900 at the age of only forty-seven). In 1897 he wrote a long article entitled "Thesis by a Russian Theologian on the *Filioque*,"[27] in which he claimed that the Holy Spirit proceeds from the Father alone, in that the Father is the source of all divinity; but the Son, through his begetting by the Father, is so united to the Father as to be the logical presupposition and objective condition for the breathing-out of the Spirit. Furthermore, the Spirit is the trinitarian condition for the begetting of the Son by the Father. In this way, relationships in the Trinity are always trinitarian: *Filioque* has to be complemented by *Spirituque*.

Paul Evdokimov, who writes with unusual insight as well as clarity, believes that we have to go beyond causal thinking in approaching the mystery of the Trinity.[28] The language of tradition is more descriptive and analogical than explanatory. He suggests we should rather start from this clause of the Creed: "We believe in the Holy Spirit . . . , who together with the Father and the Son *is adored and glorified. . . .*" This expresses the triadic relationships within the Trinity.[29] Instead of speaking of causal dialectic, Evdokimov insists, we should move on to the dialectic of revelation of the Father through the Son in the Holy Spirit, within the framework of the triple love in the Trinity. The monarchy of the Father means that he is the subject of revelation, since he is the one who ensures the unity, consubstantiality and co-eternity of the three divine Persons. It is not a matter of the Father's relationship to one or other Person, but of the relationship between the one who is revealed and those who reveal him. So *Filioque* is only justifiable if accompanied by *Spirituque*.[30]

The meaning of these two formulas is that each Person has to be contemplated simultaneously in its relationships with the other two. So the Son through his begetting receives the Holy Spirit from the Father and is then, in his being, eternally inseparable from the Holy Spirit; the Son, then, is begotten *ex Patre Spirituque*. In the same way, the Spirit proceeds from the Father and rests on the Son; this is what corresponds to *per Filium* and *ex Patre Filioque*. In all the interpersonal relationships within the Trinity, there is always an *and* and a *through*. The Father begets the Son with the participation of the Holy Spirit and breathes out the Spirit with the participation of the Son. Even the Father's unbornness involves the participation of the Son and the Holy Spirit, who witness to it by the fact of deriving from the Father as their only source.[31] This is rigorously trinitarian thinking, along the lines we have developed earlier, and points in the direction that would make a fruitful ecumenical dialogue possible, superseding the polemics of the past.

Jürgen Moltmann has equally been influenced by Boris Bolotov, especially by his concept of balance in the Trinity.[32] Moltmann starts with the Father, who is always Father of the Son. He is not Father of the Holy Spirit, but breathes out the Holy Spirit through being Father of the Son. The Son is the logical presupposition and objective condition for the procession of the Holy Spirit. The Holy Spirit proceeds from the Father of the Son: this is the most adequate interpretative formula to express our faith.[33] The Father, as the Greeks maintained, is still the source of divinity, and therefore the cause of the procession of the Holy Spirit; the Son also participates in this procession in that, as Son, he shares in the reality of the Father. So the direct relationship between the Father and the Holy Spirit is explicit. But what is the relationship of the Son to the Holy Spirit? What does the Spirit receive from the Son? Moltmann replies: "The Holy Spirit has from the Father his perfect, divine *existence* (*hypostasis, hyparxis*), and receives from the Son his relational *Gestalt* (*eidos, prosopon*)."[34] In other words: the existence of the Holy Spirit is received from the Father alone, but the specific configuration of the Spirit's existence is received from the Son of the Father. In Moltmann's own figure of speech: the Person of the Spirit proceeds from the Father; the individual aspect of the Spirit derives from the Son. This aspect is an expression of absolute beauty and a revelation of the supreme glory. *Gestalt* here means this aspect as revelation of the Person. So the Holy Spirit is always turned to the Father and the Son, who equally are always turned to the Spirit.

Moltmann concludes his exposition by accepting that both the Greek and Latin models derive from the principle of causality, which was responsible for the disputes over monopatrism (processions deriving from the Father alone) and Filioquism (the Son with the Father being responsible for the procession of the Spirit, which then has no other person deriving from it). He therefore postulates a presentation of the mystery of the Trinity that starts decisively from the interpersonal relationships between Father, Son and Holy Spirit, an approach that I share.[35]

(e) The Simultaneity of the Spirit with the Father and the Son

Going back to what was said in chapter 7 on the eternal perichoresis between the three divine Persons, we have to start with the primary *datum* of faith: the co-existence of Father, Son and Holy Spirit.[36] The Persons, while each possessing its specific property, exist with the others, through the others, in the others and for the others. Relationships of mutual revelation and recognition exist between them. As we saw, revealing themselves to each other and recognizing themselves means accepting difference. This lovingly accepted difference is the condition for communion and union.[37] What is produced in the Trinity is the eternal process of revealing reciprocal love and the mystery of the triune life. The simultaneity of the divine Three means that unbornness, begetting and procession cannot be understood as producing Persons, like a cause producing its effects.[38] Each Person is determined in relation to the other two. What theological tradition calls unbornness, begetting and procession is really a single, tri-une act of mutual recognition and mutual revelation in which each of the three Persons participates simultaneously.

The Holy Spirit reveals the gift of the Father and the Son—the Spirit itself. Through the Son, the Spirit recognizes the Father in his superabundance of life and giving. With the Father, the Spirit recognizes the Son as full expression of the Father and model of all possible creatable beings. And so one can go on forever, describing mutual and reciprocal implications between the three divine Persons.

I would like, finally, following the Greek Fathers, to recognize a certain generative function in relation to the Holy Spirit.[39] There is always a correlation between intra-trinitarian relationships and the historical-salvific mission of one of the Persons. So the New Testament recognizes the action of the Holy Spirit at the moment of the Son's incarnation; in his humanity, the Son is the work of the Holy Spirit. It is the Holy Spirit who makes Christ be born in the lives of the baptized, who lives in the just and is the breath of the Father's voice from heaven saying: "You are my beloved Son; this day have I begotten you." There is naturally an intimate relationship between the Virgin Mary and the Spirit in regard to conception, as we shall see later. The Spirit's generative mission has an intra-trinitarian correlation: engendering the Father's joy with the Son, being the one with whom the Father and the Son are in communion, the love that overflows and invites the creation of other companions for loving and living. Through the Spirit is the way from the intra-trinitarian life, and through the Spirit is the return to the trinitarian life, to the glory of the three divine Persons, now in communion with other created beings who have been caught up in a communion without end.

4. THE MISSION OF THE HOLY SPIRIT: TRANSFORMATION AND NEW CREATION

What the Holy Spirit is within the circle of the Trinity is, within the limits of time, made manifest in time. The immanent mystery is never completely revealed in history, but its shadow goes with us on our journey toward perfect freedom in the triune God.

The Spirit, as we have seen, is expansion and union, diversity and communion—in a word, the love that reveals others and is revealed in others. In the biblical and trinitarian sense, the Spirit is primarily action and transformation. We live now under the mission (the way, or law, in St Paul's terminology: Rom. 7:6; 8:2) of the Spirit. This mission is always in a dialectical relationship with that of the Son, with its final reference in that of the Father. The Father always represents the nature of mystery and inaccessible—but at the same time protective—depth. The Son, in his mission, signifies the Trinity taking root in human history, since our nature has been totally taken up into the Trinity. The Spirit acts universally in all men and women, not in just one of them, as the Son does in Jesus. It has been sent and poured out into our hearts (Gal. 4:6; Rom. 5:5). The Spirit is present in multiplicity and diversity, creating communion. Pentecost shows the dynamic of the Spirit's actions: respecting diversity and creating communion (Acts 2:11), allowing the same message to be heard in a multiplicity of languages. This presence of the Spirit engenders such enthusiasm that the Apostles appeared drunk (Acts 2:12); the ecstasy of joy and the fascination of creation are works of the Spirit.

The Spirit works in the world through action.[40] Its action flows into human actions, giving them power and making them truly creative. This is why the Spirit is hidden: it reveals human and cosmic potential; imbues the agents of history with creative powers and allows them to become true agents, not mere repeaters of some external impulse. History contains law and order, institutions and traditions, authority and the weight of facts. But it also contains revolutions, the overthrow of one sort of order and its replacement by another; it contains the making of things new, breaks with tradition and setting-up of different frames of reference implying different forms of behaviour. When the poor become conscious of their oppression, come together, organize their forces, throw over the taboos that held them in subjection, unmask the standards by which they were stygmatized, prophetically denounce those who kept them in chains; when, obliged to use force they did not want to, they face up to the violence of their oppressors and strip them of their privileges and unjust rank; when they are filled with creative imagination and plan utopias of the reconciled world in which all will have enough to eat and be able to profit from the bounty of nature, then we can say: the Spirit is at work there, being the catalyst in a conflictive situation.[41] Such historical processes are pregnant with the Spirit. The same Spirit raises up charismatic leaders who sustain enthusiasm and rekindle dormant powers in everyone. Then the creative spirit bursts out in every segment of life, in the power of the Holy Spirit: in political leadership, in the inventiveness of science and the arts, in the originality shown by the people in dealing with problems of subsistence, in the tenderness they preserve in the midst of lethal struggles and fatal dramas. The Spirit takes on a thousand faces in all these situations, the Spirit who is called faceless: its divine face is that of transfigured or humiliated humanity.

The Holy Spirit does not act only in the multiplicity of men and women, especially of the poor. Its favoured manifestation—sacrament—is in the community of those who follow Jesus. The church is the sacrament of Christ and also that of the Holy Spirit. The church contains what derives from the incarnation: institutional stability, the ordering of the community, the rule of faith, authority invested with sacred power. But it also contains the irruption of gifts and charisms (cf 1 Cor. 12; Rom. 12), of charismatic figures who shake the rigid body of the institution, who open new horizons to faith from their new experience of the divine mystery, who usher in new ways of attending to the historical needs of the community. The church stands on these two columns: the incarnate Son and the Spirit poured out on all humanity, but particularly on the church. A church without charisms, without legitimate space given to the Spirit, without the vigour and strength that give it youth and a spirit of inquiry, is not a church in the image of the Trinity, the true church of God. Without explicitly cultivating the Spirit, we shall not liberate the Christian community from the authoritarianism of its hierarchs, from domination by abstract truth, from the sterile dogmatization of dogma, from the wearisome repetition of rites which empties ceremonies of meaning. Without conscious adoration of the Spirit and respect for its divine activity, preaching loses its flavour of good news, the content of the gospel fails to release its humanizing dimension, following Jesus becomes a process of copying that narrows the mind and makes prayer mediocre.

The Spirit also acts through the sacraments, particularly confirmation and the eucharist. This is not the place to enlarge on the significance of the epiclesis (the invocation of the Holy Spirit in the eucharistic prayer).[42] Let us just note the transforming presence of the Spirit (without going into the form this presence takes) at the consecration of the bread and wine. The celebrant invokes the Holy Spirit so that the words of Christ which instituted the sacrament may take on divine efficacy. The Spirit is always the Spirit of the Son; this is why it is the Spirit that, at this holy moment, manifests the living presence of Christ under the form of bread and wine, identifying this meal with the eucharistic supper of the Lord. All celebration is directed to the Father so that the Spirit may reveal Christ present in the community and sacramentally present in the eucharistic celebration. The minister acts simultaneously *in nomine Christi* and *in persona Spiritus Sancti,* with the church.

Finally, we can ask: if the Spirit was sent by the Father together with the Son, to whom specifically was it sent? We have already seen that the answer involves a multiplicity of men and women, historical processes of change, the church, the life of the just who live a life of grace (often synonymous with the Holy Spirit in scripture). Is it possible to narrow the answer down further and seek a specific, historical person as the privileged recipient of the Spirit? Without going into detail (already dealt with in two previous works[43]), let us go straight to the point. In St Matthew, and more specially in St Luke, a close association is made between Mary and the Holy Spirit. The basic text is this: "The Holy Spirit will come upon you . . . and the power of the Most High will cover you with its shadow. And so the child will be holy and will be called Son of God" (Luke 1:35). The words of the text permit us to deduce a mission proper to the Holy Spirit, that is, a personal (hypostatic) self-communication to the Virgin Mary. This is the first time in all the scriptures when the Spirit is said to have come down directly on to a woman. Mary was thereby, as Vatican II rightly observed, "fashioned by the Holy Spirit into a kind of new substance and new creature" (LG 56b). It is natural that the "last Adam" (1 Cor. 15:45) should have the "last Eve" as mother. Only God can beget God. Mary, through the power of the Holy Spirit, is raised to the divine level so that her motherhood can be divine and herself truly, not just as a figure of speech, mother of God. Luke's phrase "the power of the Most High will cover you with its shadow" recalls the theology of the *shekinah* (tent), the palpable presence of God (cf Exod. 40:34-5), which in Judaism represented an incarnational tendency. Mary is truly made full of grace (full of the Holy Spirit), "temple of the Holy Spirit" (LG 53), daughter of Sion, the dwelling-place of God so often mentioned in the Old Testament (cf Wisd. 3:14-17).

I would say that the Holy Spirit, coming down on Mary, "pneumatized" her, taking on human form in her, in the same manner as the Son who, in a personal and unmistakable manner, set up his tent amongst us in the figure of Jesus of Nazareth (cf John 1:18). This is not official church teaching; it is a *theologoumenon* (theological hypothesis), based on correlating the biblical narrative with other related truths of faith. Thus, as truths of faith we affirm that woman as well as man is made in the image and likeness of God (Gen. 1:27); that there is a call to divinization; that femininity reveals God; that the feminine dimension present in Jesus through the incarnation was taken on hypostatically, so that a feminine element has been divinized eternally; that the feminine as well as the masculine will in eternity participate on the highest level in the communion of the Trinity. In the light of all these statements, it is legitimate to ask: as maleness was explicitly taken on by the Son in the humanity of Jesus of Nazareth (which implies a feminine dimension), could not femaleness be explicitly taken on by the Holy Spirit, given that scripture shows such an intimate connection between the Spirit and the Virgin Mary? Is there not a historical-salvific balance in the statement—made in all reverence and piety—that the whole of humanity, female and male, has become the receptacle of the self-giving of two Persons of the Trinity, sent into the world by the Father to bring men and women, with the qualities proper to each, into the communion of the Trinity? The Son divinized maleness explicitly and femaleness implicitly, to the extent that male and female are always combined and always perichoretically linked. The Holy Spirit would then have divinized femaleness explicitly and maleness implicitly, given this mutual implication of one in the other. Jesus and Mary would represent the whole of humanity; taken up within time, they would represent a blessed anticipation of the eschatological event of the full divinization of men and women in the Kingdom of God.

In such a *theologoumenon,* the Holy Spirit would have intensified its presence in Mary (whether one could talk of Mary's nature or just her person being taken on by the Holy Spirit, what name to give to this unique event in the history of salvation, and so on, would need further study) in such a real and identifiable way as to be personally present in her in the same way as the Son was incarnate in Jesus. Mary would then indeed be blessed among women, full of grace (the grace that is the Holy Spirit); not just the temple of God, but the very God of the temple, the God who dwells in her and makes her a true and living temple. What is the future destiny of humanity in its feminine embodiment? To be divinized as Mary was, to the extent proper to each person. In Mary's case this was full and immediate; all other women (and men through their feminine side) share in the process with Mary.

So from this central source—Mary—the presence of the Spirit would flood out over all the just, especially women; over the church, of which Mary is the first and most perfect member; over humanity on its journey toward the Kingdom, a journey through change and liberation processes that make creation progressively more like its ultimate goal of communion in the Trinity. If this is the case, then we can pray the Creed of our ancestors with enlightened fervour: "We believe in the Holy Spirit . . . who with the Father and the Son is adored and glorified." To the Spirit who pneumatized Mary be honour, glory and everlasting adoration now and forever! Amen!

CHAPTER XII

As It Was in the Beginning: The Immanent Trinity, in Itself

Father, Son and Holy Spirit exist in everlasting communion and are eternal. The prayer "As it was in the beginning, is now and ever shall be" seeks to express the eternity of the triune God, even though it uses the scheme of temporal succession, as the scriptures do. Its meaning, however, is not an expression of eternity as an interminable length of time, or as the coinciding of beginning, now and forever. Eternity means much more than this. It does not describe an unlimited quantity, but a new quality independent of time. Its best and shortest definition was given by Boethius (480-524): "the totally simultaneous and perfect possession of everlasting life."[1] This affirms fullness of living and of life. Because this fullness is absolute and complete (per-fected), it has always existed and will never cease to exist.

We find it difficult to imagine the eternity of God because our experience is limited to succession, to fragments of perfection or perfection threatened with extinction. What faith seeks to stress is the sovereignty of the Holy Trinity. Before the universe was, before the tiniest atom of cosmic matter moved, before time began, the Father, Son and Holy Spirit existed in themselves in an immense irruption of life and love. The immanent Trinity existed. And we, as creatures, existed in God as eternal projects, "begotten" by the

Father in the heart of the Son with the love of the Holy Spirit.

All we know of this immanent Trinity, as it is in itself, is what this Trinity has graciously shown us, in words and deeds, and most especially through the incarnation of the Son and the coming of the Holy Spirit.

1. WHEN THE ECONOMIC TRINITY IS THE IMMANENT TRINITY AND VICE-VERSA

The Trinity reveals itself to us as it is, as Trinity, and saves us by what it is in itself. This means that what we see of its saving manifestation in history—the Father revealed as the mystery of the world, the Son being incarnate and the Holy Spirit poured out into our hearts and coming down on Mary—corresponds to what the triune God actually is. If God were not Father, Son and Holy Spirit, the manifestation would have been different and human beings would never have grasped the idea of the divine Three. Therefore an axiom of modern thinking on the Trinity is: the three Unique Beings in communion who reveal themselves in the economy of salvation are the immanent Tri-unity, and vice-versa.[2]

The main argument validating this axiom is to be found in the very actions proper to the Son through the incarnation and to the Holy Spirit through its descent on the just and on the Virgin Mary. There is a presence of the Son in the world which is the immediacy of his own divine Person taking on the human reality of Jesus of Nazareth and making this the very humanity of the Son himself. Here the Son is not being just the light coming into the world that enlightens all human beings (John 1:9), nor wisdom, nor the inner meaning of all beings. Here he is himself in person bestowing himself absolutely and completely. In this moment, the person Jesus is God, who is to be adored and glorified in his own humanity. If, then, we find the Son of the Father pitching his tent amongst us—this being our experience in faith—this means that the Son of the Father exists in himself immanently.

The same holds good for the Holy Spirit: by following Jesus, believing in his words and deeds, accepting the witness of the disciples who touched the Word of life (1 John 1:1), we are imbued with the transforming power that is the Spirit, we are led by the Spirit to give ourselves to the Father, confirmed by the Spirit in our knowledge that Jesus is truly the Son and Liberator, assured by the Spirit that God is our Father and we God's sons and daughters. Furthermore, we see the Spirit come down on Mary and from a virgin make her the Mother of God; in her the Spirit is fully present in such a way that she can be called the tabernacle of the Spirit. Here is the Spirit in a unique sense manifesting itself as a divine Person, as it is. If this is how the Spirit is manifested in our history, then this means that the Holy Spirit is immanently God together with the Father and the Son. Because the triune God is revealed to us as God is, the immanent Trinity is correlated to the economic Trinity.

This correlation should not be understood in a reductionist manner, as though we were doing away with the barrier between time and eternity. What is manifested in our history is indeed God as God is, trinitarian. But the Trinity as absolute and sacramental mystery is much more than what is manifested. Its self-bestowal is made within the framework of space and time and the limits of created perception, distorted by the dark waters of sin. What the Trinity is in itself is beyond our reach, hidden in unfathomable mystery, mystery that will be partially revealed to us in the bliss of eternal life, but will always escape us in full, since the Trinity is a mystery in itself and not only for human beings. So we have to say: the economic Trinity is the immanent Trinity, but not the whole of the immanent Trinity. This is much more than has been revealed to human beings. As a further consequence of this, we also have to say that not the whole of the immanent Trinity is the economic Trinity. The correlation is perfect (which allows the "vice-versa" in the axiom) when we are dealing with the incarnation or—in my *theologoumenon*—the coming of the Spirit on Mary. Here indeed the self-communication of the Son and Holy Spirit means the presence of the eternal in time, of the divine Person as "person" in human reality. What happens on earth corresponds exactly to what exists in heaven. But the Trinity is all this and still much more.

2. THE SON AND HOLY SPIRIT COMMUNICATE THEMSELVES IN HUMILIATION

All that happens to the divine Persons in history is taken on by them: they take on human littleness, the form of a servant in

Mary's case, hunger, thirst, joy, friendship and love. Looking at the history of salvation and the way in which the Son and Holy Spirit came into the world, we have to recognize that they exalted the way of obscurity, of *kenōsis*. What we see is not the dazzle of glory, but simplicity and humility. This means that the mode of being of the immanent Trinity and that of the economic Trinity are not connatural. We recognize the Father as infinite goodness, but evil exists in the world alongside goodness, evil that affects mainly the poor and the weak; the Son is the supreme expression of Wisdom and Meaning but in his incarnation had to suffer human ignorance and the existential absurdity of being hated and persecuted. The Holy Spirit is Love and Union and yet in historical processes of change, in which it is present above all, we find the destructive fury of hatred and the dispersing power of disunity. In their coming amongst us, the Son and Holy Spirit took on human conditions subject to sin and it is from within this situation that they liberated and redeemed life and the cosmos.

This very contradiction makes the Son and Holy Spirit reveal what they are in the immanent Trinity. So the conflicts Jesus suffered, his passion and ultimate death were what demonstrated merciful love, solidarity and even identification with those who suffer in this world. This does not mean that the Son is eternally destined to crucifixion.[3] Human rejection of divine love, that love expressed in the incarnation, creates the possibility of persecution and the cross. The Son does not cease being and revealing what he is: surrender, offering of life and salvation, love for the world. But because of human rejection, this love is changed to sacrifice and an offering of forgiveness. The Son is not indifferent to human rejection. He is affected by it, since it alters his manner of being present and acting. But it does not change his love and his invitation to communion. The cross is not eternalized along with the Trinity; the cross, product of human sinfulness, is taken on, not because it represents a value, but because it allows him to show the radicalness of a love that accepts self-sacrifice rather than break his communion with others, even with his enemies. It is not the cross that bestows value; it is love that confers value on that which has none and on that which is the embodiment of anti-value.

The Holy Spirit is first and foremost life and communication of life through communion and union. This divine reality has often been experienced through contradictions in history. In the midst of the downtrodden and those condemned to die before their time, the Spirit appears as resistance, rising above all hatred, hoping against all hope. The Spirit is that little flicker of fire burning at the bottom of the woodpile. More rubbish is piled on, rain puts out the flame, wind blows the smoke away. But a thin wisp of smoke remains. Underneath everything a brand still burns on, unquenchable. Such is the Holy Spirit in the midst of human weakness and failure. The Holy Spirit will not let the reed bend to breaking-point, will not let the candle be put out. The Spirit sustains the feeble breath of life in the empire of death. The Spirit shows its strength in weakness, its communion in the midst of distorted quests for companionship and happiness. Only in the Kingdom of the Trinity will creation finally be set free, will the Son and Spirit show themselves in a way that can be fully understood by creatures, created in the image and likeness of the Trinity. Then their manifestation in the form of servants will have passed away; they will exist only in the form of God, forever united to creatures taken up and inserted into the communion of the Trinity.

3. THE ETERNAL DOXOLOGY: THE GLORY AND JOY OF THE TRINITY

Theology has generally confined itself to formal reflection on the mystery of trinitarian communion. It has tried to look with the eyes of reason into the blinding sun of the very essence of the triune God. The end term of this quest is respectful silence. Any speech that goes beyond the barriers to perception of the mystery becomes mere chatter and appears to profane the Most Holy. This is the human situation when confronted with the immanent Trinity. If we cannot and should not speak, we can nevertheless sing and praise. Reason halts, imagination takes wing. This is what happened to the mystics who received the grace of intuition of the inner life of the Trinity. Three separate beings, like the mouths of three channels without shores, flowing into a single ocean of life and love; three separate viewpoints forming a single vision; the self-giving of one to another, the nuptials of three in a single love—these produce glory and joy without end. Flux and reflux, the heartbeats of the divine Three interpenetrating, inundated in the power of everlasting communication, produce the ecstasy of love. The intertwining of the divine Persons gives rise to the intimacy, embrace and expansion of tenderness proper to eternal happiness. This happiness is the Trinity itself showing itself as a Trinity of Persons separate in the unity of a single communion, a single love and one unique life, communicated, received and given back.

All we can do is share, share and love, love and unite ourselves to the divine Persons in an eternal doxology as it was in the beginning, is now and ever shall be, from all eternity and to all eternity.

CHAPTER XIII

Now and Forever:
The Economic Trinity,
for Us

Through its inner dynamic of love and communion, the immanent Trinity manifests itself outside the intimate circle of the Trinity—though "outside" and "inside" (*ad intra* and *ad extra* workings of the Trinity) are inadequate expressions. In its omnipotence and omnipresence, the Trinity knows no restrictions; it pervades everything and everything exists in relation to the life of the Trinity. One truth, however, needs to be borne in mind: creation, the possible receptacle for the divine Persons, should not be confused with the "begetting" of the Son or the "breathing-out" of the Holy Spirit. The inner life of the divine Three is one of supreme liberty, as befits love and communion, but at the same time nothing in it is contingent. Creation is the sphere of contingency, of what is but could also not be. So how does creation relate to the Trinity? In examining this question, we need to stress the close links, though without separation or confusion, between immanent Trinity and economic Trinity, between creation eternally in the mind of the Father through the Son in the love of the Holy Spirit and its temporal actualization, in which the signs of Father, Son and Holy Spirit are apparent.

1. THE TRINITY CREATES IN ORDER TO COMMUNICATE ITSELF TO CREATION

The fourth Lateran Council declared in 1215 that the Trinity is the sole principle of the universe (*sola universorum principium:* DS 804). The Council of Florence gave a trinitarian expression to the relationship between creation and the Trinity, teaching that Father, Son and Holy Spirit are not three principles but a single principle of creation (*non tria principia creaturae, sed unum principium:* DS 1331). This formula, taken from St Augustine,[1] should be understood in line with Augustine's own clarification: "If the Father, the Son and the Holy Spirit are a single God, then a single world was made by the Father, through the Son, in the Holy Spirit."[2] The power that created the universe belongs to the whole Trinity; each divine Person contributes in accordance with the properties and order of that Person,[3] and the processions of the Persons lie behind the logic of production of creatures with attributes of understanding and will.[4] So how should the creation of the universe by the Trinity be understood? Theology has been divided into two main tendencies on this point.

The first, which is more monotheistic than trinitarian in expression, states that creation stems from the free exercise of the divine will. God is omnipotent and absolutely free; God can create what God wants, subject to no coercion, internal or external; creation takes nothing from God, and adds nothing to God, as many liturgical texts state.[5] Everything that flows from God's almighty Word is good and gracious, since it corresponds to the essential goodness of God. In this view, creation is really something *ad extra* (something made outside the trinitarian circle). The universe is a manifestation of divine play, of the overflowing glory of the eternal Being.

The second tendency starts from the very mystery of love and perichoretic communion between the divine Three. Love—God's nature—is of itself communicative and effusive; so the God-Trinity is by nature creator and originator of different beings as an expression of the superabundance of God's being-in-communion. The *idea* of creation, as a transfusion of trinitarian communion, is eternal, co-eternal with the Trinity. The Father loves the Son eternally; the Son responds eternally with love, the love received from the Father. The Holy Spirit loves the Father and the Son from the beginning and together they join in a single movement of self-giving and love.

As we have seen earlier, the Father, in projecting himself in the Son, also projects all beings different from himself, the whole possible creation, the image and likeness of himself and the Son in whom, by whom, with whom and for whom everything exists. The communion and love that circulate between Father, Son and Holy Spirit are a communion and love between co-equals, co-eternals. They are not yet love and communion for other, different beings. From a trinitarian perspective, temporal creation is just the manifestation of trinitarian love and communion for what is not God, for the utterly other than God: creatures. This is where the expression "*opera ad extra amoris Trinitatis*" fits in: insofar as creation is the *idea* of the Father in the Son with the love of the Holy Spirit, it is eternal and a work of the Trinity *ad intra;* inasmuch as this idea is embodied, drawn from nothing, brought into being and formed in the image and likeness of the Trinity, it is a work *ad extra*. In effect, the Trinity creates out of nothing that which was not and which, through the act of creation, comes into being. The Trinity limits itself[6] by the fact of creating from nothing, in that it brings something distinct from itself into being. Creation is of the Trinity, comes from the Trinity, goes to the Trinity, reflects the Trinity, but is not the Trinity.

Creation never ceases to be contingent and totally dependent on the Trinity, but this does not make it a snap decision of an arbitrary will that might just as well have decided not to create as to create. The divine logic can better be seen by starting from the very essence of the three divine Persons: perichoretic communion and love. Creation, without being necessary (nothing is imposed on God), is con-natural with the divine essence. This means it is also free. It prolongs and reflects the outpouring of life and love that eternally constitute the being of Father, Son and Holy Spirit. To use anthropomorphic language: the Trinity does not wish to live alone in its splendid trinitarian communion; the three divine Persons do not love just one another, but seek companions in communion and love. Creation arose from this wish of the three divine Persons to meet others (created by them) so as to include them in their eternal communion. Creation is external to the Trinity only so as to be brought within it. Action *ad extra* is ordered to action *ad intra* because the origin of actions *ad extra* is to be found in actions *ad intra*. In other words, creation, before being temporal, was eternal in the Father's plan; before being embodied "outside" God, it was a plan "inside" God.

2. CREATION BY THE FATHER THROUGH THE SON IN THE HOLY SPIRIT

St Thomas Aquinas has a famous passage which stresses the trinitarian nature of creation:

> The causality concerning the creation of things answers to the respective meaning of the coming forth each Person implies. . . . God is the cause of things through his mind and will, like an artist of works of art. An artist works through an idea conceived in his mind and through love in his will bent on something. In like manner God the Father wrought the creature through his Word, the Son, and through his Love, the Holy Ghost. And from this point of view, keeping in mind the essential attributes of knowing and willing, the comings forth of the divine Persons can be seen as types for the comings forth of creatures.[7]

This passage shows that all three divine Persons, in their trinitarian order, participate in the single act of creation. The Father is the first cause, acting through intelligence (the Son), and love (the Spirit). The goodness and wisdom of creatures find their supreme example in the Spirit and the Son, who are always referred to the Father. In this way creation refers not only back simply to the triune God, without distinction of Persons, but to each Person acting personally, through the properties of each individual hypostasis. So St Thomas can say: "the comings forth of the divine Persons can be seen as types for the comings forth of creatures." So creation is trinitarian in character, and being trinitarian is being in permanent perichoresis.

This will be clearer if we recall what was said earlier about the Father-Son relationship: the Father, in his infinite love, "begets" the Son and in him projects the eternal expression of all creatures. These are always *through* the Son and so possess a filial, brotherly and sisterly, dimension because of their trinitarian origin. The Son signifies the infinite response to the Father's wisdom and love, and with his response goes that of all creatures, especially of rational creatures who can see "the first of many brothers" and sisters in the Father their creator and the historical Jesus, eternally destined to be the incarnate Son of God. Creation should be seen as the *proper* (not just *appropriated*) work of the Father, who, in "begetting" the Son, expresses in him all possible images and likenesses of the Father and the Son in the Holy Spirit.

The Father creates through the Son *in* the Holy Spirit. This means that creation is introduced into trinitarian communion by the Holy Spirit, which is always active in creation. Without the Spirit and its transforming power, creation would cease to exist (cf Ps. 104:29, 30). The Spirit is "poured out on all mankind" (Joel 2:28-32; Acts 2:17), especially "into our hearts" (Rom. 5:5). The whole of creation groans to be united and set free (cf Rom. 8:22ff); the Spirit unites what is different in communion and love. So the whole of creation is created in the Spirit to make up the Kingdom of the Trinity.

Creation is first and foremost the proper work of the Father, in which he associates the Son and the Spirit. So the whole Trinity shares in creation and is mirrored in it. All that is mystery in creatures, however transparent, is the Father making himself present; all that is reason, logic, wisdom in creatures is the Son revealing himself in them; all that is love, giving, integrating in creatures is the Holy Spirit acting in them. The whole of creation is a majestic sacrament of the Trinity.

3. TRACES OF THE TRINITY IN CREATION

As there are traces of the Trinity in the whole cosmic order, so there are in human lives. Every human being is undoubtedly a mystery, with unfathomable depths not communicated to oneself or to others; this is the presence of the Father as deep, inner mystery in every human person. All men and women possess a dimension of truth, self-knowledge and self-revelation, the light and wisdom of their own mystery; this expresses the presence of the Son (Word and

Wisdom) acting in them, developing the communication of their mystery. All human beings feel an urge to commune with others and be united in love; the Holy Spirit is present in this desire and in the joy of its fullfilment in this life. Mystery, truth and communion live together in each individual; they are interwoven realities that together make up the unity of life. They provide a reflection of trinitarian communion and are the ultimate foundation for humanity being the image and likeness of the Trinity.

When we live in the love of the Mystery (are in a state of grace), the three divine Persons truly live in our hearts. The more righteously we live, the more we allow the mystery of life (the Father) to shine out, the truth of life (the Son) to glow, and the love of life (the Spirit) to radiate. As the Trinity is a living, ever-active mystery, we can say with the mystics that the lives of the just show the Father continually "begetting" the Son and inserting his adoptive sons and daughters in the Son; Father and Son continually bestowing themselves on each other in love, pouring themselves out in love for other creatures and drawing them to themselves; that is, Father and Son continually "breathing out the Holy Spirit" in the depths of their lives.

This view, however, concentrates too much on human individuality. In the Bible, people are essentially social, beings-in-communion. Living a human life always means living with others; it is in the exercise of co-humanity that an individual is fully personalized. Genesis presents humanity as made in the image and likeness of God. Now we see God as communion and love in eternal perichoresis. So humanity becomes an image of the Trinity through establishing community and relationships of giving and receiving. Adam, Eve and the product of their mutual love, their son Seth, are an image of the Trinity: Father (Adam), Son (Eve) and the unnamed but present "*co-dilectus*" (so called by Richard of St Victor), the Holy Spirit (Seth). Obviously the analogy is not intended to compare sexual characteristics, but the type of relationship between the Three, a relationship of living reciprocity and communion.

So human life is intrinsically bound up in the communion of the Trinity. This structure applies both to the order of creation and to the order of grace. We can live the order of grace consciously, though in this life we cannot palpably feel what this truth means in joy and happiness; acted out in faith, hope and love, it remains veiled in darkness; in eternity we shall be the created part of the mystery of the Father, the begetting of the Son, the breathing-out of the Holy Spirit, consciously, in sharing and joy.[8]

The Trinity is present too in the course of history and the progress of society, though the nature of society and above all the existence of structural sin mean that this presence is not easily detected. Our faith, however, tells us that the Trinity is present in a specially close way in the struggles of the oppressed for their liberation. In every upheaval that leads toward more life-giving forms of society, the Son is being socio-historically "begotten" in the bosom of the Spirit that inspires and promotes life. The Father in his mystery hides in the underlying meaning of history which, in the final analysis, escapes our grasp. When the oppressed unite, when interests converge for the common good, when men and women take heart to face up to age-old threats to their lives and freedom, show solidarity and even identification with the cause of the oppressed, they are shot through with the hidden presence of the Spirit of life, prophecy and liberation. Human history does not cease to be human: its agents of change (and conservation), its conflicts, alliances, advances and setbacks are all human. But the Trinity lives in it, in a mysterious but nonetheless effective way, giving heart to the struggle, power to resist, skill to create and the will to be free of everything that threatens these shoots of new life. History is the theatre for the possible glory of the Trinity, now in types and shadows, but at the end of time in full evidence and unending celebration.

The Trinity is present in a special way too in that section of humanity that the Spirit moves to accept Jesus as liberator and incarnate Son: the church.[9] The two missions, those of the Son and the Holy Spirit, are carried out in the church. So the church is founded both on Jesus, the incarnate Son, and the Holy Spirit, who came down on Mary at the Annunciation and on the Apostles and Mary at Pentecost. In this life, the church lives on the communion of the Trinity; its unity derives from the perichoresis that exists between the three divine Persons. As Vatican II so well expressed it: "Thus, the church shines forth as 'a people made one with the unity of the Father, Son and Holy Spirit.' "[10]

The church is first and foremost a communion of believers. The

Son and the Spirit, sent by the Father, who for all time sustain and give life to this community, make it into the body of Christ. Communion in Christ and in the Spirit and the communion among the faithful themselves make up the one church, which is a communion of gifts and services (cf 1 Cor. 12:4), all ordered to the building up of the body of Christ. Paul, speaking of the gifts that give concrete form to the community, refers to the Three, the Father, Christ the Lord (the Son) and the Spirit. And this is as it has to be, because the community of those who follow Jesus is, in the enthusiasm infused into them by the Spirit revealing the Father and the Son, a reflection of the communion of the Trinity: *ecclesia de Trinitate.*[11]

The august mystery of the Trinity is present in creation and history in a thousand different ways. The universe is pregnant with this unutterable mystery, so close we can even touch it, transcendent because it surrounds us on every hand, intimate because it dwells in us as in its own temple and home.

CHAPTER XIV

Forever and Ever: The Trinity in Creation and Creation in the Trinity

The meaning of creation lies in its being a receptacle capable of holding the manifestation of the Trinity and, on the human level, of being a temple for the self-communication of the Son (in Jesus of Nazareth) and the Holy Spirit (in Mary and the lives of the just, in our *theologoumenon*). Creation was the start of creative action by the three divine Persons beyond their intra-trinitarian life. Throughout the course of time, this action goes on developing outward till it continues in eternity, on the plane of glory and perfection. We should not think that the creative process of the Trinity ceases in eternity. The very theological concept of creation supposes that the three divine Persons act in perpetuity to ensure that beings continue in being and do not fall back into the nothing from which they came. The Trinity is eternally carrying out the creation of what is different in order to manifest itself and give itself. In this way, creation is inserted in the very life, communion and "history" of the Trinity.[1] Creation is the basis on which the Trinity has a history. In eternity pure and simple, there is no history, though there is movement in eternal life, renewal of revelation of one divine Person to the others. But these processes are simultaneous and eternal; they always were, are and always will be. They form the *nunc stans,* the eternal "now" of the perichoretic love between the divine Three.

Let us look at the meaning of creation inserted in the Trinity, in the plenitude of glory, and starting from the irruption of the parousia at the end of the eschatological process (which begins in time and ends in eternity). This insertion is the blessed end of what began in time. Creation is only in the Trinity because the Trinity is first in creation. Let us look at these two aspects.

1. THE AGE OF THE FATHER, SON AND HOLY SPIRIT: PROVIDENCE, LIBERATION, INDWELLING

I am not using the term "age" here in the sense given it by Joachim of Fiore, that of a specific time within time, to be succeeded by another that overcomes it and embraces it.[2] He said that the age of the Father was to be followed by the age of the Son, which, in turn, would give place to the age of the Holy Spirit. I am using "age" in the trinitarian sense that all time is the time of Father, Son and Holy Spirit. However, this does not mean there is no distinction of dimensions within the presence of the divine Three in their creation. The Three are present with their hypostatic properties in each dimension. But we can distinguish one particular presence in particular events, without denying the action of the others. So one can talk of the age of the Father, the age of the Son and the age of the Holy Spirit.

When we speak of the "age of the Father," we emphasize creation in its aspect of open system, on its way to completion in the age of the Trinity, in eschatological glory. God the Father provides for his creation, created through his Son in the love of his Spirit. This providing means the maternal and paternal providence that watches over all created beings; it watches over creation to ensure it does not sink back into itself but remains directed toward the future fullness that is to come. The Father-and-Mother-God watches over human destiny, so often handed over to the diabolical forces of oppression by the strong of the weak; ensures that the impoverished do not completely lose their feeling for life and hope in a freedom without prisons. The heavenly Father-Mother shows endless patience in the face of human failures and shows his/her omnipotence by drawing good from evil and a more glorious life from death itself (cf Rom. 4:17). The universe is governed not by a judge, but by the Father-Mother of the beloved Son who with the Spirit of love makes up eternal goodness. It is the Father-Mother full of mercy who teaches us the parable of the prodigal son (Luke 15:11-32); it is the Father-protector of the poor who always takes their side and makes them the privileged recipients of revelation (cf Matt. 11:25-7).[3]

The "age of the Son" emphasizes the time of liberation of humanity corrupted by the abuse of human freedom, which blocks the achievement of humanity's first calling, which is to give glory to the Trinity. The Son reveals the filial, brotherly and sisterly nature of all beings, as expressions of the Father's love and wisdom in the Spirit. He became incarnate to bring life in all its abundance (cf John 10:10); by virtue of this mission, he sounds the knell for all systems that destroy life, oppress through their legalism, through subjecting some to others. The incarnate Son died as a protest against the slaveries imposed on God's sons and daughters. In himself and in the community of his followers he brought in the clearest anticipation of the Kingdom of freedom. He shows himself to creation as the great liberator, in that he liberates life from all the oppressions that beset it, setting it free primarily for us to serve one another as brothers and sisters, fully and freely. This liberation of his begins with the most needy, those who are historically oppressed by economic exploitation, political marginalization and religious and cultural alienation. The Son continually gives himself in the form of servant, of prophet-martyr, of crucified; his sacrificial love and forgiveness thereby gain the Kingdom of liberty and life for himself and his brothers and sisters. For this he was raised up and made Lord.

The "age of the Holy Spirit" continues and interiorizes—in individuals and social movements—the new life won by the Son. The Spirit makes the universe transparent to the Trinity; it fills all historical reality (cf John 2:28; Acts 2:16); the love of God is poured into our hearts by the Spirit (Rom. 5:5). In the Spirit we are reborn to our divine calling (cf John 3:3, 5). Through the Spirit, the Trinity dwells amongst human beings. The Spirit's presence in the community is shown by all sorts of gifts and services for the common good (1 Cor. 12); people's bodies become temples of the Spirit (1 Cor. 6:13-20). The new heaven and new earth are fruits of the Spirit which makes the universe ready to become the temple of the Trinity (cf Rev. 22:17; 21:3). The Spirit dwells in the heart of creation, which bears the seed of the renewal brought by the Son.

So to sum up we can say that the Trinity is in creation because the Father creates all things from the inexhaustible source of his life and love, through the Son in whom all things are enclosed as in an eternal prototype, by the power of the Holy Spirit which unites all things from their heart and leads them back to the Father. So we can praise and thank Father, Son and Holy Spirit. The age of the Father contains the age of the Son and of the Spirit; so the Three are equally adored and glorified. The age of the Son encloses the age of the Father and that of the Spirit, just as the age of the Spirit includes the age of the Father and that of the Son. This perichoretic inclusiveness makes honour and glory due to Father, Son and Holy Spirit forever and ever, since in their love and desire for communion they inundate the entire universe.

2. CREATION AS THE BODY OF THE TRINITY

The Trinity in creation seeks to insert creation in the Trinity. The providence of the Father, the liberation brought by the Son and the indwelling of the Holy Spirit are ordered to the transfiguration of the universe. This is the age of the Trinity. After the millions and millions of years since its origin, the development of its latent forces, the cosmic crisis in which the universe was subjected to the whole weight of human ignominy and perversity projected on to history and the structures of nature, creation will finally reach the age of the Trinity. Starting with the transforming power of the Spirit, through the liberating action of the Son, the universe will finally come to the Father. This is when the true history of creation with its trinitarian creator will begin. The whole mystery of creation will meet the mystery of the Father; all created beings will be confronted with their eternal prototype in the Son; the communion and union that binds all together will be seen as an expression of the Holy Spirit. Creation will be united forever to the mystery of life, love and communion of Father, Son and Holy Spirit.

Men will find themselves taken up, in the likeness of Jesus of Nazareth, into the Person of the Son.[4] Then they will everlastingly be adopted sons in the eternal Son, expressions of the love, wisdom and life of the Father. Women will find themselves taken up, in the likeness of Mary of Nazareth, into the Holy Spirit, and will reveal the eternal Father-Mother and the only-begotten Son; they will be united to the divine Three in love and tenderness so as to be united in tenderness and love to all created beings. The universe in the triune God will be the body of the Trinity, showing forth, in the limited form of creation, the full possibility of the communion of the divine Three.

This is the festival of the redeemed.[5] It is the celestial dance of the freed, the banquet of sons and daughters in the homeland and household of the Trinity, of Father, Son and Holy Spirit. In trinitized creation, we shall leap and sing, praise and love the Father, Son and Holy Spirit. And we shall be loved by them, praised by them, invited to dance and sing, sing and dance, dance and love forever and ever, amen.

CHAPTER XV

Amen:
The Whole Mystery
in a Nutshell

At the end of this journey in faith and thought, all that is left for us to say is a biblical *Amen*. *Amen* is a Hebrew expression of assent (cf Deut. 27:14ff; 1 Cor. 14:16) deriving from *amin,* which means believing in, accepting and handing oneself over to God and God's plan. *Amen* is humankind's response to the revelation of the triune God: So be it! How good that it should be so! Come, most holy Trinity, come! It is pronounced in an atmosphere of worship and reverence for the unspeakable mystery. But before finally praying *Amen* and falling respectfully silent in the face of the august Trinity, let us give reason one last turn, in an attempt to sum up in a number of propositions the basis of the trinitarian doctrine developed above:

1. By "God" in the Christian faith we should understand the Father, the Son and the Holy Spirit in communion with each other, in such a way that they form a one and only God.

2. In relation to the Trinity, doxology precedes theology. First we profess faith in Father, Son and Holy Spirit in prayer and praise (doxology). Then we reflect on how the divine Three are one single God in perichoretic communion between themselves (theology).

3. In theological reflection, the economic Trinity precedes the immanent Trinity. By "economic Trinity" we mean the manifestation (the self-communication in the case of the Son and Holy Spirit) of the divine Three in human history, whether together or separately, for the purposes of our salvation. By "immanent Trinity" we mean Father, Son and Holy Spirit in their inner, eternal life, considered in itself. Starting with the economic Trinity, we can glimpse something of the immanent Trinity. Only by referring to the incarnation of the Son and the sending of the Holy Spirit can we say that the economic Trinity is the immanent Trinity and vice-versa. Outside these historic, salvific events, the immanent Trinity remains an apophatic mystery.

(i) The Trinity is revealed in the life of Jesus of Nazareth and the manifestations of the Holy Spirit as these were witnessed by the communities of disciples and recorded by them in the New Testament. The triadic expressions found in the Old Testament have trinitarian meaning only on the basis of a Christian reading of them in the light of the New Testament.

(ii) As they appear in the New Testament, Father, Son and Holy Spirit are always mutually related and reciprocally implied. The Father sends the Son into the world; the Son feels himself of one being with the Father; the Holy Spirit is also sent into the world by the Father, at the Son's request. The Holy Spirit takes what is of the Son and enables us to know the Son; it teaches us to cry "Abba, Father."

(iii) The triadic formulas of the New Testament, especially that in Matthew 28:19, show a way of thinking that always associates the divine Three in the work of salvation. This and similar formulas helped in the later elaboration of trinitarian doctrine.

4. The central problem of trinitarian doctrine is this: how to express the fact that the divine Three are one God. Faith says: Father, Son and Holy Spirit are really three and distinct; but they are always related; they are one God. How to equate trinity in unity and unity in trinity?

5. Three solutions put forward are unacceptable to Christian faith because they fail either to preserve trinity, or to maintain unity, or to keep the equality between the Three.

(i)*Tritheism:* affirms the existence of three gods, separate and distinct, each eternal and infinite. This interpretation preserves trinity; however, besides containing serious philosophical errors, it destroys unity.

(ii) *Modalism:* Father, Son and Holy Spirit are three pseudonyms of the same, single God, or three modes of presentation (masks) of the same divine substance. God would be three only for us, not in God's self. This interpretation (Sabellianism) preserves unity, but abandons trinity.

(iii) *Subordinationism:* Strictly speaking, there is only one God—the Father. The Son and Holy Spirit receive their divine substance from the Father in subordinate form, so that they are not consubstantial with the Father but rather creatures adopted (*adoptionism*) to share in his life. This interpretation (Arianism) denies the equality of the Three, since the Son and the Holy Spirit are not fully divine.

JW's

6. The orthodox Christian reply is expressed in basically philosophical terms drawn from the prevailing culture and says: God is one nature in three Persons, or, God is one substance in three hypostases. The concepts *nature* and *substance* (or essence) denote unity in the Trinity; the concepts *person* and *hypostasis* safeguard trinity in unity.

7. There are three classic currents of thought that seek to deepen this expression of faith by elaborating a doctrine of the Trinity: Greek, Latin and modern.

(i) *Greek:* This starts from the Father, seen as source and origin of all divinity. There are two ways out from the Father: the Son by begetting and the Spirit by proceeding. The Father communicates his whole substance to the Son and the Holy Spirit, so both are consubstantial with the Father and equally God. The Father also forms the Persons of the Son and of the Holy Spirit in an eternal process. This current runs the risk of being understood as subordinationism.

(ii) *Latin:* This starts from the divine nature, which is equal in all three Persons. This divine nature is spiritual; this gives it an inner dynamic: absolute spirit is the Father, understanding is the Son and will is the Holy Spirit. The Three appropriate the same nature in distinct modes: the Father without beginning, the Son begotten by the Father, and the Spirit breathed out by the Father and the Son. The three are in the same nature, consubstantial, and therefore one God. This current runs the risk of being interpreted as modalism.

(iii) *Modern:* This starts from the Trinity of Persons—Father, Son and Holy Spirit. But the Three live in eternal perichoresis, being one in the others, through the others, with the others and for the others. The unity of the Trinity means the union of the three Persons by virtue of their perichoresis and eternal communion. Since this union is eternal and infinite, we can speak of one God. This interpretation runs the risk of being seen as tritheism. We follow this current: first, because it starts from the *datum* of faith—the existence of Father, Son and Holy Spirit as distinct and in communion; and second, because it allows a better understanding of the universe and human society as a process of communication, communion and union through the interpenetration of creatures with one another (perichoresis). This interpretation strengthens the cause of the oppressed struggling to liberate themselves so that there can be greater sharing and communion.

8. Trinitarian language is highly figurative and approximative, the more so in that the mystery of the Trinity is the deepest and most absolute mystery of the Christian faith. Expressions such as "cause" referring to the Father, "begetting" referring to the Son, and "breathing-out" applied to the Holy Spirit, like "processions," "mission," "nature" and "persons" are analogical or descriptive and do not claim to be causal explanations in the philosophical sense. The inner meaning of such expressions shows the diversity that exists in the divine reality on one hand, and the communion on the other. We use terminology hallowed by tradition and also biblical terminology because they are less ambiguous and because they are used by some modern theologians. Some of those terms are: revelation, acceptance, communion.

9. The conceptual language of devout reason is not the only means of access to the mystery of the Trinity. The church has also developed the symbolic language of imagery. This emphasizes the significance the Trinity has for human existence, particularly in its longing for wholeness. This wholeness is the mystery of the Trinity. It is best expressed through symbols which spring from the depths of the individual and collective unconscious, or from humanity's common religious stock. Symbolic language does not replace conceptual language, but is basic to the formation of religious attitudes.

10. Humanity, male and female, was created in the image and likeness of the triune God. Male and female find their ultimate raison d'être in the mystery of trinitarian communion. Though the

Trinity is trans-sexual, we can use male and female forms in speaking of the divine Persons. So we can say "maternal God-Father" and "paternal God-Mother."

11. The *Filioque* question (the Holy Spirit breathed out by the Father and the Son, or through the Son) is bound up with the theological sensitivity of the Eastern church vis-à-vis the Western, as is a certain type of terminology adopted by one or the other (the Father as source or principle of all divinity—Eastern; or the Son as sourced source—Western). Another theological strand starting from the perichoresis of the divine Persons would have not only *Filioque,* but *Spirituque* and *Patreque* as well, since in the Trinity everything is triadic.

12. By virtue of perichoresis, everything in the Trinity is trinitarian—shared by each of the divine Persons. This does not preclude there being actions proper to each of the Persons, through which the property of each person is shown.

(i) The proper action of the Father is creation. In revealing himself to the Son in the Spirit, the Father projects all creatable beings as expressions of himself, of the Son and of the Holy Spirit. Once created, all beings express the mystery of the Father, have a filial nature (since they come from the Father), a brotherly and sisterly nature (since they are created in the Son) and a "spiritual" nature (meaning full of meaning, of dynamism, since they were created by the power of the Holy Spirit).

(ii) The action proper to the Son is the incarnation in Jesus of Nazareth, through which he divinizes all creation and redeems it from sin. Through the Son, maleness shares in divinity.

(iii) The action proper to the Holy Spirit is the "pneumatization" through which created life is inserted into the mystery of the life of the Trinity, and redeemed from all threat of death. Through the Holy Spirit, femaleness is introduced into the divine mystery.

13. From the perichoresis-communion of the three divine Persons derive impulses to liberation: of each and every human person, of society, of the church and of the poor, in the double —critical and constructive—sense. *Human beings* are called to rise above all mechanisms of egoism and live their vocation of communion. *Society* offends the Trinity by organizing itself on a basis of inequality and honours it the more it favours sharing and communion for all, thereby bringing about justice and equality for all. The *church* is more the sacrament of trinitarian communion the more it reduces inequalities between Christians and between the various ministries in it, and the more it understands and practises unity as co-existence in diversity. The *poor* reject their impoverishment as sin against trinitarian communion and see the inter-relatedness of the divine "Differents" as the model for a human society based on mutual collaboration—all on an equal footing—and based on individual differences; that society's structures would be humane, open, just and egalitarian.

14. The universe exists in order to manifest the abundance of divine communion. The final meaning of all that is created is to allow the divine Persons to communicate themselves. So in the eschatological fullness, the universe—in the mode proper to each creature, culminating in man and woman in the likeness of Jesus of Nazareth and Mary—will be inserted into the very communion of Father, Son and Holy Spirit. Then the Trinity will be all in all.

15. The Holy Trinity is a sacramental mystery. As *sacramental,* it can be understood progressively, as the Trinity communicates itself and the understanding heart assimilates it. As *mystery* it will always remain the Unknown in all understanding, since the mystery is the Father himself, the Son himself and the Spirit itself. And the mystery will last for all eternity.

Glossary

ACTION—*ad extra:* Describes the actions of the Trinity directed outside the circle of the Trinity, such as creation, revelation, salvation of human beings.

ACTION—*ad intra:* Describes intra-trinitarian actions, within the circle of the Trinity, such as the begetting of the Son and breathing-out of the Holy Spirit.

ACTION—appropriated: An action attributed to one of the divine Persons, though carried out jointly by the Three; it is attributed to one Person because of the affinity of that action to the properties of that Person. So, creation is attributed to the Father, redemption to the Son and sanctification to the Spirit.

ACTION—proper: An action specific to a particular Person, such as the incarnation of the Son or the coming of the Holy Spirit on Mary at the moment of Jesus' conception.

AFFIRMATION—essential: An affirmation based on the divine essence, equal and unique in the three Persons. E.g.: stating that God is merciful, infinite, eternal, meaning that the divine essence is to be merciful, infinite, eternal.

AFFIRMATION—notional: An affirmation based only on the Persons in their distinction one from another. There are four: the Father begets, the Son is begotten, the Father and the Son (or the Father through the Son) breathe out the Holy Spirit, the Spirit is breathed out by the Father and the Son (or through the Son).

ANAMNESIS: Literally means "memorial"; the calling to mind, after the consecration of the bread and wine, of the passion, death, resurrection and ascension of Christ.

ANAPHORA: Literally means "offering"; the central part of the eucharistic celebration, including consecration, anamnesis and communion.

APOPHATIC: From the Greek meaning "negative": the attitude the theologian must take to the divine mystery—after saying all that can be said, keeping a respectful silence. We speak of an "apophatic theology," meaning one that ends in the silence of veneration and adoration.

ARCHĒ: Greek expression for the fact that the Father is origin, source and sole cause in the begetting of the Son and the breathing-out of the Holy Spirit.

ARIANISM: The heresy propagated by Arius (250-336), a priest of Alexandria. Arius affirmed subordinationism: the Son and the Holy Spirit are subordinate to the Father; they are sublime creatures, created before the universe, but they are not God. Subordinationism is also adoptionist: the Son was adopted as Son through the grace of the Father, but he does not share the same nature as the Father.

BREATHING-OUT: The act by which the Father, together with the Son, makes the person of the Holy Spirit proceed (according to Latin theology) as from one source. The Greeks make the Spirit proceed only from the Father of the Son or from the Father through the Son.

CHARISM: From Greek meaning "grace"; it is a gift or facility given by the Spirit to an individual for the sake of the common good.

CIRCUMINCESSION: The active interpenetration of the divine Persons between themselves, due to the eternal communion between them. *See* "Perichoresis."

CIRCUMINSESSION: The being or dwelling of one Person in another, since each divine Person exists only in the others, with the others, through the others and for the others. *See* "Perichoresis."

DOXOLOGY: Formula of praise, from Greek *doxa.* Generally appears at the end of prayers, giving thanks to the Father through the Son in the unity of the Holy Spirit.

ECONOMY: *Oeconomia:* organization, distribution. The various phases of the working-out of God's plan in history, or of the progressive revelation of God's self by God. In relation to the Trinity, it means the order of procession in relation to the Father: first comes the Son, then the Holy Spirit.

EK: Greek particle corresponding to Latin *ex* or *de,* meaning the proceeding of one divine Person from another. So, the Son is begotten by (*ek, ex* or *de*) the Father; the Holy Spirit proceeds *from* the Father and *from* the Son (in Latin theology).

EKPOREUSIS: Greek term designating the proceeding of the Holy Spirit from the Father, who is always Father of the Son; corresponds to Latin *spiratio.*

EPICLESIS: Celebration in which the Holy Spirit is invoked, used particularly of the part of the eucharistic prayer preceding the consecration.

ESSENCE—divine: What constitutes the triune God, divinity: being, love, goodness, truth, reciprocal communion, in absolute and eternal form. *See* "Nature," "Substance."

FILIOQUE: Literally "and from the Son"; doctrine by which the Spirit proceeds from the Father *and from* the Son as from one source. This doctrinal interpretation is sometimes known as "Filioquism"; it is common among Latin theologians.

GENNĒSIS: Greek term expressing the begetting of the Son by the Father.

GESTALT—relational: Term used by the German theologian Jürgen Moltmann to express the contribution made by the Son to the breathing-out of the Spirit together with the Father: the person of the Holy Spirit comes from the Father, while the specific configuration (*Gestalt*) of the person of the Holy Spirit derives from the Son. "Relational" because the Persons are always turned to one another and are within one another.

HOMOIOUSIOS: Literally "of like nature"; a heresy which held that the Son was not equal to the Father, but only like the Father in nature.

HOMOOUSIOS: Literally "of the same or equal nature"; the Son and Holy Spirit are said to have one same and equal nature with the Father; the Persons are consubstantial.

HYPOSTASIS: Greek term used to denote a divine Person. *See* "Person" and "*Prosopon*."

KENŌSIS: Greek term meaning "annihilation" or "emptying"; the way in which the divine Persons of the Son and Holy Spirit chose to communicate themselves in history. Opposite to *doxa,* which indicates the way of glory.

KOINŌNIA: Greek equivalent of Latin *communio;* the proper way persons, including the divine Persons, relate one to another.

MISSION: In trinitarian theology means the self-communication of the Person of the Son to the human nature of Jesus of Nazareth, and of the Holy Spirit to the just, to Mary and to the church. It implies the enthronement of humanity in the bosom of the Trinity.

MODALISM: Heretical doctrine in which the Trinity consists of three human ways of regarding the one and only God, or three ways (masks) in which this one and only God is revealed to human beings; God would not be a Trinity within God's self, but strictly one and unique.

MONARCHIANISM: Denial of the Trinity in the name of a rigid monotheism.

MONARCHY: In trinitarian language, implies the single causality of the Father; the Father alone begets the Son and, being Father of the Son, breathes out the Holy Spirit: a typical expression of Greek Orthodox theology.

MONOTHEISM: The affirmation of the existence of a one and only God. The Old Testament professes a pre-trinitarian monotheism, previous to the revelation of the Trinity. There can also, after the revelation of the mystery of the Trinity, be an a-trinitarian monotheism: speaking of God without taking the Trinity of Persons into account, as though God were a single reality and existed only in substance. There is also trinitarian monotheism, in which God is one and only because of the same substance existing in Father, Son and Holy Spirit, or because of the eternal communion and perichoresis that have always existed between the three Persons.

MYSTERY: In the strict sense means the reality of the Holy Trinity being inaccessible to human reason; even once it has been communicated, it can be known incompletely without ever being fully grasped by the human mind. The triune God is a mystery, not only to the human mind, but as a concept in itself, since the Trinity is essentially infinite and eternal. As it affects salvation in history, the concept of the triune God is a sacramental mystery, a mystery communicated by the actions and words of Jesus and the actions of the Holy Spirit in the church community and in human history.

NATURE—divine: The one and only divine substance in each of the three Persons; it concerns the unity or union in God.

NOTION: the characteristics proper to each of the Persons, which differentiate them one from the others: the fatherhood and unoriginatedness of the Father, the sonship of the Son, the breathing-out by the Father and the Son, the being breathed out by the Holy Spirit. There are therefore five notions.

PATREQUE: Literally "and by the Father"; in the Trinity, all relationships are triadic: the Son relates to the Holy Spirit together with the Father or through the Father; in the same way, the Holy Spirit loves the Son through and together with the Father and so on.

PĒGĒ: Greek expression designating the Father as single and infinite *source* from which the Son and the Holy Spirit both spring.

PERICHORESIS: Greek term meaning literally that one Person contains the other two (static sense) or that each Person interpenetrates the others, and so reciprocally (active sense). The derived adjective "perichoretic" defines the type of communion obtaining between the divine Persons. *See* "Circumincession" and "Circuminsession."

PERSON: In trinitarian language means what is distinct in God: the individuality of each Person, existing simultaneously in and for that Person's self and in eternal communion with the other two. See "Hypostasis" and "Substance."

PROCESSION: The derivation of one Person from another, but consubstantially, in the unity of one same nature, substance, essence or divinity.

PROSOPON: Literally means mask or faceguard; in trinitarian theology a Greek word used to designate the individuality of a Person. Synonymous with "hypostasis." *See* "Person."

RELATIONSHIP: In trinitarian language means the ordering of one Person to the others, or the eternal communion between the divine Three. There are four relationships: fatherhood, sonship, breathing-out and being breathed out.

SABELLIANISM: The heresy of Sabellius (early second century in Rome), also called modalism (q.v.). The Son and the Spirit would be simply modes of manifestation of the divinity, not distinct Persons.

SPIRITUQUE: Literally "and by the Spirit"; as relationships in the Trinity are always triadic, the Father is said to beget the Son together with the Spirit, the Son to recognize the Father together with the Spirit.

SUBSISTENCE: One of the synonyms of "Person" or "hypostasis"; since nothing in the Trinity is accidental, the relationships between the Persons are said to be subsistent; each Person is considered as a subsistent relationship.

SUBSTANCE: In the context of the Trinity denotes what unites in God and is identical in each of the Persons. *See* "Essence" and "Nature."

SYMBOL: Used technically in classical theology to denote the formularies in which the church officially summed up its belief: synonym of "Creed."

THEOGONY: Process by which divinity arises, or explanation of the mystery of the Trinity in such a way as to give the impression that the Persons are not co-eternal and co-equal, but produced one by another.

THEOLOGY: In the context of the Trinity denotes the Trinity in itself, prescinding from its manifestation in history; its "theology" is thereby opposed to its "economy" (q.v.).

TRIAD: From Greek *trias,* used to designate the Trinity of Persons.

TRINITY—economic: The Trinity as it reveals itself in the history of humanity and acts with a view to our participation in the communion of the Trinity.

TRINITY—immanent: The Trinity considered in itself, in its eternity and perichoretic communion between Father, Son and Holy Spirit.

UNORIGINATEDNESS: The exclusive property of the Father: being neither born nor derived from anyone; the unsourced source.

Notes

I. IN THE BEGINNING IS COMMUNION

1. Cf R. Schulte, "La préparation de la révélation trinitaire," in *Mysterium Salutis*, vol. 5 (Paris, 1970), pp. 71–119; many references in J. Brinktrine, *Von der göttlichen Trinität*, vol. 2 of *Die Lehre von Gott* (Paderborn, 1954), pp. 183–212; B. de Margerie, *La Trinité chrétienne dans l'histoire* (Paris, 1975), pp. 24ff: Eng. trans., *The Christian Trinity in History* (Still River, Mass., and Leominster, 1982).

2. Cf S. Arce Martínez, "El desafío del Dios trinitario de la Iglesia," *La teología como desafío* (Havana, 1980)—one of the first studies from Latin America on the Trinity; it views the Trinity in the light of the Latin American and socialist reality of Cuba.

3. Cf D. Barbé, "A Trindade e a política," in *A graça e o poder* (São Paulo, 1983), pp. 76–84: Eng. trans., *Grace and Power* (Maryknoll, N.Y., 1987), pp. 41–61.

4. R. Panikkar, *The Trinity and the Religious Experience of Man* (Maryknoll, N.Y., and London, 1973), esp. pp. 9–39; J. Moltmann, *Trinität und Reich Gottes* (Munich, 1980), pp. 144–68: Eng. trans., *The Trinity and the Kingdom of God* (London and San Francisco, 1981); J. Daniélou, *Théologie du judéo-christianisme* (Paris, 1958), pp. 169–96: Eng. trans., *The Theology of Jewish Christianity* (London and Chicago, 1966); see also note 7, below.

5. Cf G. Gutiérrez, *Hablar de Dios desde el sufrimiento del inocente: Una reflexión sobre el Libro de Job* (Lima, 1986): Eng. trans., *On Job: God-Talk and the Suffering of the Innocent* (Maryknoll, N.Y., 1987).

6. I. Kant, *Der Streit der Fakultäten*, vol. 8 (Berlin, 1917), pp. 38–9.

7. Cf Y. Congar, "Classical Political Monotheism and the Trinity," *Concilium* 143 (1981), pp. 31–6; F. Dvornik, *Early Christian and Byzantine Political Philosophy: Origins and Backgrounds*, 2 vols. (Washington, D.C., 1966); E. Peterson, "Der Monotheismus als politisches Problem," in *Theologische Traktate* (Munich, 1951), pp. 45–149; Moltmann, *Trinität*, pp. 207–20.

8. Moltmann quotes the example of political-religious absolutism provided by Genghis Khan, who said: "In heaven there is but one God, and on earth but one Lord, Genghis Khan, the son of God" ("The Inviting Unity of the Triune God," *Concilium* 177 [1985], pp. 50–58).

9. The social paternalism and political patriarchalism of Latin American societies find a permanent ideological support in a certain type of Christian preaching of God as one Lord (celestial boss). Donoso Cortés, part of this anti-democratic tradition, taught: "All for the people, but nothing by the people." Abraham Lincoln, on the other hand, said: "Government . . . by the people, and for the people."

10. Cf Y. Congar, *L'ecclésiologie du Haut-Moyen-Age* (Paris, 1978), pp. 388–9.

11. Cf the investigations by F. Mayr, "Trinitätstheologie und theologische Anthropologie," *Zeitschrift für Theologie und Kirche* 68 (1971), pp. 427–77; idem, "Die Einseitigkeit der traditionellen Gotteslehre," in *Erfahrung und Theologie des Heiligen Geistes*, ed. C. Heitmann and H. Mühlen (Munich, 1974), pp. 239–72.

II. HOW THE HOLY TRINITY WAS REVEALED TO US

1. Irenaeus, *Adv. Haer.* V, 6,1. *Sources Chrétiennes,* 153, pp. 72–81.

2. Cf A. Hamman, "La Trinité dans la liturgie et la vie chrétienne," in *Mysterium Salutis*, vol. 5 (Paris, 1970), pp. 185–204.

3. Justin, *Apologia* I, 67.

4. Cf F. J. Schierse, "La révélation de la Trinité dans le Nouveau Testament," in *Mysterium Salutis*, vol. 5 (Paris, 1970), pp. 121–83; A. Wainwright, *The Trinity in the New Testament* (London, 1962); various, *La Trinidad en la Biblia* (Salamanca, 1973); F. Pastor, "Kerygma bíblico e ortodoxia trinitária," *Semântica do mistério* (São Paulo, 1982), pp. 5–22.

5. Cf W. Marchel, "Abba, Père," *Anal. Bibl.* 19 (Rome, 1966); L. Boff, *The Lord's Prayer: The Prayer of Integral Liberation* (Maryknoll, N.Y., 1985).

6. Cf Y. Congar, *I Believe in the Holy Spirit* (New York and London, 1983).

7. Cf H. Echegaray, *The Practice of Jesus* (Maryknoll, N.Y., and Melbourne, 1984); C. Duquoc, *Dieu différent: Essai sur la symbolique trinitaire* (Paris, 1977), pp. 43–60.

8. For details of this analysis, cf Schierse, "La révélation."

9. Ibid.

10. Detailed analysis in Wainwright, *The Trinity*.

11. Cf J. Kelly, *Early Christian Creeds* (London, 1972), pp. 23ff.

12. Cf R. Schulte, "La préparation de la révélation trinitaire," in *Myste-*

rium Salutis, vol. 5 (Paris, 1970), pp. 71–119; R. Panikkar, *The Trinity and the Religious Experience of Man* (Maryknoll, N.Y., and London, 1973), pp. 9ff.

13. The plural formula in Gen. 1:26: "Let *us* make man in our image and likeness" (cf 3:22; 11:17; Isa. 6:8) is not trinitarian; some would call it a royal plural, others a "deliberative" plural: God is deliberating with himself; the plural is merely stylistic. The triple "Holy" of the seraphim in Isa. 6 is not trinitarian either; the threefold repetition is a stylistic device for emphasizing the transcendence and lordship of God. Despite this, these passages were very significant for the Fathers in their working out of trinitarian doctrine.

14. See my little essay "O dogma da Santíssima Trindade na Sagrada Escritura," *Sponsa Christi* 19 (1965), pp. 264–9.

III. EFFORTS AT UNDERSTANDING THE TRUTH OF THE TRINITY

1. See the main Creeds collected in Denzinger-Schönmetzer (DS), *Enchiridion Symbolorum, definitionum et declarationum de rebus fidei et morum*, 36th ed. (Freiburg, Rome, Barcelona, 1976), nos. 1–76.

2. For this period see various histories of dogma, especially: L. Scheffczyk, "L'élaboration du dogme dans le Christianisme primitif," *Mysterium Salutis*, vol. 5 (Paris, 1970), pp. 211–300; J. Lebreton, *Histoire du dogme de la Trinité*, 2 vols. (Paris, 1927–8); Th. de Régnon, *Etudes de théologie positive sur la Sainte Trinité*, 4 vols. (Paris, 1892–8); A. Adam, *Lehrbuch der Dogmengeschichte,* vol. 1 (Gütersloh, 1965); B. de Margerie, *La Trinité chrétienne dans l'histoire* (Paris, 1975): Eng. trans., *The Christian Trinity in History* (Still River, Mass., and Leominster, 1982); G. Prestige, *God in Patristic Thought* (London, 1952); E. Hoornaert, *A memória do povo cristão* (Petrópolis, 1986): Eng. trans. in preparation for this series.

3. For their defence of the Trinity against both monotheism and polytheism, Christians were sometimes accused of atheism; hence the protest of Athenagoras, a second-century apologist: "Who would not be astonished at hearing those who profess one God the Father, one Son of God, one Holy Spirit, who show their power in unity and their distinction in order, called atheists?" (*Legatio pro christianis* 10: W. Schoedel [ed.] [Oxford, 1972], pp. 22ff).

4. We would not go as far as E. Bloch, who wrote: "To think is to transgress. The best thing about religion is that it creates heretics" (*Atheismus in Christentum* [Frankfurt, 1968], p. 15). Such an attitude can be applied only to the advance of knowledge without regard for the faith of the faithful.

5. Cf other examples in Scheffczyk, "L'élaboration."

6. A. Harnack, *Dogmensgeschichte*, vol. 1 (Tübingen, 1909), pp. 250ff, regards the Gnostics as the first Christian theologians (though heretical); they were also the first to reflect on the Trinity: cf A. Orbe, *Hacia la primera teología de la procesión del Verbo*, I/1 (Rome, 1958), p. 4; cf de Margerie, *Trinité*, pp. 102–4. But what they developed was a theogony and a cosmogony rather than a genuine doctrine of the Trinity, as can be seen from the Christian theologians who opposed them, such as Irenaeus and Tertullian.

7. The texts of the period, with a modern bibliography, are given in F. Pastor, *Semântica do mistério* (São Paulo, 1982), pp. 47–80, esp. 51–54.

8. See the interesting study by J. Lebreton, "Le désaccord de la foi populaire et de la théologie savante dans l'Eglise chrétienne du IIIme siècle," *Rev. Hist. Ecc.* 19 (1923), pp. 481-506; 20 (1924), pp. 5–37.

9. Roscellinus Compiègne (d. 1125) also thought of the divine Persons as three autonomous natures, "like three souls or three angels" (cf Anselm of Canterbury, *De incarnatione Verbi* 1); in regard to their nature, Gilbert of Poitiers (d. 1154) viewed the Persons as so autonomous that the result was a quaternity. He was condemned by the Council of Rheims in 1148 (DS 745). See G. di Napoli, "La teologia trinitaria di Gioacchino da Fiore," *Divinitas* 23 (1979), pp. 281ff.

10. There is a good summary of Irenaeus's trinitarian theology in C. Folch Gomes, *A doutrina da Trindade eterna: O significado da expresão "três pessoas"* (Rio de Janeiro, 1979), pp. 219-31.

11. See note 6, above.

12. Irenaeus, *Demonstratio* 6, *Sources Chrétiennes*, 62 (Paris, 1959), pp. 39–40.

13. Idem, *Adv. Haer.* II, 25, 3.

14. Idem, *Adv. Haer.* IV, 14, 1.

15. Idem, *Epid.* 10.

16. Cf J. Daniélou, *Origène* (Paris, 1948), pp. 243–58: Eng. trans. in *The Gospel Message and Hellenistic Culture* (London and Pennsylvania, 1973); there is also a good summary in J. Barbel, *Der Gott Jesu im Glauben der Kirche* (Aschaffenburg, 1976), pp. 65-8.

17. Origen, *Contra Celsum* 8, 12; *Com. in Johan.* 2, 10, 75.

18. Other similar formulations are: Tertullian, *De pudicitia* 21: "tres personae unius divinitatis"; idem, *Adv. Prax.* 25: "tres unum sunt, non unus"; ibid. 2: "tres autem gradu . . . forma . . . specie, unius autem substantiae et unius status et unius potestatis."

19. See the following studies: J. Moingt, *Théologie trinitaire de Tertullien*, vols. 1-3 (Paris, 1966); Th. Verhoeven, *Studien over Tertullianus' "Adversus Praxean"* (Amsterdam, 1948).

20. Tertullian, *Adv. Prax* 2: CCL 2, 1161.

21. Cf M. Gomes Mourão de Castro, *Die Trinitätslehre des hl. Gregor*

von Nyssa (Freiburg, 1938); A. Ritter, *Das Konzil von Konstantinopel und sein Symbol* (Göttingen, 1965).

22. Gregory Nazianzen, *Or. theol.* V, 5: *PG* 36, 137.

23. Augustine, *De Trinitate* I, 6, 10 and 11; cf O. du Roy, *Intelligence de la foi en la Trinité selon Augustin* (Paris, 1966).

24. *De Trin.* VII, 6, 12; XV, 4, 6.

25. Ibid. IX.

26. Ibid. X, 14–15.

27. Ibid. VII, 6, 11.

28. Ibid. V and VII.

29. Ibid. VIII, 8, 12.

30. Cf Thomas Aquinas, *ST* I, q. 2, prol.; cf P. Vanier, *Théologie trinitaire chez St. Thomas d'Aquin* (Paris, 1953); F. Bourassa, "Note sur la traité de la Trinité dans la Somme Théologique de St. Thomas," *Science et Esprit* 27 (1975), pp. 187ff.

31. Thomas Aquinas, *ST* I, q. 28, a. 2.

32. Idem, *De potentia* q. 9, a. 4.

33. Tertullian, *Adv. Prax.* 3: *PL* 2, 180.

34. For this whole question, see Folch Gomes, *A doutrina*, which is entirely devoted to an examination of what "three Persons" meant in classical times and means in modern thought. Cf also R. Cantalamessa, "The Evolution of the Concept of a Personal God in Christian Spirituality," *Concilium* 103 (1977), pp. 57–66; Prestige, *God*, pp. 157–68.

35. The replacement of *hypostasis* by *ousia* was facilitated by the Council of Nicaea, which had defined Christ as being of the same *ousia* as the Father (*homoousios*), that is, of the same nature and essence as the Father.

36. At the Synod of Alexandria in 362, at which St Athanasius presided, the formula *treis hypostaseis* was declared legitimate. Its meaning was also clarified: *treis hypostaseis* are not synonymous with *treis ousiai* (three essences) since this would be tritheism (three gods). If *hypostasis* is still regarded as synonymous with *ousia*, we should say: in God there is only one *hypostasis* or *ousia* (nature, substance or essence).

37. Augustine, *De. Trin.* V, 9, 10; cf VII, 6, 11.

38. Cf C. Andresen, "Zur Entstehung und Geschichte des trinitarischen Personenbegriffes," *Zf NT Wiss.* 52 (1961), pp. 1–39; B. Studer, "Zur Entwicklung der patristischen Trinitätslehre," *Th. und Glaube* 74 (1984), pp. 81–93, which is a favourable critique of Andresen.

IV. DOGMATIC UNDERSTANDING OF THE TRINITY

1. Augustine, *De Trinitate*, I, 6, 12; XV, 4, 6. Cf F. Bourassa, "Théologie trinitaire chez St. Augustin," *Gregorianum* 58 (1977), pp. 675–725.

2. John Damascene, *De fide orthodoxa* I, 12: *PG* 94, 849.

3. Ibid., 832–3.

4. Cf P. Evdokimov, *L'Esprit Saint dans la tradition orthodoxe* (Paris, 1969), p. 56.

5. *The Pope Speaks* 17 (1972), pp. 66–7.

6. See St Augustine's wise warning, valid for all who deal with this august mystery: "There is no matter concerning which error is more dangerous, investigation more arduous and discovery more fruitful" (*De Trin.* I, 3, 5). St Thomas advises approaching this treatise on the Trinity "with caution and modesty" (*ST* I, q. 31, a. 2).

7. This classification, with its attendant simplification, was first suggested by Th. de Régnon, *Etudes de théologie positive sur la Sainte Trinité*, vol. 1 (Paris, 1892), pp. 335–40, 428–35. Cf also X. Pikaza, "Trinidad y ontología en torno al planteamiento sistemático del misterio trinitario," *Estudios Trinitarios* 8 (1974), pp. 189–236, esp. 200–205; H. Barré, *Trinité que j'adore* (Paris, 1965), pp. 21–54.

8. For a more detailed explanation of what is a formal distinction, particularly in Duns Scotus, and its application to the Trinity, see M. Schmaus, *Der Glaube der Kirche*, vol. 1 (Munich, 1969), pp. 577ff: Eng. trans., *Dogma*, 6 vols. (London and New York, 1968–77).

9. Gregory Nazianzen, *Oratio* 42, 15: *PG* 36, 476.

10. John Damascene, *De fide orthodoxa* 18: *PG* 94, 828.

11. Basil, *Tract. de Spiritu Sancto* 17, *Sources Chrétiennes* (Paris, 1945), pp. 190ff.

12. Evdokimov, *L'Esprit Saint*, p. 44.

13. Gregory Nazianzen, *Oratio* 40: *PG* 36, 4l7B, 4l9B.

14. John Damascene, *De fide* I, 8: *PG* 94, 828–9.

15. God is God not through possessing divinity as Peter is human through possessing humanity, which is also in John and Mary, and so on. God is God by very divinity (*Deus est ipsa deitas: Deus est quod habet*). The divine substance exists in absolute numerical unity (uniqueness); it therefore exists once only, though under three real modes of appropriation or subsistence, which are the three divine Persons.

16. The scholastics expressed this as : *indivisum in se, divisum ab omni alio*; meaning an individual existing in itself and distinct from all others.

17. Augustine, *De Trin.* V, 9, 10.

18. Ibid. VII, 4, 7.

19. Cf F. Bourassa, "Personne et conscience en théologie trinitaire," *Gregorianum* 55 (1974), pp. 471–93, 677–719; idem, "Sur la Trinité: Dogme et théologie," *Science et Esprit* 24 (1972), pp. 257–84; there is a good summary of the scholastic position in C. Folch Gomes, *A doutrina da Trindaae eterna* (Rio de Janeiro, 1979), pp. 310–70.

20. Augustine, *De Trin*. VII, 4, 9. Augustine takes full cognizance of the problem and difficulties inherent in using the term "person" for the three names (Father, Son and Holy Spirit). Each Person is a unique being. How to apply a common noun—person—to Father, Son and Holy Spirit? "We merely have to admit," he says "that these expressions are born of the need to face up better to the errors of the heretics."

21. The breathing-out by the Father and the Son, which makes the Spirit proceed, constitutes a property of the Father and the Son. It also constitutes an opposition in relation to the third Person. Through the trinitarian logic of relationships it should constitute a personality in itself. But this does not happen because breathing-out is not conceived as an origin unique to the Holy Spirit (the Son also receives being an origin from the Father). Being breathed out is the property of the Holy Spirit, and does not produce another person because the Holy Spirit constitutes the union between the Father and the Son, thus closing the trinitarian circle. This being the case, we must say: there are only three relationships that constitute persons: fatherhood, sonship, and being breathed out.

22. Anselm, "In Deo omnia sunt unum, ubi non obviat relationis oppositio," *De processione Spiritus Sancti* 2. The Council of Florence adopted this axiom (DS 1330). For a study of the meaning and origin of this axiom, see M. Schmaus, *Dogma*, vol. 1 (London and New York, 1968); H. Mühlen, "Person und Appropriation. Zum Verständnis des Axioms: 'In Deo omnia . . . ' ," *Münchener ThZ* 16 (1965), pp. 37–57.

23. This aspect will be examined in detail in ch. 7.

24. See "Dieu Trinité," in *Mysterium Salutis*, vol. 5, pp. 13–40; there is a critical analysis of the application and limits of this axiom in W. Kasper, *Der Gott Jesu Christi* (Mainz, 1982), pp. 333–7: Eng. trans., *The God of Jesus Christ* (London and New York, 1984).

V. THE TRINITY IN THEOLOGICAL IMAGERY

1. St Augustine, who was responsible for the great anthropological image of the Trinity, was very conscious that we are never dealing with analogical truths, but with approximate images, in which what differs is greater than what approximates (cf *Sermo*. 52, 10, 23: *PL* 38, 364).

2. Gregory of Nyssa, *Oratio catechetica magna* 2, 1; cf A. Hamman, "La Trinidad en la catequesis de los padres griegos," *La Trinidad en la catequesis* (Salamanca, 1978), pp. 87–101.

3. Ignatius of Antioch, *Ad Ephesios* 9, 39–40.

4. For this section see A. Hamman, "La Trinité," in *Mysterium Salutis*, vol. 5 (Paris, 1970), pp. 185–204.

5. Augustine, *De Trin*. IX–XV. See the classic study by M. Schmaus,

Die psychologische Trinitätslehre des hl. Augustinus (Münster, 1927), and the corrective criticism of this in A. Turrado, "Trinidad," in *Gran Enciclopedia Rialp* 22 (Madrid, 1975), pp. 775–82; B. de Margerie, *La Trinité chrétienne dans l'histoire* (Paris, 1975), pp. 397–417: Eng. trans., *The Christian Trinity in History* (Still River, Mass., and Leominster, 1982); A. van den Berg, "A SS. Trindade e a existência humana," *Rev. Ecl. Bras.* 33 (1971), pp. 629–48; 36 (1976), pp. 323–46; M. Sciacca, "Trinité et unité de l'esprit," *Augustinus Magister*, vol. 1 (Paris, 1954), pp. 521–33.

6. For a detailed study of this image see de Margerie, *La Trinité*, pp. 368–90.

7. Tertullian, *De baptismo* VI, 1 CCL: 1, 282.

8. Cf Y. Congar, "La Tri-unité de Dieu et L'Eglise," *La Vie Spirituelle* 604 (1974), pp. 687–703; B. Forte, *La Chiesa icona della Trinità* (Brescia, 1984), pp. 27–59.

9. Cf C. Kaliba, *Die Welt als Gleichnis des dreieinigen Gottes* (Salzburg, 1952), pp. 165–99.

10. John Damascene, *De fide orthodoxa* IV, 16: *PG* 44, 1172; Thomas Aquinas, *ST* III, q. 25, a.3, ad 1.

11. See the criticisms by Karl Barth of the doctrine of *Vestigium Trinitatis* in *Church Dogmatics* I/1 (Edinburgh, 1969), pp. 383–99.

VI. THE DOCTRINE OF THE TRINITY IN A CHANGED CULTURAL SITUATION

1. There are classified bibliographies in C. Folch Gomes, *A doutrina da Trindade eterna* (Rio de Janeiro, 1979), pp. 15–162, 310–52; B. Grom and J. Guerrero, *El anuncio del Dios cristiano* (Salamanca, 1979), pp. 34–57; J.-M. Alonso, "La reflexión teológica trinitaria hoy," *La Trinidad hoy* (Salamanca, 1984), pp. 165–202; B. de Margerie, *La Trinité chrétienne dans l'histoire* (Paris, 1975), pp. 335–420; C. Welch, *The Trinity in Contemporary Theology* (London, 1953); W. Breuning, "Trinitätslehre," *Bilanz der Theologie* 3 (Freiburg, 1970), pp. 21–36; U. Ruh, "Das unterscheidend Christliche in der Gottesfrage," *Herderkorrespondenz* 36 (1982), pp. 187–92; various, *Trinidad y vida cristiana* (Salamanca, 1979); B. Forte, *Trinità come storia* (Turin, 1985), pp. 68–88.

2. P. Schoonenberg, "Trinität—der vollendete Bund," *Orientierung* 37 (1973), pp. 115–7.

3. K. Rahner, "Dieu Trinité: Fondament transcendant de l'histoire du salut," *Mysterium Salutis*, vol. 6 (Paris, 1970), pp. 13–140.

4. To name only some of the best-known in trinitarian studies: C. Folch Gomes, R. Guardini, M. Schmaus, B. Lonergan, F. Bourassa, H. Mühlen, G. Lafont, G. Ebeling, E. Brunner.

5. See three learned studies by F. Bourassa, "Personne et conscience en

théologie trinitaire," *Gregorianum* 55 (1974), pp. 471–93; "Sur la Trinité: Dogme et théologie," *Science et Esprit* 24 (1972), pp. 257–84; *Questions de théologie trinitaire* (Rome, 1970).

6. B. Lonergan, *Divinarum personarum conceptio analogica* (Rome, 1956), p. 165.

7. Cf R. Garrigou-Lagrange, "Le clair-obscur da la Sainte Trinité," *Revue Thomiste* 45 (1939), p. 659.

8. H. Mühlen, *Der Heilige Geist als Person* (Münster, 1963), p. 164; idem, *Una mystica persona* (Paderborn, 1967).

9. I am thinking particularly of K. Rahner, "Dieu Trinité," and Barth, *Kirchliche Dogmatik*, I/1 (Zurich, 1964), pp. 165ff: Eng. trans., *Church Dogmatics* (Edinburgh, 1969).

10. K. Barth, *Kirchliche*, I/1, p. 379. This expression was used by St Basil and other Fathers; St Thomas himself describes the person as a *modus existendi* (*De pot.* 9, 4c). For patristic texts that use this expression, see G. Prestige, *God in Patristic Thought* (London, 1964), pp. 242–64; esp. 245–9.

11. Barth, *Kirchliche*, I/1, pp. 379ff; cf C. Welch, *Trinity*, 190ff.

12. Rahner, "Dieu Trinité," pp. 136–8.

13. M. de França Miranda, *O mistério de Deus em nossa vida: A doutrina trinitária de Karl Rahner* (São Paulo, 1975), p. 178.

14. The central thesis of F. Taymans d'Eypernon, *Le mystère primordial: La Trinité dans sa vivante image* (Paris, 1950), esp. pp. 56–62.

15. Grom and Guerrero, *El anuncio*, pp. 36, 99–106; cf A. Greck, "Socialtheologie," *Lexikon für Theolgie und Kirche* 9, pp. 925ff.

16. M.J. Scheeben, *Handbuch der katholischen Dogmatik*, vol. 4 (Freiburg, 1948), no. 1038, p. 439. There is a surprisingly forthright statement in G. Gordon, *Ultimate Conceptions of the Faith* (Boston, 1903), p. 354: "The real question is to know whether God is a social being or a solitary being, if he is an eternal egoist or an eternal socialist. If God is an eternal egoist, he stands in contradiction to humanity. If he is an eternal socialist, then in him is beginning and hope."

17. Cf B. Fraigneau-Julien, "Réflexion sur la signification religieuse du mystère de la Sainte Trinité," *Nouv. Rev. Th.* 87 (1965), pp. 673–87; G. Salet, "Charité trinitaire et charité des chrétiens," *Christus* 6 (1959), pp. 362–76; L. Lochet, "Charité fraternelle et vie trinitaire," *Nouv. Rev. Th.* 78 (1956), pp. 113-34.

18. His classic work is *Trinität und Reich Gottes* (Munich, 1978): Eng. trans., *The Trinity and the Kingdom of God* (London and New York, 1981); see also "The Inviting Unity of the Triune God," *Concilium* 177 (1985), pp. 50–58; idem, "La dottrina sociale della Trinità," *Sulla Trinità* (Naples, 1982), pp. 15–40.

19. Moltmann, *Trinität*, p. 174.

20. Cf R. Radford Ruether, *Religion and Sexism* (New York, 1974); for an overall view of the problem, see M. Hunt and R. Gibellini, eds., *La sfida del femminismo alla teologia* (Brescia, 1980).

21. M. Daly, *Beyond God the Father* (Boston, 1973), esp. pp. 34ff.

22. Cf M. Lucchetti Bingemer, "A Trindade a partir da perspectiva da mulher," *Rev. Ecl. Bras.* 46 (1985), pp. 73–99.

VII. THE COMMUNION OF THE TRINITY AS BASIS FOR SOCIAL AND INTEGRAL LIBERATION

1. Cf G. Gutiérrez, *El Dios de la vida* (Lima, 1982); V. Araya, *El Dios de los pobres* (San José, Costa Rica, 1982): Eng. trans., *God of the Poor* (Maryknoll, N.Y., 1987); for the biblical dimension, see R. Bultmann, "Zao, zoē," *ThWNT* 2 (1935)pp. 833–37.

2. Cf P. Tillich, "Die Zweideutigkeiten des Lebens in der geschlichtichen Dimension," in *Systematische Theologie*, vol. 3 (Stuttgart, 1978), pp. 388–97; F. Jacob, *Die Logik des Lebenden* (Frankfurt, 1972); J. Schröder, *Was ist Leben?* (Munich, 1971); P. Jordan and K. Rahner, *Das Geheimnis des Lebens* (Freiburg, 1968).

3. Aristotle, *De anima* II, 4, 415B; cf Thomas Aquinas, *Super III Sent.* d.35,q.1,a.1; I,q.18,a.1; *Contra Gentiles* I,97-8.

4. Pope St Dionysius, writing to his namesake, the Bishop of Alexandria, in 259, used the following image: "The Holy Trinity must reduce and collect itself into a peak, into one, that is, the almighty God of the universe" ("adeoque divinam Trinitatem in unum, quasi in quendam verticem, hoc est Deum universorum omnipotentem reduci atque colligi") (DS 112).

5. C. Folch Gomes, *Deus é comunhão. O conceito moderno de pessoa e a teologia trinitária* (Rome, 1978); it is unfortunate that this work does not include any development of the concept of communion.

6. Among works on this subject are: F. Pastor, *Semântica do mistério* (São Paulo, 1982), pp. 81–106; Moltmann, "Dottrina sociale," *Sulla Trinità* (Naples, 1982), pp. 15–40; idem, "Inviting Unity," *Concilium* 177 (1985), pp. 50–58; J. Bracken, "The Holy Trinity as a Community of Divine Persons," *Heythrop Journal* 15 (1974), pp. 166–88; A. van den Berg, "A SS. Trindade e a existência humana," *Rev. Ecl. Bras.* 33 (1973), pp. 629–48; 36 (1976), pp. 323–46; P. Bori, *Koinonía: L'idea della comunione nell'ecclesiologia recente e nel Nuovo Testamento* (Brescia, 1972); J. Hamer, *L'Eglise est une communion* (Paris, 1962): Eng. trans., *The Church Is a Communion* (London and New York, 1964).

7. Cf F. Hauck, "Koinonía," *ThWNT,* vol. 3 (1938), pp. 789–810.

8. Cf A. Acerbi, *Due ecclesiologie: Ecclesiologia giuridica ed ecclesiologia di communione nella Lumen Gentium* (Bologna, 1975).

9. A. Antoniazzi, "Comunhão e a participação (Rio de Janeiro, 1980).

10. Cf Richard of St. Victor, *De Trinitate* III, 3, 4: *PL* 196, 917–23.

11. The main bibliographies on this subject: Th. de Régnon, *Etudes de théologie positive sur la Sainte Trinité*, vol. 1 (Paris, 1892), pp. 409ff; A. Deneffe, "Perichoresis, circumincessio, circuminsessio," *ZKTh* 47 (1923), pp. 497–532; G. Prestige, "Perichoreo and Perichoresis in the Fathers," *Journal of Theological Studies* 29 (1928), pp. 242–52; idem, *God in Patristic Thought* (London, 1952), pp. 291–9; J. Scheeben, *Katholische Dogmatik,* vol. 2, pp. 1036–8; A. d'Alés, *De Deo uno et trino* (Paris, 1934), pp. 249–57.

12. Deneffe, "Perichoresis," pp. 531–2; see also Petavius, *De Incarnatione Verbi* IV, 14,8; Kasper, *The God of Jesus Christ* (London and New York, 1903).

13. The most complete study, explaining all the intricacies of the term, is Prestige, *God in Patristic Thought*, 291–9.

14. The classic instances of the term in St John Damascene are: *De fide orthodoxa* 1, 8: *PG* 94, 829A; 1, 14: *PG* 94, 860B; 3, 5: *PG* 94, 1000B; 4, 18: *PG* 94, 1476B; *De natura composita contra Acephalos* 4: *PG* 95, 118D.

15. Some Latin synonyms of *circumincessio/circuminsessio* are: *circuitio, commeatio, immanio, immanentia, assessio, inexistentia, circuminexistentia, accessio*; and the verbs: *permeare, pervadere* and *circumdare*. The term *circumincessio* was coined by the first translator of St John, Judge Burgundio of Pisa, in the mid-twelfth century.

16. The usage is explicit in Gregory of Nyssa, *Ep.* 101, 6: *PG* 37, 181; and in Maximus the Confessor, *Disputatio cum Pyrrho: PG* 91, 337C.

17. Cf M. Schmaus, *Der Glaube der Kirche*, vol. 1 (St Ottilien, 1979), pp. 208–9.

18. See Moltmann's pervasive criticism of this in *Trinität und Reich Gottes*, pp. 24ff, 155–61.

19. Augustine, *De Trinitate* VII, 4, 7.

20. Ibid, V, 9, 10.

21. P. Evdokimov, *L'Esprit Saint dans la tradition orthodoxe* (Paris, 1969), p. 43.

22. See the essay by A. Turrado, in various, *La Trinidad en la catequesis* (Salamanca, 1978), pp. 105–7.

23. Augustine, *De symbolo s. ad catech.* 2, 4: *PL* 40, 629.

24. Augustine, *Sermo* 182,3,3: *PL* 38, 986.

25. Cf Turrado, in *La Trinidad*, and Augustine's texts. In *De Trinitate* VII, 6, 11, Augustine says that if being is for itself and in itself, then

"person" means relationship to others: *"Nam si esse ad se dicitur, persona, vero, relative."*

26. *De Trinitate* VI, 10, 12.

27. Thomas Aquinas, *In Joann.* 17, lectio V, 2.

28. John Damascene, *De fide orthodoxa* I, 8, 14: *PG* 94, 829–60. St Gertrude (d. 1302), quoted in W. Dehl, *Deutsche Mystiker*, vol. 2, p. 90, expressed her experience of the Trinity like this: "Then the three persons jointly shed a marvellous light; each one appeared to throw his flame through the others and all joined one with another." This is a vision of a perichoretic relationship between the Persons.

29. J. Moltmann, "La dottrina sociale della Trinità," *Sulla Trinità* (Naples, 1982), p. 36; "Inviting Unity," *Concilium* 177 (1985), 50–58.

30. L. Boff, "A Igreja como mistério e a teologia da libertaçâo," *A Igreja se fez povo* (Petrópolis, 1986), pp. 12–15.

31. Y. Congar, "La Tri-unité de Dieu et l'Eglise," *La Vie Sprituelle* 604 (1974), pp. 687–703, with bibliography; J. Moltmann, "Criticism of Political and Clerical Monotheism," in *The Trinity and the Kingdom of God*; B. Forte, *La Chiesa icona della Trinità* (Brescia, 1984).

32. Pope St Symmachus, in a letter to Aronius of Arles, about 500, alluded to the trinitarian reference in the same priesthood shared by all the bishops: *Epist.* 3: *PL* 62, 51A.

VIII. GLORY BE TO THE FATHER, AND TO THE SON AND TO THE HOLY SPIRIT

1. For a doxological reflection, see A. Hamman, *Mysterium Salutis*, vol. 5 (Paris, 1970), pp. 185–204; *Trinidad y vida cristiana* (Salamanca, 1979); E. Schlink, "Trinität," in *Religion in Geschichte und Gegenwart*, vol. 6 (Tübingen, 1962), 1032–43; J. Moltmann, *The Trinity and the Kingdom of God* (London and New York, 1981).

2. A. Michel, "Trinité," *Dict. de Théol. Cath.*, vol. 15 (Paris, 1950), p. 1783.

3. The New Testament gives the divine names in different orders: Father, Son, Holy Spirit (Matt. 28:19; Rom. 8:11; 15:16); Holy Spirit, Son, Father (1 Cor. 12:1–6; Eph. 4:4–6); Son, Father, Holy Spirit (2 Cor. 13:13); Holy Spirit, Father, Son (Heb. 20:28); Father, Holy Spirit, Son (2 Thess. 2:13–14; 1 Pet. 1:1–2); Son, Holy Spirit, Father (Eph. 2:18; 1 Cor. 6:11). St Gregory Nazianzen asked: "Why this variation in order?" and replied: "In order to show the equality of nature" (*Oratio* 34, 15: *PG* 36, 253). Theodoretus, a great fifth-century theologian of christological and trinitarian questions, said that the changes in order were to "teach that the difference does not mean any difference of dignity . . . : it is to call

attention to the equality of glory in the bosom of the Trinity" (*Haereticorum fabularum Compendium* 3: *PG* 83, 456).

4. The Greek word *mysterion* was translated into classical Latin as *sacramentum;* see the detailed examination of its meaning in L. Boff, "O que significa sacramento," *Rev. Ecles. Bras.* 34 (1974), pp. 860–95.

5. See the apposite reflections of M. Scheeben, "The Mystery of the Holy Trinity," chap. 2 of *The Mysteries of Christianity* (St. Louis and London, 1946); K. Rahner, "On the Concept of Mystery in Catholic Theology," in *Theological Investigations*, vol. 4 (London and Baltimore, 1966); A. Milano, "Trinidad," *Dicc. teol. interdisciplinar*, vol. 4 (Salamanca, 1983), pp. 587–8; A. Brunner, *Dreifaltigkeit* (Einsiedeln, 1976), pp. 20–21.

6. Hilary of Poitiers, *De Trinitate* III, 1 *CCL* 62,73.

7. K. Barth, *Church Dogmatics*, II/1 (Edinburgh, 1970).

8. See Augustine's long prayer at the end of *De Trinitate* XV, 28, 51.

9. Thomas Aquinas, *In Boet. de Trinitate*, Problem. q.2, a.1, ad.6.

IX. GLORY BE TO THE FATHER: ORIGIN AND GOAL OF ALL LIBERATION

1. The different approaches are summed up in H. Tellenbach, *Das Vaterbild im Mythos und Geschichte* (Stuttgart, 1976); the classic work on the subject is J. Jeremias, *The Central Message of the New Testament* (London and New York, 1965); see also L. Boff, *The Lord's Prayer* (Maryknoll, N.Y., 1985).

2. Cf L. Bouyer, *Le Père invisible* (Paris, 1976); J. Galot, "Pour une théologie du Père," *Esprit et Vie* 94 (1984) and 95 (1985); the entire number 143 of *Concilium* (1981), *God as Father*.

3. See the reflections of P. Aubin, *Dio-Padre-Figlio-Spirito* (Turin, 1978), pp. 83ff.

4. C. Duquoc, "Jésus le non-théologien," *Dieu différent: Essai sur la symbolique trinitaire* (Paris, 1977), pp. 43–60.

5. Meister Eckhart, *Deutsche Predigten und Traktate*, ed. J. Quint (Munich, 1977), p. 185.

6. H. du Lubac, *The Drama of Atheist Humanism* (London, 1969); C. Fabro, *Introduzione all'ateismo moderno* (Rome, 1964); various, *El ateísmo contemporáneo*, 5 vols. (Madrid, 1971–3).

7. Cf J. Moltmann, "The Motherly Father," *Concilium* 143 (1981), pp. 51–6; "Ich glaube an Gott der Vater," *Evangelische Theologie* 43 (1983), pp. 397–415; L. Armendáriz, "El Padre maternal," *Estudios Ecles.* 58 (1983), pp. 249–75; see also the well-known book by M. Daly, *Beyond God the Father* (Boston, 1973).

8. See John Paul II, encyclical *Dives in misericordia*, 4, n. 52, with biblical texts on this motherly aspect of God.

9. Basil, *De Spiritu Sancto*, 6ff.

10. Hilary of Poitiers, *De Trinitate* II, 9.

11. Gregory of Nyssa, *Oratio* 29, 8.

12. P. Ricoeur, "La paternité, du fantasme au symbole," *Le Conflit des Interprétations* (Paris, 1969), pp. 458–86.

13. J. Pohier, *Au nom du Père* (Paris, 1972).

X. GLORY BE TO THE SON:
MEDIATOR OF INTEGRAL LIBERATION

1. The Catholic theologian W. Kasper writes: "There is now broad agreement among exegetes on the faith of the disciples in the resurrection of Jesus, the Crucified, as starting-point and foundation of New Testament christology. Their thesis is that before Easter there was no express christological belief. All the christological titles in the Bible: Christ (Messiah), Redeemer, Servant of God, Son of God, etc., are post-Easter confessions, which Jesus himself never explicitly claimed for himself" (*Der Gott Jesus Christi* [Mainz, 1982], p. 210): Eng. trans., *The God of Jesus Christ* (London and New York, 1984).

2. See L. Boff, *Jesus Cristo Libertador*, 10th ed. (Petrópolis, 1985), pp. 153–172: Eng. trans., *Jesus Christ Liberator* (Maryknoll, N.Y., 1978).

3. Cf J. Sobrino, *Christology at the Crossroads* (Maryknoll, N.Y., 1978), chaps. 4–5; idem, "La aparición del Dios de vida en Jesús de Nazaret," in *La lucha de los dioses* (San José, Costa Rica, 1980), pp. 79–121.

4. G. Gutiérrez, *Beber no próprio pozo* (Petrópolis, 1984), pp. 48–62: Eng. trans., *We Drink from Our Own Wells* (Maryknoll, N.Y., 1985).

5. Cf H. Echegaray, *A prática de Jesus* (Petrópolis, 1983), 62–67: Eng. trans., *The Practice of Jesus* (Maryknoll, N.Y., and Melbourne, 1984).

6. See M. Lucchetti Bingemer, "A Trindade a partir da perspectiva da mulher," *Revista Eclesiástica Brasileira* 46 (1986), pp. 73–99, with ample bibliography. The feminine attributes of Jesus—tenderness, gentleness, love for outcasts, the image of feeding with milk—did not go unnoticed in Christian piety, which at some periods venerated Jesus as mother: cf A. Cabasut, "Une dévotion médiévale peu connue: La dévotion à 'Jésus notre Mère'," *Rev. Asc. et Myst.* 25 (1949), pp. 234–45; see also C. Walker Bynum, "Jesus as Mother and Abbot as Mother: Some Themes in Twelfth-century Cistercian Writings," *The Harvard Theological Review* 70 (1977), pp. 257–84.

7. Cf P. Evdokimov, *L'Esprit Saint dans la tradition orthodoxe* (Paris, 1969), p. 71.

8. There is a good summary in Kasper, *God*, pp. 199-245.

9. Evdokimov, *L'Esprit Saint*, p. 72.

10. There is a brief summary of the question in Moltmann, *Trinität und Reich Gottes* (Munich, 1980), pp. 129-33; Eng. trans., *The Trinity and the Kingdom of God* (London and San Francisco, 1981).

11. See L. Boff, *O evangelho do Cristo cósmico* (Petrópolis, 1971), pp. 103-8; idem, "O promogênito da criaço: Principios teológicos do Baeto J. Duns Scotus para uma teologia da criacão," *Vozes* 69 (1966), pp. 34-9; C. Koser, "Cristo-Homen, razão de ser da criação," *Vozes* 69, pp. 23-34.

12. There is a more detailed account in L. Boff, *Natal: A humanidade e a jovialidade de nosso Deus* (Petrópolis, 1978).

XI. GLORY BE TO THE HOLY SPIRIT: DRIVING FORCE OF INTEGRAL LIBERATION

1. There is now a vast literature on the subject, inspired by the Catholic charismatic movement. Among the most valuable titles are: Y. Congar, *I Believe in the Holy Spirit* (London and New York, 1983); J. Comblin, *O tempo da ação: Ensaio sobre o Espírito e a história* (Petrópolis, 1978) and *O Espírito no mundo* (Petrópolis, 1978); H. de Lima Vaz, H. Harada, L. Boff and others, *O Espírito Santo* (Petrópolis, 1973); H. Brandt, *O rísco do Espírito* (São Leopoldo, 1977); CLAR, *Vida segundo o Espírito nas comunidades religiosas da América Latina* (Rio de Janeiro, 1973); the whole no. 128 of *Concilium* (1979): *Conflicts about the Spirit*; H. Mühlen, *Una mystica persona* (Paderborn, 1967); S. Verges, *Imagen del Espiritu de Jesús* (Salamanca, 1974); "Esprit," G. Kittel, *Dict. biblique* (Geneva, 1971).

2. Cf K. Lehmann and W. Pannenberg, *Glaubensbekenntnis und Kirchengemeinschaft* (Freiburg-Göttingen, 1982).

3. For a short summary of the question, see D. Ritschl, "The History of the Filioque Controversy," *Concilium* 128 (1979), pp. 3-14.

4. Cf R. Laurentin, *Catholic Pentecostalism* (London, 1977); P. de Oliveira, J. Liboanie and others, *Renovação carismática católica* (Petrópolis, 1978); H. Mühlen, *Die Erneuerung des christlichen Glaubens* (Munich, 1976); C. Heitmann and H. Mühlen, *Erfahrung und Theologie des Heiligen Geistes* (Munich, 1977).

5. Cf E. Schweizer, *The Holy Spirit* (Philadelphia, 1980; London, 1981); C. Barrett, *The Holy Spirit and the Gospel Tradition* (London, 1981).

6. X. Pikaza, "El Espíritu Santo y María en la obra de San Lucas,"

Ephemerides mariologicae 28 (1978), pp. 151-68; idem, *María y el Espíritu Santo* (Salamanca, 1981); A. Feuillet, "L'Esprit Saint et la Mère du Christ," *Bulletin de la Société Française d'Études Mariales* 25 (1968), pp. 39–64.

7. Cf GS 26.

8. Cf Paul VI's apostolic letter *Octogesima adveniens* (1971), n. 37.

9. For this aspect, see L. Boff, *Church: Charism and Power* (New York and London, 1985), pp. 144–53; Y. Congar, "L'Esprit, Esprit du Christ: Christomonisme et Filioque," *La Parole et le Souffle* (Paris, 1984), pp. 162–87.

10. Relevant works on this aspect are: M. Lucchetti Bingemer, "A Trindade a partir da perspectiva da mulher," *Rev. Ecl. Bras.* 46 (1985), pp. 73–99; Y. Congar, "The Motherhood of God and the Femininity of the Holy Spirit," *I Believe in the Holy Spirit* (London and New York, 1983); L. Boff, *The Feminine Face of God* (New York, 1987); idem, *A Ave-Maria: O feminino e o Espírito Santo* (Petrópolis, 1980).

11. See the examples given by L. Bouyer, *Le trône de la sagesse: Essai sur la signification du culte marial* (Paris, 1957), p. 272.

12. Cf Congar, "Motherhood of God."

13. Cf R. Murray, "The Holy Spirit as Mother," *Symbols of Church and Kingdom: A Study in Early Syrian Tradition* (Cambridge, 1975), pp. 312–20.

14. These and other texts are given in J. and E. Moltmann, *Dieu, homme et femme* (Paris, 1984), p. 120.

15. Lémonnyer, *Notre vie divine* (Paris, 1936), pp. 66ff.

16. Gregory Nazianzen, *Oratio* 31, 7: *PG* 36, 140-6.

17. Jerome, *In Isaiam* 49, 9–11: *PL* 24, 419B.

18. Cf E. Wurz, "Das Mütterliche in Gott," *Una Sancta* 32 (1977), pp. 261–72; G. Kaltenbrunner, "Ist der Hl. Geist weiblich?," *Una Sancta* 32 (1977), pp. 273–9.

19. There is a good summary in Congar, *I Believe*.

20. Cf Comblin, *O tempo da ação,* pp. 112–53.

21. See Augustine, *De Trinitate* XV, 17, 29; 26, 47; *Sermo* 71, 26: *PL* 38, 459. This expression can be found earlier in Tertullian, *Adv. Prax* 3 and also, in similar formulations, in Ambrose and Hilary.

22. The Fathers of the third century, battling against subordinationism and those who denied the divinity of the Holy Spirit, had particular difficulty in showing how the Spirit proceeded from the Father if not by begetting, since it is begetting that ensures sameness of essence. The analogy of Eve was often used. Eve is not Adam's daughter; she did not come through begetting but shares his same nature. For this question see A. Orbe, "La Procesión del Espíritu Santo y el origen de Eva," *Gregorianum* 45 (1964), pp. 103–18.

23. See P. Evdokimov, *L'Esprit Saint dans la tradition orthodoxe* (Paris, 1969), pp. 56-7.

24. W. Kasper gives a good account of the different models used by Greek and Latin theology to represent the procession of the Holy Spirit— see *The God of Jesus Christ* (London and New York, 1984), pp. 264-72.

25. Cf Epiphanius of Salamis, *Anacoratus* 8: *PG* 43, 29; Cyril of Alexandria, *Thesaurus de Trinitate* 34: *PG* 75, 585.

26. Cf R. Slenczka, "Das Filioque in der neueren ökumenischen Diskussion," in K. Lehmann and W. Pannenberg, *Glaubensbekenntnis,* pp. 80-99.

27. *Rev. Int. de Théologie* 5 (1898), pp. 681-712; republished in *Istina* 17 (1972), pp. 271-89; summary in Congar, *I Believe.*

28. Evdokimov, *L'Esprit Saint*; idem, "Panagion et panagia," *Bull. de la soc. fr. d'études mariales* 27 (1970), pp. 59-71.

29. Evdokimov, *L'Esprit Saint*, p. 70.

30. Ibid., p. 71.

31. Ibid., p. 72.

32. J. Moltmann, *Trinität und Reich Gottes* (Munich, 1980), pp. 194-206: Eng. trans., *The Trinity and the Kingdom of God* (London and New York, 1981).

33. Ibid., p. 201.

34. Ibid., p. 202.

35. Ibid., pp. 204-6.

36. C. Duquoc, *Dieu différent* (Paris, 1977), pp. 96-124.

37. Cf E. Fortman, *The Triune God* (London, 1972), where this idea appears frequently.

38. Evdokimov tackles this question, convincingly in my view, in *L'Esprit Saint*, pp. 74-5.

39. Cf S. Bulgakov, *Le Paraclet* (Paris, 1969).

40. This is Comblin's basic and valid thesis in *O tempo da ação.*

41. See the whole of *Lumière et Vie* 173 (1985) on the Holy Spirit as Liberator.

42. There is a clear account in L. Bouyer, *Le Consolateur* (Paris, 1980), pp. 339-54; see also Congar, *I Believe.*

43. L. Boff, *El rostro materno*, esp. pp. 99-127; idem, *A Ave-Maria*, pp. 41-6, 81-5.

XII. AS IT WAS IN THE BEGINNING: THE IMMANENT TRINITY, IN ITSELF

1. Boethius, *De consolatione philosophiae* V, 6: "Interminabilis vitae tota simul et perfecta possessio."

2. This axiom is given detailed treatment by K. Rahner in "Dieu

Trinité," *Mysterium Salutis*, vol. 6, pp. 13–140; see also M. de França Miranda, *O mistério de Deus em nossa vida* (São Paulo, 1975), pp. 151–60; Moltmann, *Trinität und Reich Gottes* (Munich, 1980), pp. 175–9; and Kasper, *Der Gott Jesu Christi* (Mainz, 1982), pp. 333–7.

3. Moltmann has a deep analysis of the relation between the cross and the Trinity, seeing the crucifixion as an intra-trinitarian gesture—see *The Crucified God* (London, 1977); see his comments on the same aspect in *Trinität* and my critique of him in *Paixão de Christo—Paixão do Mundo* (Petrópolis, 1978), pp. 138–41: Eng. trans., *Passion of Christ, Passion of the World* (Maryknoll, N.Y., 1987).

XIII. NOW AND FOREVER: THE ECONOMIC TRINITY, FOR US

1. Augustine, *De Trinitate* V, 14, 15.

2. Augustine, *In Johannem* 20, 9: *PL* 35, 1561.

3. B. de Margerie discusses this point on the basis of texts from Augustine and Thomas Aquinas, in *The Christian Trinity in History* (Still River, Mass., and Leominster, 1982).

4. Thomas Aquinas, *ST* I, q. 45, a.6.

5. See for example the Preface for Ordinary Time.

6. See the opportune reflections by Moltmann in *Trinität*, pp. 123–7.

7. Aquinas, *ST* I, q. 45, a. 6.

8. For a more detailed account, see L. Boff, *Liberating Grace* (Maryknoll, N.Y., 1979).

9. Detailed account in Y. Congar, "La Trinité de Dieu et l'Eglise," *La Vie Spirituelle* 604 (1974), pp. 687–703.

10. LG 4; Cyprian, *De Cath. Ecclesiae unitate* 7; *De orat. dominica 23: PL* 4, 553; Augustine, *Sermo* 71, 33: *PL* 38, 463ff.

11. Cf B. Forte, "Ecclesia de Trinitate," in *La Chiesa icona della Trinità* (Brescia, 1984), pp. 9–22.

XIV. FOREVER AND EVER: THE TRINITY IN CREATION AND CREATION IN THE TRINITY

1. See J. Moltmann, "Die trintarische Geschichte Gottes," in *Zukunft der Schöpfung* (Munich, 1977), pp. 89–96.

2. The two main works dealing with this question are *Concordia Novi ac Veteris Testamenti* (Venice, 1519) and *Expositio in Apocalypsium* (Venice, 1527); see H. du Lubac, *La posterité spirituelle de Joachim de Fiore* (Paris-Namur, 1979); E. Benz, *Ecclesia spiritualis* (Stuttgart, 1934); idem,

"Creator Spiritus: Die Geistlehre des Joachim von Fiore," in *Eranos-Jahrbuch* (1956), pp. 285–355.

3. Cf V. Araya, *El Dios de los pobres* (San José, Costa Rica, 1982): Eng. trans., *God of the Poor* (Maryknoll, N.Y., 1987); M. Díaz Mateos, *El Dios que libera* (Lima, 1985); G. Gutiérrez, *Hablar de Dios desde el sufrimiento del inocente* (Lima, 1986): Eng. trans., *On Job: God-Talk and the Suffering of the Innocent* (Maryknoll, N.Y., 1987); G. Pixley and C. Boff, *Opção pelos pobres* (Petrópolis, 1986): Eng. trans. in preparation for this series.

4. Cf L. Boff, "Además del cielo, ¿qué podemos esperar?", in *La fe en la periferia del mundo* (Santander, 1985), pp. 103–11.

5. H. Cox, *The Feast of Fools* (Cambridge, Mass., 1969).

Select Bibliography

CLASSICAL SOURCES

Augustine, St. *De Trinitate*, Corpus Christ. 50, 50A. 2 vols. Turnhout, 1968. Eng. trans.: *On the Trinity*, Fathers of the Church, vol. 45. Washington, D.C., 1963.

Cyril of Alexandria. *Dialogus de sancta et consubstantiali Trinitate*. Fr. trans.: *Dialogues sur la Trinité*. Sources chrétiennes, 237, 246. Paris, 1976, 1978.

Hilary of Poitiers. *On the Trinity (De Trinitate)*. Philosophia Patrum. Leiden, 1982.

Marius Victorinus. *Traités théologiques sur la Trinité*. Sources chrétiennes, 58, 69. Paris, 1960.

Richard of St Victor. *The Trinity*. Classics of Western Spirituality, vol. 3. London and New York, 1979.

Tertullian. *Adversus Praxean. PL* 2, 175–219.

Thomas Aquinas, St. "On the Trinity," *Summa Theologiae* I: q. 27–43. Latin text and Eng. trans., London and New York, 1964–76.

BOOKS AND ARTICLES

Andresen, C. "Zur Entstehung und Geschichte des trinitarischen Personenbegriffes." *Zeitschrift für Neutestamentliche Wissenschaft* 52 (1961), pp. 1–39.

Araya, V. *El Dios de los pobres*. San José, Costa Rica, 1982. Eng. trans.: *God of the Poor*, Maryknoll, N.Y.: Orbis, 1987.

Arce Martínez, S. "El desafío del Dios trinitario de la Iglesia." In *La teología como desafío*. Havana, 1980, pp. 45–54.

Baget-Bozzo, G. *La Trinità*. Florence, 1980.

Bardy, G. "Trinité." In *Dictionnaire de Théologie Catholique*, vol. 15. Paris, 1950, pp. 1545–1702.

Barré, H. *Trinité que j'adore: Perspectives théologiques*. Paris, 1965.

Barth, K. *Die kirchliche Dogmatik*. Zollikon-Zurich. Eng. trans.: *Church Dogmatics*, I, II. Edinburgh: T. & T. Clark; New York: Scribner's, 1969.

Boff, L. *A atualidade da expêriencia de Deus*. Rio de Janeiro, 1974.

———. *O Pai-Nosso: A oração da libertação integral*. Petrópolis: Vozes, 1979. Eng. trans.: *The Lord's Prayer: The Prayer of Integral Liberation*. Maryknoll, N.Y.: Orbis, 1984.

Bonnin, E. *Espiritualidad y liberación en América Latina*. San José, Costa Rica, 1982.

Bourassa, F. *Questions de théologie trinitaire*. Rome, 1970.

———. "Personne et conscience en théologie trinitaire." *Gregorianum* 55 (1974), pp. 471–93.

Bouyer, L. *Le consolateur: Esprit Saint et vie de grâce*. Paris, 1980.

Bracken, J. A. "The Holy Trinity as a Communion of Divine Persons." *Heythrop Journal* 15 (1973), pp. 629–48; 257–70.

Breton, V. M. *The Blessed Trinity: History, Theology, Spirituality*. London, 1934.

Breuning, W. "La Trinité." *Bilan de la théologie du XXème siècle*. Tournai: Casterman, 1970, pp. 252–67.

Camelot, T. "Le dogme de la Trinité: Origine et formation des formules dogmatiques." *Lumière et Vie* 30 (1956), pp. 9–48.

Cantalamessa, R. "The Development of the Concept of a Personal God in Christian Spirituality." *Concilium* 103 (1977), pp. 57–66.

Coda, P. *Evento pasquale: Trinità e storia*. Rome, 1984.

Comblin, J. *A tempo da ação: Ensaio sobre o Espírito e a história*. Petrópolis: Vozes, 1982.

———. *El Espírito Santo y la liberación*. Madrid: Paulinas, 1986. Eng. trans. in preparation for this series.

Congar, Y.-M. *Je crois en l'Esprit Saint*. 3 vols. Paris: du Cerf, 1979–80. Eng. trans.: *I Believe in the Holy Spirit*. New York: Seabury Press; London: Geoffrey Chapman, 1983.

———. "La Tri-unité de Dieu et l'Eglise." *La Vie Spirituelle* 604 (1974), pp. 687–703.

———. "Classical Political Monotheism and the Trinity." *Concilium* 143 (1981), pp. 31–6.

Daniélou, J. *La Trinité et le mystère de l'existence*. Bruges, 1968.

Deneffe, A. "Perichoresis, circumincessio, circuminsessio." *Zeitschrift für katholische Theologie* 47 (1923), pp. 497–532.

Díaz Mateos, M. *El Dios que libera*. Lima, 1985.

Duchesne-Guillermin, J. "En el nombre del Padre, del Hijo y del Espíritu Santo." *Communio* 5 (1980), pp. 466–77.

Duquoc, C. *Dieu différent: Essai sur la symbolique trinitaire*. Paris, 1977.

Echegaray, H. *A prática de Jesus*. Petrópolis: Vozes, 1982. Eng. trans.: *The Practice of Jesus*. Maryknoll, N.Y.: Orbis; Melbourne: Dove Communications, 1984.

Estudios Trinitarios. Review dedicated to the subject of the Trinity, beginning in 1966. The Trinitarian Secretariat of Salamanca also publishes excellent books on the subject and organizes frequent conferences.

Evdokimov, P. *L'Esprit Saint dans la tradition orthodoxe.* Paris: du Cerf, 1969.

Fernández Ardanaz, S. "El problema del dinamismo trinitario en Orígenes." *Angelicum* 49 (1972), pp. 67–98.

Folch Gomes, C. *Deus é comunhâo: O conceito moderno de pessoa e a teologia trinitária.* Rome, 1978.

———. *A doutrina da Trindade eterna: O significado da expresão "tres pessoas."* Rio de Janeiro, 1979.

Forte, B. *La Chiesa icona della Trinità.* Brescia: Queriniana, 1984.

Fortmann, E. *The Triune God.* London; Philadelphia: Westminster, 1972.

Galot, J. "Pour une théologie du Père." *Esprit et Vie* 94 (1984), pp. 479–503, 661–9, 95 (1985), pp. 295–304.

Garrigou-Lagrange, R. "Le clair-obscur de la Sainte Trinité." *Revue Thomiste* 45 (1939), pp. 647–64.

———. *De Deo Trino et Creatore.* Turin, 1944.

Gendron, L. *Le mystère de la Trinité et symbolique familiale.* Rome, 1975.

Gironés, G. "La divina arqueología: Apuntes para un tratado de la Trinidad." *Anales Valentinos* 8 (1982), pp. 1–18.

Gomes Mourão de Castro, M. *Die Trinitätslehre des hl. Gregor von Nyssa.* Freiburg: Herder, 1938.

González de Cardedal, O. *Misterio trinitario y existencia humana.* Madrid: Rialp, 1965.

Gutiérrez, G. *Beber en su propio pozo.* Salamanca: Sígueme, 1984. Eng. trans.: *We Drink from Our Own Wells.* Maryknoll, N.Y.: Orbis, 1985.

———. *El Dios que libera.* Lima, 1982.

———. *Hablar de Dios desde el sufrimiento del inocente.* Lima, 1986. Eng. trans.: *On Job: God-Talk and the Suffering of the Innocent.* Maryknoll, N.Y.: Orbis, 1987.

Hamman, A. "Existe-t-il un langage trinitaire chez les Pères apostoliques?" *Augustinianum* 13 (1973), pp. 455–8.

———. "La Trinité dans la liturgie et la vie chrétienne." *Mysterium Salutis*, vol. 5. Paris, 1970, pp. 183-204.

Isaac, J. *La révélation des personnes divines.* Paris, 1968.

Jüngel, E. *Gott als Geheimnis der Welt.* Tübingen, 1977. Eng. trans.: *God as the Mystery of the World.* Grand Rapids: Eerdmans; Edinburgh: T. & T. Clark, 1978.

Kaiser C. "Discerning the Trinity on the Basis of Empirical Situations." *Scottish Journal of Theology* 28 (1975), pp. 449–60.

Kaliba, C. *Die Welt als Gleichnis des dreieinigen Gottes*. Salzburg, 1952.

Kasper, W. *Der Gott Jesu Christi*. Mainz, 1982. Eng. trans.: *The God of Jesus Christ*. London: SCM Press; New York: Crossroad, 1983.

Lebreton, J. *Histoire du dogme de la Trinité*. 2 vols. Paris, 1919.

Libânio, J. B. *Libertar para a comunhâo e a participação*. Rio de Janeiro, 1980.

Lonergan, B. *De Deo Trino*. 2 vols. Rome, 1964.

———. *Divinarum personarum conceptio analogica*. Rome, 1957.

Lucchetti Bingemer, M. C. "A Trindade a partir da perspectiva da mulher." *Revista Eclesiástica Brasileira* 46 (1986), pp. 73–99.

Margerie, B. de. *La Trinité chrétienne dans l'histoire*. Paris, 1975. Eng. trans.: *The Christian Trinity in History*. Still River, Mass.: St. Bede's; Leominster: Fowler Wright, 1982.

Miranda, M. de França. *O mistério de Deus em nossa vida: A doutrina trinitária de Karl Rahner*. Sâo Paulo, 1975.

Moingt, J. *Théologie trinitaire de Tertullien*. 4 vols. Paris, 1966–9.

Moltmann, J. *Trinität und Reich Gottes*. Paderborn, 1978. Eng. trans.: *The Trinity and the Kingdom of God*. London: SCM Press; San Francisco: Harper and Row, 1981.

———. "The Inviting Unity of the Triune God." *Concilium* 177 (1985), pp. 50–58.

Muñoz, R. *El Dios de los cristianos*. Madrid: Paulinas, 1987.

Nédoncelle, M. "*Prosopon* et *persona* dans l'Antiquité classique: Essai de bilan linguistique." *Revue des Sciences Religieuses* 22 (1948), pp. 277–99.

Orbe, A. "La procesión del Espíritu Santo y el origen de Eva." *Gregorianum* 45 (1964), pp. 103–18.

Panikkar, R. *The Trinity and the Religious Experience of Man*. Maryknoll, N.Y.: Orbis; London: Darton, Longman and Todd, 1973.

Pannenberg, W. "El Dios de la historia: El Dios trinitario y la verdad de la historia." *Salmanticensis* 24 (1977), pp. 259–77.

Pastor, F. *Semântica do mistério: A linguagem teológica da ortodoxia trinitária*. São Paulo, 1982.

Penido, M. T. L. "Prélude grec à la théorie 'psychologique' de la Trinité." *Revue Thomiste* 45 (1939), pp. 665–74.

Pikaza, X. "Experiencia religiosa, historia de Jesús y revelación trinitaria." *Estudios Trinitarios* 13 (1979), pp. 19–93.

———. "Trinidad y ontología en torno al planteamiento sistemático del misterio trinitario." *Estudios Trinitarios* 8 (1974), pp. 189–236.

Prestige, G. L. *God in Patristic Thought*. London: SPCK, 1952.

Prete, S. "Confessioni trinitarie in alcuni Atti dei martiri del sec. II." *Augustinianum* 13 (1973), pp. 469–82.

Rabeneck, J. "Primera persona divina." *Estudios eclesiásticos* 102 (1952), pp. 353–63.

Rahner, K. "Dieu Trinité: Fondament transcendant de l'histoire du salut." *Mysterium Salutis*, vol. 6. Paris, 1970, pp. 13–140.

Régnon, Th. de. *Etudes de théologie positive sur la Sainte Trinité*. 4 vols. Paris, 1892–8.

Rius Camps, J. *El dinamismo trinitario en la divinización de los seres racionales según Orígenes*. Rome, 1970.

Scheffczk, L. "L'élaboration du dogme dans le Christianisme primitif." *Mysterium Salutis*, vol. 5. Paris, 1970, pp. 211–300.

———. "Reflexión teológica sobre la inhabitación de la Trinidad en el hombre." *Estudios Trinitarios* 13 (1979), pp. 293–303.

Schierse, F. J. "La révélation de la Trinité dans le Nouveau Testament." *Mysterium Salutis*, vol. 5. Paris, 1970, pp. 121–83.

Schmaus, M. *Die psychologische Trinitätslehre des hl. Augustinus*. Münster, 1927.

———. *God in Revelation*, vol. 1 of *Dogma*. London and New York: Sheed & Ward, 1968.

Schulte, R. "La préparation de la révélation Trinitaire." *Mysterium Salutis*, vol. 5. Paris, 1970, pp. 71–119.

Segundo, J. L. *Our Idea of God*, vol. 3 of *A Theology for Artisans of a New Humanity*. Maryknoll, N.Y.: Orbis, 1974.

———. *Jesus of Nazareth Yesterday and Today*. 5 vols. Maryknoll, N.Y.: Orbis; London: Sheed & Ward, 1984–8.

Sobrino, J. *Jesús en América Latina*. San Salvador: UCA, 1982. Eng. trans.: *Jesus in Latin America*. Marynoll, N.Y.: Orbis, 1987.

———. *Cristología a partir de América Latina*. Salamanca: Sígueme, 1982. Eng. trans.: *Christology at the Crossroads*. Maryknoll, N.Y.: Orbis, 1978.

———. *Resurrección de la verdadera Iglesia*. Santander: Sal Terrae, 1981. Eng. trans.: *The True Church and the Poor*. Maryknoll, N.Y.: Orbis, 1984.

Solano Ramírez, L. *El misterio salvífico del Dios Trinidad*. Bogotá: USTA, 1979.

Studer, B. "Zur Entwicklung der patristischen Trinitätslehre." *Theologie und Glaube* 74 (1984), pp. 81–93.

Tavard, G. H. *The Vision of Trinity*. Washington, D.C.: University Press of America, 1981.

Trigo, P. "La Trinidad como fundamento del método teológico." *Nuevo Mundo* 104 (1979), pp. 135–53.

Various. *Trinidad y vida cristiana*. Salamanca, 1979.

———. *El misterio trinitario a la luz del Vaticano II*. Salamanca, 1979.

————. *Trinidad y vida comunitaria.* Salamanca, 1980.

————. *Trinität: Actuelle Perspektiven der Theologie.* Freiburg: Herder, 1984.

Vidigal de Carvalho, J. *A devoção da Santísima Trindade na época colonial.* Viçosa, Brazil, 1979.

Vives, J. "El Dios trinitario y la comunión humana."*Estudios Eclesiásticos* 52 (1977), pp. 129–37.

————. "Creer en Dios, Padre, Hijo y Espíritu Santo." *Estudios Trinitarios* 16 (1982), pp. 81–104.

Wainwright, A. W. *The Trinity in the New Testament.* London: SPCK, 1962.

Welch, C. *The Trinity in Contemporary Theology.* London, 1963.

Index